D0812458

Joseph Conrad's comments about his works have until now been dismissed as theoretically unsophisticated, while the critical notions of James, Woolf and Joyce have come to shape our understanding of the modern novel. Richard Ambrosini's study of *Conrad's Fiction as Critical Discourse* makes an original claim for the importance of his theoretical ideas as they are formed, tested, and eventually redefined in "Heart of Darkness" and *Lord Jim*. Setting the narrator's discourse in these tales in the context of the dynamic interplay of Conrad's fictional with his non-fictional writings, and of the transformations in his narrative forms, Ambrosini defines Conrad's view of fiction and the artistic ideal underlying his commitment as a writer in a new and challenging way.

Conrad's innovatory techniques as a novelist are shown in the continuity of his theoretical enterprise, from the early search for an artistic prose and a personal novel form, to the later dislocations of perspective achieved by manipulation of conventions drawn from popular fiction. This reassessment of Conrad's critical thought offers a new perspective on the transition from the Victorian novel to contemporary fiction.

CONRAD'S FICTION AS CRITICAL DISCOURSE

CONRAD'S FICTION AS CRITICAL DISCOURSE

RICHARD AMBROSINI
Department of English, University of Rome

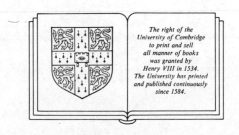

The right of the
University of Cambridge
to print and sell
all manner of books
was granted by
Henry VIII in 1534.
The University has printed
and published continuously
since 1584.

CAMBRIDGE UNIVERSITY PRESS
Cambridge
New York   Port Chester
Melbourne   Sydney

Published by the Press Syndicate of the University of Cambridge
The Pitt Building, Trumpington Street, Cambridge CB2 1RP
40 West 20th Street, New York, NY 10011–4211, USA
10 Stamford Road, Oakleigh, Melbourne 3166, Australia

First published 1991

Printed in Great Britain at the University Press, Cambridge

British Library cataloguing in publication data
Ambrosini, Richard
Conrad's fiction as critical discourse.
1. Fiction in English. Conrad, Joseph, 1857–1924
I. Title
823.912

Library of Congress cataloguing in publication data
Ambrosini, Richard.
Conrad's fiction as critical discourse / Richard Ambrosini.
p.   cm.
Includes bibliographical references and index.
ISBN 0 521 40349 9
1. Conrad, Joseph, 1857–1924 – Criticism and interpretation.
2. Conrad, Joseph, 1857–1924 – Aesthetics.   I. Title.
PR6005.O4Z5465   1991
823'.912 – dc20   90–45645   CIP

ISBN 0 521 40349 9 hardback

To my mother and father

Contents

Acknowledgments

The initial impetus behind my work on Conrad was the feeling I had of the integrity of Conrad's thinking – which was so clear when I read his fiction but then got blurred whenever I tried to set forth my response to those moral concerns which touched me so deeply. If I have been able in some way to transform my respect and love for Conrad into a solid understanding of his work, the source of my success is to be found in two persons who helped me find the way to adapt the tools of literary criticism to the ideas I wanted to express. Professor Agostino Lombardo of the University of Rome taught me through his Shakespearean and Conradian readings that ethical criticism is not just another school but a way of making worthwhile a life commitment to the study of literature. At the University of Ottawa the intellectual rigor and human sympathy of my supervisor, Professor Camille René La Bossière, were the driving force behind this work.

A project like this, which took shape across the Atlantic, would not have been possible without the help of both institutions and individuals. The faculty and staff of the English Department and the School of Graduate Studies of the University of Ottawa extended their support and encouragement throughout my sojourn. In Canada I must thank in particular David L. Jeffrey, John Hill, April London and Frans De Bruyn, who made my work at the University of Ottawa such an interesting and enriching experience. Thanks to them, and to Mrs Miriam Magner of Ottawa, I was pleasantly surprised to find what a warm place Canada really is. Here in Italy I am deeply indebted to Professor Piero Boitani, who believed in the worth of my work and helped me transform it into a book. I am also grateful to Professor Mario Curreli, who helped me with the kindness that is so characteristic of him. Also the loving encouragement of Cristina, Elizabeth and Federico must not be overlooked. Finally, I wish to thank Claudia, who believed so much in the value of what I was doing that she married me even before the work was finished.

Abbreviations

The following abbreviations are used in the course of the book to refer to individual texts by Joseph Conrad. Page references to Conrad's works are to the Dent 21-volume *Collected Edition*.

C	*Chance*
CL	*Collected Letters*, ed. Frederick R. Karl and Laurence Davies
LE	*Last Essays*
LJ	*Lord Jim*
LL	*Joseph Conrad: Life and Letters*, ed. G. Jean-Aubry
MoS	*The Mirror of the Sea*
N	*Nostromo*
NLL	*Notes on Life and Letters*
NoN	*The Nigger of the "Narcissus"*
PR	*A Personal Record*
SA	*The Secret Agent*
T	*Typhoon and Other Stories*
TU	*Almayer's Folly and Tales of Unrest*
UWE	*Under Western Eyes*
Y	*Youth, Heart of Darkness and The End of the Tether*
WtT	*Within the Tides*

Introduction

The re-evaluation of Joseph Conrad's work in the second half of this century has uncovered in his texts complex narrational forms and startling perceptions of the darkness in Western consciousness. That scholarly enterprise has discarded, apparently for good, several simplistic labels that earlier, less-refined approaches had attached to his fiction. Conrad's admission to the modernist pantheon, however, has not substantially redefined the earlier casting of the writer as a mature sailor who had spent his formative years in a world foreign to literary circles. The very assumptions which have made possible Conrad's re-evaluation are largely grounded on the notion that the valuable parts of his texts have to be rescued from their author's tampering with the product of his creative imagination. As a result, the comments he makes about his own art in his fiction, letters and essays are dismissed as perfunctory self-defenses. According to Douglas Hewitt, for example, Conrad seems to be "unaware of what qualities make him a great novelist."[1] Reasoning along these lines, critics have felt that in assessing Conrad's greatness they were formulating for the first time the theoretical implications of his artistic choices.

In the long run, however, the assumptions which have guided Conrad's reassessment have actually impeded understanding of the complexity of his work. The dismissal of the theoretical relevance of Conrad's comments about his work has frustrated the kind of discussion by which other modernist writers have gained considerably. Henry James, Virginia Woolf and James Joyce all introduced critical terms which have shaped the very notion of the modern novel.[2] Their reflections on their craft have provided ever new contexts for the rereading of their novels because their speculations tally with the theoretical assumptions they themselves helped to establish. Joyce, in particular, understood clearly that the "*ad hoc*

genre" he created entailed "an *ad hoc* critical tradition." With that
understanding in mind, he enlisted Valery Larbaud's aid in putting
"the phrase 'interior monologue' into circulation, and many
sequences cleared up when the readers knew that was what to call
them. He also urged Eliot to circulate a phrase coined in conversation, 'two plane,' but Eliot never got around to it."[3] The reading
pattern thus given currency has proved to be intellectually
stimulating because it has made possible a conversation in which
critics and their subjects share the same language. But when, as in
Conrad's case, the ideas the author suggests for interpreting his
novels are "honor" and "fidelity" – hardly the stuff of current
fashion – his statements of literary intention have not come to be
valued as contributing to critical discussion of the modern novel.

Conrad, like Joyce, recognized the important assistance a critic
can provide for the shaping of an appropriate response to the
artist's work. In 1923, while Richard Curle was preparing a review
of the Uniform Edition of his works for *The Times Literary Supplement*,
Conrad sent his friend a letter in which he "suggests" what he
would like to read in an article on himself. He is worried about
"how the public mind fastens on externals";[4] and, to counteract
"the danger of precise classification, either in the realm of exotism
or of the sea" (*LL* II, 320), he wishes to point out what is peculiar
to his work. In an offhand manner, he proposes as an opening for
the article some "general observation on authors and their
material, how they transform it from particular to general, and
appeal to universal emotions by the temperamental handling of
personal experience. You might also say that not everybody can do
that" (*LL* II, 321). Conrad is vindicating here the originality of his
literary achievement, by indicating in this "appeal" the personal
form of expression which he has worked to develop throughout his
career as artist: he never separated the moral implications of the
commitment to memory which underlies his "handling of personal
experience" from his aesthetic concern about the effectiveness of a
medium aimed at touching "universal emotions." But this last
effort to make explicit his literary intention did not meet with
success. Curle certainly was not an appropriate mouthpiece for
such a rejection of biographical criticism, as Conrad's barely
camouflaged displeasure at his friend's unperceptive reviews makes
plain enough. But, even if Curle had been a Valery Larbaud and
had served as a more effective broker for the critical terms sug-

gested, what reception could notions such as "universal emotions" and "temperamental handling" have had among, say, the Bloomsbury coterie or among the Imagist poets? Obviously, Conrad does not use, here or in any other piece, a readily identifiable theoretical language. And this is the main reason why his ideas about fiction have not attracted much critical interest.

Given the critics' lack of interest in the ideas Conrad articulates in his fictional and non-fictional writings, the recent marked decline in the number of scholarly works devoted to him comes as no surprise. A statistical analysis of this decline brings David Leon Higdon to consider the possibility that "Conrad simply no longer [occupies] the central position in modernism we once believed."[5] Or is it that "modernism" is not as comprehensive a term as "we once believed," leaving Conradian criticism to find its own way to the recognition of Conrad's originality?

Samuel Hynes' "Conrad and Ford: Two Rye Revolutionists"[6] is emblematic of the problems that Conrad's formulation of his convictions raises for an historian of ideas; and of why, as a consequence, the writer is made to seem like a lightweight in comparison with authors such as Henry James. Hynes, as the author of a well-known scholarly work about the intellectual environment Conrad lived in, *The Edwardian Turn of Mind*,[7] is well qualified to judge the value of Conrad's position in a cultural context. The minatory conclusion he draws regarding the value of Conrad's thought is therefore particularly damaging: "though Conrad was an emotionally complex man, he was intellectually simple. His aesthetic principles, like his philosophical principles, were few and plain: a half-page of note paper would contain all the ideas he had" (49). By contrast, Hynes reckons that a theoretical conception of the novel is "illuminated" by the Jamesian notion of art as pure "artifact, the unique creation of the considering mind" (51). Conrad is incapable of such theorizing, because, for him, "art was subject to the same pressures and uncertainties as life, and was to be lived in the same way. Consequently his thoughts about fiction are thoughts about life – interesting for what they reveal about Conrad's mind at work, but not generally illuminating of the novel as a genre" (51). Hynes' distinction between "thoughts about life," significant only as biographical information, and ideas, which have theoretical value only if expressed according to an already recognized system, suggests an extremely mechanical conception of the novel. New insights and a new language resulting from changes in the novel genre, deriving from its interacting with the "pressures and uncertainties of life," seem not to have theoretical status.

The theoretical assumption underlying Hynes' approach becomes evident when he tries to come to terms with Conrad's particular form of expression. While the critic finds that the "forms of Conrad's novels are . . . difficult and obscure by intention," he defends such an intention even against James' famous stricture against *Chance*: "Conrad had set out to render experience as he perceived it, with all the limitations and difficulties of perception built into it." Hynes, then, recognizes it was no accident that Conrad built that limit of perception which characterizes stream of consciousness novels and much of twentieth-century poetry into his narrative forms. But that recognition does not alter his assumption, since, for him, "the central point about Conrad as a thinker-about-fiction [is] that his forms emerged from his vision of things, and not from theories" (51). By setting in opposition theories and "vision of things," Hynes effectively diminishes the value of his own insights. As an historian of ideas, he does not allow space for critical ideas which have no direct and obvious reference to established philosophical or aesthetic tradition. He elects to use Henry James' literary criticism as a crystal-like "lens" (49), and this despite the fact that the American writer's prefaces have led only to an impossible standard for the evaluation of novels.[8] What Hynes misses is the opportunity to interpret the theoretical implications which Conrad's representation of his "vision of things" has for the idea of the novel.

Hynes, at least, does address Conrad's ideas, if only to dismiss them as theoretically irrelevant. Other critics, more often than not, emphasize the apparent contradictions and inconsistencies in Conrad's comments on his work to justify their reluctance to engage the ideas he set out in his non-fictional writings. The gradual dissociation of contemporary critical expectations from the traces of the author's living mind at work in Conrad's tales originates with the tendency to distinguish the value of these tales from the ideas at work in them. However, the record of the attempts made in the past to separate Conrad's intellectual powers from his worth as a novelist suggests that his critics' rejection of his ideas springs from a deeply entrenched resistance to the novels themselves.

E. M. Forster's scathing review, in 1921, of *Notes on Life and*

Letters, the only collection of essays Conrad published during his lifetime, foreshadows later critiques of Conrad's "philosophy": "These essays," Forster writes, "do suggest that he is misty in the middle as well as at the edges, that the secret casket of his genius contains a vapour rather than a jewel."[9] The wide range of the responses these remarks have invited – from laudatory confirmations to disdainful rejections of his "infamous evaluation"[10] – suggests that Forster has touched on something vital in the effect which Conrad's fiction has on the reader. Forster, in fact, is playing on the disquieting effect produced by much of Conrad's work in order to attack his critical language. And, rather than addressing what Conrad actually says, he offers with this rationalization an easy way out from the issues raised. A "heart of darkness" does not exist: Conrad simply does not know what he is talking about.

The sentence which follows the remark regarding mistiness confirms that Forster's response to Conrad's ideas is influenced by his reading of the latter's fiction. Conrad, it would seem, does not have a creed, only "opinions, and the right to throw them overboard when facts make them look absurd. Opinions held under the semblance of eternity, girt with the sea, crowned with the stars, and therefore easily mistaken for a creed."[11] The language Conrad uses to express his ideas so fits the seaman persona projected in the works which Forster privileges that all possible difficulties in interpreting that language can be easily resolved by referring to the author's intellectual simplicity.

When, in 1948, F. R. Leavis gave a decisive impulse to Conrad's re-evaluation with *The Great Tradition*, Forster's assessment became useful for the screening of what was worth saving in the writer's work. Leavis' attitude is basically censorious, prompted as it is by his conviction that Conrad's obscurity is "a disconcerting weakness or vice" rather than "something simply and obviously deplorable."[12] He actually goes so far as to set the "good Conrad" (218) against the bad: the novels written between 1902 and 1915, "Typhoon" and *The Shadow Line* have virtue, the other works none.

Leavis objects in the first place to Conrad's use of Marlow to articulate his personal commentary in the fiction, which he sees as spoiling the concreteness of the impressionistic account. The workings of Conrad's rhetoric are ignored, and the possibility of a connection between the passages left unanalyzed and the ones deemed fit for critical evaluation is left unconsidered. Leavis uses Forster to dismiss Conrad's indication of a further meaning beyond a physically concrete representation of events in "Heart of Darkness": Conrad, he considers, "is intent on making a virtue out of not knowing what he means" (207). And again, like Forster, Leavis rests comfortably on the assumption that Conrad "was in some respects a simple soul" (209), without suspecting that the privatives in "Heart of Darkness" are an indication of the theoretical problems raised by a "realistic" rendition of a subjective experience.

The difference between Forster and Leavis is that the latter applies the former's categories to Conrad's fiction rather than to his essays. Thus, Forster's characterization of Conrad's "philosophy" evolves into, as it helps produce, a critique of what is worth reading in the writer's canon. Conrad's "genius," which, according to Leavis, "was a unique and happy union of seaman and writer" (217), is to be found in his straightforward, concrete rendition of physical reality. But Conrad, it is clear, ought not to dabble with more weighty matters. Leavis and other critics predisposed to "realism" censor those portions of the texts which do not meet the moral or aesthetic standards they have set up for the simple seaman turned writer. In the Marlow tales, however, the author's probing of the problematic aspects of his writing is the source of the text's ambiguities. To dismiss these ambiguities such critics juxtapose Conrad's vigorous, seaman-like prose to its vague and obscure *doppelgänger*, and thus refuse to interpret Marlow's commentary.

Leavis' "re-evaluation" was followed, in 1952, by Douglas Hewitt's "reassessment." The critic set out to establish the centrality of the texts themselves in opposition to symbolic interpretations, and his study is certainly one of the most successful attempts to synthesize the symbolic and literal meanings of Conrad's tales. Hewitt, like Leavis, feels that it is necessary to separate the good from the bad Conrad. However, he is more concerned with the unreliability of the artist's autocriticism than with expunging portions of single texts. As he writes in *Conrad: A Reassessment*, his study "grew very largely from reflection on the marked inferiority of most of Conrad's later works to his earlier ones and on the unhelpfulness of his own comments in prefaces and letters."[13] The decline in intellectual and creative power that he finds in Conrad's works is simply a more comprehensive application of Forster's and Leavis' approach.

Later, in the preface to the 1975 edition, Hewitt explains why he does not "want to disclaim" his "share of paternity" of the "Achievement-and-Decline school of Conrad criticism." Back in 1952 it had seemed important to point out Conrad's decline in the second half of his career as writer so as to "emphasise the nature of his achievement"; and still today, "to contrast the good and the bad remains a useful way of defining the nature of the good."[14] Hewitt's repeated emphasis on the positive side of his achievement-and-decline hypothesis tacitly acknowledges that it has been used to undermine the integrity and intelligence of Conrad's works. But he does not seem to realize why his own work has given place to a negative perception of Conrad himself. In fact, as a justification of his "reassessment," he writes in the same 1975 preface that he had concentrated on "the possible reasons" for the decline only because "Conrad was often misunderstood . . . he often appeared to misunderstand in retrospect what was valuable in his own work, and . . . it was necessary, therefore, to free our view of him both from many of his own comments and also from inferior works."[15] Unfortunately, later critics used the achievement-and-decline theory without Hewitt's respect toward the author, giving a psychological interpretation of Conrad's comments: the author was dissembling, covering up the decline of his creativity, when, in later years, he tried to explain his literary intention.[16] Hewitt wanted to root in "the literal world" the "symbolic and metaphorical effects" of Conrad's texts, in opposition to "the strange logic of archetypes"[17] at work in so many Freudian and Jungian interpretations. Ironically, however, the achievement-and-decline theory provided common ground for "realist" critics and the symbolist critics Hewitt was reacting against: a shared disregard for the conscious portion of Conrad's fictional language.

Critics who have traced the emergence of unconscious material in the imaginative process have made a great contribution to the understanding of Conrad's works. The best Freudian work on Conrad, Bernard C. Meyer's *Joseph Conrad: A Psychoanalytic Biography* (1967),[18] recommends itself by the consistency of its logical argument even for readers who do not share its theoretical postulates. Freudian criticism working on a "clinical" notion of subconsciousness defines for itself the limits beyond which a symbolic interpretation based on an assumed model of mental processes should not go. It is worth remembering, though, that, according to the Freudian model, the unconscious material does not emerge directly from a dream, but from the patient's rendering of that dream in the waking state.[19] It is the patient's interpretation of his dream – his associating – that allows the translation of dream images into words. If so, it is not the individuation of a certain primordial image that leads to a "preconscious" intention on the writer's side. The emergence of material from the author's subconsciousness is traceable in the literal surface of a text, which is created by the interplay between unconscious material and the interpretation of that material in its given rhetorical shape.[20]

When, as in many symbolic and archetypal readings, the interconnection between conscious and unconscious production is utterly uprooted from its linguistic representation, abstract notions are substituted for linguistic processes as the source of literary creation. Once a critic argues, for example, the possibility that "the primal plot may operate in a work of art not only without the artist's conscious knowledge but almost against his will,"[21] he is freed from any obligation to demonstrate in terms of the text itself the difference between conscious and unconscious portions of the fictional language. It is because most commentators have felt that their readings did not have to be held to Conrad's own remarks that the concerns voiced by the authorial strain in the texts have not raised any doubts as to the validity of so many a priori assumptions.

Critics attentive to the theoretical implications of their own imaginative responses to the tales have been compelled to acknowledge the difficulty of reconciling universal categories with Conrad's texts. The classic formulation of the dilemma which the personal authorial strain poses for a critic can be found in the first lines of Albert J. Guerard's *Conrad the Novelist* (1958):

The purest criticism attends only to the text, which it conceives as floating in a timeless vacuum: a text and meaning immutable, created by no flesh-and-blood writer and without flesh-and-blood readers in mind. This book cannot hope to achieve such purity. For Joseph Conrad was one of the most subjective and most personal of English novelists.[22]

The same tension between theoretical purity and fidelity to the actual reading experience is apparent in Ian Watt's *Conrad in the Nineteenth Century* (1979). Watt recognizes in his preface the "difficulties and dangers of biographical criticism." But, he argues, "the justification for its use in the present case is that although Conrad was not a directly autobiographical writer, his fictional world is an intensely personal one."[23] Neither Watt nor Guerard, though, relies on biographical criticism to interpret Conrad's tales. If they launch their studies by acknowledging the personal strain resonant in Conrad's fiction, it is because neither attempts to explain away on theoretical grounds the effect peculiar to his texts. Rather, they adapt their critical assumptions to the task of interpreting the living tension that the author has imprinted on his fiction.

A critic participates in the creation of a text's meaning only by reacting to the textual language, even though by so doing he or she historicizes that purely verbal structure, referring it to the literary conventions and critical expectations of a new community of readers. But if the critic's reading counteracts the presence of the living mind at work in the original text, by opposing to the effect of this presence a critical language referable first of all to his or her own preconceptions, criticism becomes a vain contest over a dead body of words.[24] This is arguably what has happened in Conradian studies. Important questions have remained unanswered, even unasked, because commentators have been perhaps too daunted by the "intentional fallacy" to come to terms with what is particular to Conrad's art: the author's presence in the text, active both as a voice and as a conscious manipulator of different kinds of discourses.

An awareness of the particular quality of Conrad's critical language is necessary if his critics are more fully to engage his ideas and assess critically that sense of moral seriousness which his personal voice evokes.[25] Perhaps Virginia Woolf gets as close as possible to explaining her response to this voice when she writes that, in Conrad's prose, "the beauty of surface has always a fibre of morality within."[26] Her spatial metaphor makes plain why it is so problematic to transform this response into a critical evaluation. Since the "fibre of morality" lies somewhere beyond the reader's analytical power, and its effect can be evaluated only in aesthetic terms, these same moral values would seem beyond the reach of literary criticism. A critical language which can synthesize the "fibre" within with the "beauty" on the surface would seem not to exist.

However, Conrad did in fact attempt to articulate such a

language. Woolf's insight does not lead to a critical evaluation of his fictional language because it distinguishes the reader's moral response from the aesthetic. Conrad's narrative and linguistic choices, instead, were designed to reach the source of an emotional response the existence of which was, for him, a moral postulate. This approach is reflected in the form he adopted to discuss his literary purpose: a synthesis of the moral and aesthetic aspects of his view of fiction through a metaphorical mode of expression. This book is intended to uncover and engage the theoretical implications of this metaphorical discourse by linking the expression of Conrad's own convictions with the appeal he makes to the readers in his tales.

The distinction often made between the value of Conrad's novels and the significance of the ideas at work in them is based on notions of theory and writing which do not take into account Conrad's own approach. Conrad's literary theory is, first and foremost, the expression of an author's interpretation of his own writing. It is in the heat of creation that he finds answers to theoretical issues, only to go on subsequently to test them in different forms and verbal structures.[27] The frame narrative structure, his authorial commentaries or, in general, the "personal" presence he projects through his rhetorical statements, all set in the foreground those segments of the fictional language in which he articulates his critical discourse.[28] In particular, in the works which immediately concern the present study, Conrad builds an intellectual drama into the fictional language of his tales, and uses his authorial strain to direct the reader's attention toward the theoretical implications of this drama. The very effect he was aiming at in these works was based on a critical discussion designed to involve the reader.

Conrad's statements about his art are largely glosses on discoveries he made about his medium as he tried to create an effect which would prompt in his readers an instinctive recognition of a common set of values. Though "there can be no fellowship with a great multitude whose voice is a shout," he once wrote, "every mute individual of it can and does make his appeal straight to a heart aware of our common fate."[29] The fact that, as Zdzisław Najder notes, Conrad "seems to be a sort of self-translating author: a writer who conveys the experiences and conventions of one culture in the language of another"[30] makes this recognition particularly problematic. The convictions he tried to remain faithful to may very well have been untimely and difficult to translate. However, the lucidity with which Conrad concentrated on the language and structure of his fiction, so as to prompt their recognition in his readers, invites more attentive study of his efforts. Conrad anticipated Marshall McLuhan's insight into the essentially rhetorical quality of literary works.[31] He consciously devised fictional worlds aimed at establishing some line of communication with his readers. This is why he concerned himself, first of all, with the specific means of giving universal effectiveness to the language of fiction. There are depths of meaning beneath the "appeal to universal emotions" (*LL* II, 321) and the other, allegedly naive, critical terms Curle was invited to introduce in Conradian criticism. That depth is lost if commentators do not set these terms within the frame of the unity and dynamic interplay of Conrad's fictional with his non-fictional writings.

Fiction allowed Conrad to express his concerns in terms which made them significant in relation to everyday life. Conrad's letters and essays bear witness as to how intensely he participated in the political and cultural discussion of his time. But when it came to setting down his most deeply felt convictions, he strove after a synthesis of abstract principles and life experience. Consequently, he did not separate the theoretical issues raised by writing from the language he employed to tell stories about living and suffering men and women. Understandably, then, the method of the historian of ideas to describe Conrad's participation in the literary circles or currents of his time is not useful for a reading of Conrad's critical discourse. The difference, rather than contiguity, between Conrad and the theoretical language of his contemporaries constitutes the frame of reference which gives cogency to the words he uses as critical terms.

The two arguments scholarship has used generally to dismiss the value of Conrad's comments on his art – their theoretical irrelevance[32] and their unreliability for an interpretation of his fiction[33] – are based on a reluctance to interpret these comments. Two major factors have contributed to this attitude. On the one hand, there is the search to discover aesthetic concerns independent of a "personal" point of view, a search which is inevitably frustrated by Conrad's synthesizing of aesthetic and moral concerns; on the other hand, there is the fact that his comments constantly emphasize the continuity in his production, an affirmation which is contradicted, apparently, by the evolution of his art. When, for example, he asserts in 1919 that his "convictions in the main remain the same"[34] as in the preface to *The Nigger of the "Narcissus,"* the first impulse is to conclude that these "convictions" did not have much influence on his writing. Otherwise, why should *The Arrow of Gold* (1919) be so different from the 1897 deep-sea tale? Nor do Conrad's remarks prove to be much more illuminating on the subject of the evolution of his art. An apparent inconsistency seems to underlie the claim he made in 1903 (to J. B. Pinker, August 22) that *Nostromo* "is more of a novel pure and simple than anything I've done since Almayer's Folly" (*CL* III, 55). What does "pure" mean? What do *Almayer's Folly* and *Nostromo* have in common with each other but not with *Lord Jim*? The articulation of a critical discourse common to both Conrad's tales and his non-fictional writings can help answer these and other questions raised by Conrad's comments. It makes possible an interpretation of these comments which simultaneously takes into account Conrad's vindication of the continuity of his convictions and his transformation of subjects and narrative forms.

Conrad's comments, in the preface to *The Shorter Tales of Joseph Conrad* (1924), on the illusions which grounded his early works help define the nature of these convictions. Here, Conrad sets out to provide his American readers with a key to his shorter fiction, but he feels he has to return to the early years, "when I launched my first paper boats in the days of my literary childhood." Forgiveness is due to this "grandiloquent image," as a sign of indulgence toward "the lofty ambitions of well-meaning beginners." "Much time has passed, since," he writes,

and I can assure my readers that I have never felt more humble than I do to-day while I sit tracing these words, and that I see now, more clearly than ever before, that indeed those were but paper boats, freighted with a grown-up child's dreams and launched innocently upon that terrible sea that, unlike the honest salt water of my early life, knows no hope of changing horizons but lies within the circle of an Eternal Shadow. (*LE*, 142–143)

Is Conrad being carried away by his highfalutin tone and passion for sea metaphors, or has the revisitation of his first tales led to a moment of truth? For the achievement-and-decline critic, the question can be easily dismissed: since Conrad wrote the preface in

1924, it is just another sign of "the deterioration of his art."[35] And yet a certain momentousness in Conrad's tone, in the description of himself "tracing these words," calls out for a greater attention to his use of these apparently hackneyed images. He is not being careless in their handling. He is organizing them according to that figurative alliance of writing and sailing used to vindicate the continuity of his life in *A Personal Record*. The artistic ideal which impelled his first works was that fiction could bring a shift in the horizon of a reader's everyday life, by suggesting a world of possibilities alternative to actuality. In editing his earlier tales, however, the writer finds that he can see, with self-revelatory lucidity, that this was but a dream.

Conrad's artistic self-awareness, as expressed in his 1924 comments, offers a new context for the evolution of his art and provides a perspective on the ideas he articulates in his fictional and non-fictional writings.[36] This book argues that the writer's "dream" was that ideal standard of craftsmanship which he first set out in the preface to *The Nigger*. By using in the preface two parallel discourses to articulate the moral and aesthetic aspects of this "dream," he established the rhetorical pattern which underlies those clusters of words and themes – of which the writing/sailing metaphor is the most important – common to his essays, letters and Author's Notes. The examination of this continuing discourse in Chapter 1 concentrates on the five major critical terms which Conrad uses to synthesize the aesthetic and moral implications of his artistic intention: the tropes of WORK, IDEALISM, FIDELITY, EFFECT and PRECISION. Other equally important critical terms introduced by Conrad in the preface – such as "solidarity" or "temperament" – are given less attention precisely because they are not used to express figuratively the author's aesthetic concerns. The continuity of these tropes shows that Conrad was still reacting imaginatively to his earlier convictions in his later years, still elaborating on the tropes running through his critical discourse.[37]

Following the 1897 preface to *The Nigger*, the writer's "dream" was carried out, tested, and eventually redefined in "Heart of Darkness" and *Lord Jim*, his "paper boats." Chapter 2 analyzes the impact that Conrad's commitment to authorship had on his writing, by clarifying how the writer "freighted" his "paper boats" with formal experimentations, authorial self-questioning and figurative language. The readings of *The Nigger*, "Karain" and

"Youth" – the tales he was working on before, during and shortly after he wrote the 1897 preface – trace the origin and first modifications of the strategies which allowed him to articulate his artistic ideal in the critical discourse of "Heart of Darkness" and *Lord Jim.*

This ideal centered on the search for a language which would allow the writer, by its "magic suggestiveness" (*NoN*, ix), to express that universal content deposited in the subjectivity of personal experiences. These readings argue, however, that the author had started experimenting with the structure of his narratives before he tried to put into practice the ideal of a universally effective language. Thus, Conrad's later use of Marlow to draw the reader's attention to the workings of his ideal prose is actually a development of the rhetorical skills he acquired while writing *The Nigger.*

Marlow, the imaginative sea captain aware of the dangers lurking below the surface of the sea, enabled Conrad to construct around the writing/sailing metaphor a personal novel form. The internal narrator's preoccupation with the inexpressible side of experience dramatizes the author's groping for words, his quest for a poetically effective prose. However, only after Marlow's first appearance in "Youth," the narrative frame becomes a rhetorical structure which allows the author to articulate a meta-narrative commentary on the theoretical issues being tested in his writing. The intellectual drama built into the fictional language of "Heart of Darkness" and *Lord Jim* sets Marlow's function in the context of Conrad's expectations of how a critical language is to act on readers. Marlow is not a character who voices the author's convictions, but a specialization of the frame technique for a particular purpose. His personality matters only in so far as it gives a moral texture to the world of objective reality, by transforming visual impressions into individual memory. In trying to remain faithful to his memory, Marlow's moral concerns become a questioning of the very possibility of communicating his past experiences. Conrad can thus make explicit the theoretical dimension of his own struggle to transform his own memories into visual impressions, through his internal narrator's addresses to his audience.

Chapter 3 examines the writer's use of the narrative frame in "Heart of Darkness" as a means to probe the audience's resistance to the disquieting revelations which the tale brings to the surface.

Marlow's commentary in the African story draws a line between the sayable and the unsayable, thus enabling Conrad to distinguish the *story* of the events from the *tale* of the effect those events had on the narrator. The interplay of these two levels of language creates a suggestively impressionistic language.

Chapter 4 offers an analysis of how Conrad forces a sense of the reality of Jim's predicament on his readers through Marlow's interpretation of the young man's figurative language. This interpretation is aimed at translating the expression of a subjective experience into a statement of its universality. However, the author's concern in *Lord Jim* with the narrative structure's potentialities for bridging the communication gap with his readers suggests an alternative to the strategy based on a linguistic effect. It will be in the shift between Marlow's inquiry into the *Patna* case and the Patusan romance that a reliance on the effectiveness of particular narrative structures comes to supersede the model for an artistic fiction envisaged in the preface to *The Nigger*.

Chapter 5 argues that, by presenting Marlow's sending of Jim to Patusan as the outcome of his interpretation of the young man's case, Conrad is suggesting that only a fictional world can create that "suspension of disbelief" which makes a fictional character exist in the eyes of the readers. As the end of the novel discloses, the Patusan fiction-within-the-fiction is at one and the same time the result of Marlow's interpretation of Jim's case and his greatest failure. Marlow's commentary is an extra-fictional linguistic segment which hinders the "existence" of a fictional world. Marlow's written chronicle signals Conrad's relinquishing of an involved narrator voicing the author's reflection on fiction and foretells the change in settings and narrative techniques after *Lord Jim*.

In the "Postscript" the link between the *Patna*/Patusan shift and the change after *Lord Jim* opens a range of possibilities for interpreting Conrad's later fiction in the light of the critical discourse and of the "dream" freighting his "paper boats." By putting Marlow temporarily aside, Conrad did not capitulate to more conventional novel forms. Rather, it was the author's ongoing quest for an original novel form that brought about a re-adjustment in the balance between form and language conceived in the initial formulation of his artistic ideal. He had to transform his narrative forms to remain faithful to his convictions.

Once Conrad relinquished the metaphorical possibilities offered by his narrator, he came to rely on the distortions created by the narrative structure for the referentiality of his fictional worlds. The result was a series of experiments in genre which replaced Conrad's earlier experiments with language. From *Nostromo* on, through *The Secret Agent*, *Under Western Eyes* and *Chance*, he applied the narrative techniques elaborated in his "paper boats" to dislocate the meaning of stories which ostensibly respected sub-generic contexts. This book does not include the later novels because Conrad is not finding there new terms to express his literary theory, as is the case with "Heart of Darkness" and *Lord Jim*. However, the critical discourse underlying these later novels mainly reflects that concern with EFFECT which – as Chapter 1 argues – becomes of overriding importance after the early Marlow tales.

The evolution thus outlined shows that out of a commitment to untimely convictions and an alien inheritance Conrad shaped a vision and a means of communication at once original and innovative. His mastery of his craft finally enabled him to create worlds in which the reality of his convictions could be vindicated. With an awareness of the metaphorical quality of the writer's critical language and of the implications of his "dream," further study on the critical discourse of his later tales may very well show that his effort to carry out that solidarity which underlay his sense of craftsmanship ever since he wrote the preface to *The Nigger* can help chart a path connecting the Victorians with contemporary fiction.

CHAPTER I

The critical discourse: five tropes

Continuity in thought was responsible for the evolution of Conrad's art. Whenever he addressed the principles underlying his craft, he invariably returned to the formed convictions he carried into literary life. It was this constant *nostos* that inspired his search for more effective novel forms. Therefore, the key to understanding his artistic evolution lies in the dynamic process set in motion by his strenuous efforts to remain faithful to his personal convictions. As Conrad writes to Barrett H. Clark (May 4, 1918),

I am a man of formed character. Certain conclusions remain immovably fixed in my mind, but I am no slave to prejudices and formulas, and I shall never be. My attitude to subjects and expressions, the angles of vision, my methods of composition will, within limits, be always changing.

His "writing life . . . has been a time of evolution" (*LL* II, 204). It is precisely in Conrad's willingness to change subjects and methods that he demonstrated his fidelity to his convictions. The artistic intention which guided Conrad's artistic evolution must be understood, not by interpreting these convictions against a set of "prejudices and formulas," but by uncovering, in his fiction, his effort to bring them to bear on the narrative and stylistic choices involved in the creative process. The articulation of a critical discourse common to both Conrad's tales and his non-fictional writings allows an interpretation of his theoretical statements which simultaneously takes into account Conrad's vindication of the continuity of his convictions and his transformation of subjects and narrative forms.

The thematic and chronological reading of Conrad's non-fictional writings in this chapter considers the writer's own comments on his art in the light of the convictions that direct his quest for ever more effective narrative forms. The close reading of the preface to *The Nigger* and the examination of the five tropes which synthesize his central concerns reveal that Conrad was still reacting imaginatively to his earlier convictions in his later years, still elaborating on the tropes running through his critical discourse. Conrad uses WORK to reassert his primary moral memento: the writer's craft is not different from the everyday activities of his fellow human beings. IDEALISM is associated for the most part with the author's probing of fiction's paradoxical nature: the more illusionary it is, the more effective it will be. In FIDELITY Conrad articulates the moral implications of his craftsmanship, by connecting the continuity of his writing with his commitment to memory. The fourth trope, EFFECT, is the central concern of that sense of craftsmanship which prompted Conrad ever to search for new ways to reach out to his audience. PRECISION, like EFFECT, is used more frequently in the later writings, to express the writer's awareness of the originality of the techniques he had learned to master after his experimentations in his "paper boats."

THE PREFACE TO *THE NIGGER OF THE "NARCISSUS"*

In recent years, several commentators have subjected the preface to a highly sophisticated scrutiny to illuminate the intellectual sources of Conrad's ideas. By setting the preface in the perspective of the cultural conversation of the later nineteenth century, they have investigated Conrad's use of terms derived from his contemporaries. Frederick Karl, Ian Watt and others have made a number of possible contexts available for words such as "impressionism" and "temperament," and concepts such as "Art for Art's sake."[1] These studies attempt to bridge the gap separating Conrad from the critical expectations of the present times, but at the price, ultimately, of belittling the personal appeal which runs through the 1897 preface.

Too exclusive a concentration on the literary and philosophical influences converging on Conrad at the time he became a writer leads to a juxtaposition of the reference assigned to a particular word with the context in the preface's literal surface. As a result, hypothetical frame references become objective data more significant than the text itself. It is because of this juxtaposition that a critic can rely on the fact that "even so shrewd a critic as Ian Watt finds Conrad's use of [solidarity] equivocal," to contend that "Conrad did not know what he was talking about in the preface."[2]

If this last remark appears a rather extreme case of misreading the way in which Conrad's argument actually shapes the preface's text, it is not far removed from the mainstream view of Conrad's (un)reliability as a theorist. The very recognition of the preface's importance carries the inevitable undertone that Conrad's effort to express his ideas there is an exception. In no other essay, article or Author's Note, according to most commentators, does Conrad articulate his thought in terms which can be connected with the formulation of 1897. Frederick Karl, in his influential "Joseph Conrad's Literary Theory" (1960), uses the achievement-and-decline theory to explain why he finds "an almost total lack of that 'aesthetic feel' running through the Preface to *The Nigger*" in the 1919–1920 Author's Notes.[3] Samuel Hynes, in 1965, is even more drastic in evaluating the central position of the preface in Conrad's canon: "The *Nigger* Preface contains Conrad's whole aesthetic: he wrote it very early in his career, but he never evolved beyond its propositions."[4] In 1974, Ian Watt, drawing sustenance from Karl and Hynes, writes that the preface remains "by default the most reliable" statement of Conrad's literary intention.[5] These critics approach the preface with the assumption that Conrad was incapable of articulating an original point of view on fiction; or, as Karl phrases it, with Conrad's own realization that "he lacked the type of mind required for sustained literary criticism."[6] They are willing to take into consideration Conrad's reflections in the preface on an intellectual level, because there the writer uses a language which is ascribable to his contemporary literary theory. But when, in later writings, Conrad expresses his views as thinker-about-fiction in a more personal language, the same critics lose any interest in his ideas.

Karl draws out the inference built into the assumptions he is working from when he writes that the preface is a "statement of Conrad's bearing in relationship to various late-nineteenth century critical traditions," but that "we cannot view it as intrinsic to the growth of Conrad's literary imagination in the crucial period from 1899 to 1904."[7] Is Conrad's "literary imagination" a faculty beyond his rational control, a no man's land over which the critic exercises absolute power, or is the novelist aware of the theoretical dimension of his transformation of imaginative stimuli into literary forms? The preface, far from being a mere rehearsal of received ideas, is Conrad's most explicit attempt to clarify the moral and aesthetic implications of his creative process. Not only is the piece "intrinsic to the growth of Conrad's literary imagination": it is the author's statement of his control over the evolution of his art in the works he wrote near the turn of the century.

The creative process involved for Conrad a constant questioning of the moral and aesthetic principles underlying the writer's craft. That he could make plain the interrelation between these two aspects in an interlocking discourse only proved that it was possible to convey his personal view. Under the influence of his definitive commitment to authorship following the completion of *The Nigger*, Conrad tried to express in the preface his newly found awareness of the potentialities of fiction. In so doing, he was working on an abstract notion of the relationship he could establish between his audience's sensibility and the untimely values at the heart of his convictions. It is in the parallel development of a moral and an aesthetic discourse in the preface's rhetorical structure that Conrad shapes his particular formulation of the artist's task. He will then use the strategy he devised to enunciate his artistic intention to adapt the novel form to the communication of his personal appeal. The distortions of the fictional language's linearity in the early Marlow tales are the result of Conrad's articulation of his moral and aesthetic concerns in a fictional context. The parallel discourse of the 1897 preface set the pattern for interweaving rhetorical commentaries and fictional language. The combination of discourses by which the author answers the basic questions concerning his art – the artistry of the novel and the artist's social responsibility – underlies the critical discourse of both his fictional and nonfictional writings.

In the first line of the preface, Conrad acknowledges that an ideal craftsmanship is required to enlarge the potentialities of prose language: "A work that aspires, however humbly, to the condition of art should carry its justification in every line" (*NoN*, vii). This statement answers the question Flaubert had first raised in the nineteenth century: how can a work of prose become, like poetry, an artistic medium? Flaubert's higher standard of craftsmanship for the novel called for a greater concern for the novel's language.[8] This greater awareness revealed fiction's potentialities as an artistic form of expression. It is not surprising, then, that in voicing his commitment to authorship in the 1897 preface Conrad pays allegiance to Flaubert's "ascetic . . . devotion to his art" (*PR*, 3), which had guided his own literary apprenticeship.

What is remarkable, however, is the position of Conrad's statement. By asserting conclusively the aesthetic dimension of Flaubertian craftsmanship at the beginning of his own artistic apology, Conrad is implicitly taking for granted the critical discussion which evolved from the master's teachings. Conrad's reflection on fiction starts from the conclusion reached by those writers and thinkers who connected the novelist's endeavor for a more precise expression and the search of contemporary poets for the aural suggestiveness of the written word. All that follows in the preface is appropriately read as Conrad's definition of the differences between his point of view and that of other writers and thinkers. By introducing for the first time many of the critical terms which will recur in his critical discourse, he is pointing out a new direction for his contemporaries' reflections on fiction.

Following the opening statement on the artistry of the novel, Conrad embarks on a definition of "art itself" – "a single-minded attempt to render the highest kind of justice to the visible universe, by bringing to light the truth, manifold and one, underlying its every aspect" (vii). So obtrusive is this statement, encumbered as it is with unwieldy matters such as "truth" and "visible universe," that most commentators have singled it out as Conrad's notion of art. It is not surprising that David Goldknopf, on reading the opening paragraph of the preface, finds that one's "head bobs beneath the volley of rhetorical words and phrases." Goldknopf feels that the "onerous expectation" raised by this opening definition is inevitably disappointed when "the ground quickly shifts" and all he finds are "repeated statements of faith in visualization, embodied in a hodgepodge of platonic, positivistic, and romantic sentiments."[9] As a matter of fact, Goldknopf misses the intrinsically metaphorical function of Conrad's critical language. To understand how Conrad's language adapts to the critical task in the preface, it is first necessary to examine its underlying rhetorical structure. A close reading foregrounding the dynamic relationship of images, similes and words makes possible a more coherent discussion of Conrad's *ars poetica*. Since the argument of the preface is organized in eleven paragraphs, it is unreasonable to expect a full answer from the first lines. Conrad simply did not write that way.

The organization of his paragraphs and the successive qualification[10] of his critical terms will help interpret the shift which occurs after the first sentence of the preface. Conrad's expansion of the initial discussion of a work's "justification" certainly undermines the first sentence's relevance. At the same time, however, his vindication of the kind of truth that art can achieve introduces the term "appeal": "The artist, then, like the thinker or the scientist, seeks the truth and makes his appeal." Thus, the comparison which follows is between the appeal made by the artist and that made by scientists and philosophers. Through the term "appeal," Conrad alters the line of his argument from an abstract notion of art to the specific condition he tries to achieve in his work. This shift in argument enables him to enunciate his sense of social responsibility as if this were part of his answer to the issue of the artistry of the novel.

Conrad was fully aware of the potential risks of the Art-for-Art's-sake concept.[11] Early symbolist poets such as Baudelaire, Rimbaud and Verlaine did not distinguish between their social position and the kind of poetry they were writing. They accepted their marginality as a result of the artist's dislocation in society.[12] With Mallarmé, this awareness of the freedom granted by the poet's not being tied to an audience evolved into an intentional obscurity.[13] But the social critique implicit in the *symbolistes*' rejection of any social responsibility had lost much of its significance by the time Conrad wrote the preface. Moreover, "*la suggestion*" postulated by Mallarmé and the other *symboliste* writers had never been achieved. Therefore, especially in Britain, where *symbolisme* was understood by its dandy epigones to be a *décadent* aestheticists' movement,[14] the idea of an artistic novel had to be qualified in opposition to elitism and obscurity.[15] In articulating this double rejection, Conrad found the terms for expressing his personal view of fiction.

Conrad explains why his artistic prose should not be obscure by suggesting that the effectiveness of the art form he is striving for is based on the universality of its appeal. He proceeds with the comparison based on the different kinds of appeals: "Impressed by the aspect of the world," scientists and philosophers find the terms of their appeal in ideas and facts (vii). Their appeal is persuasive because they help man adapt to the "visible universe." By contradistinction, the artist "descends within himself" to find the terms of an appeal which is made to "that part of our nature which . . . is necessarily kept out of sight within the more resisting and hard qualities" (viii). He speaks "to our less obvious capacities," and to "that part of our being which is not dependent on wisdom." But whereas the "changing wisdom of successive generations discards ideas, questions facts," his appeal's "effect endures forever." He speaks, in fact, "to the latent feeling of fellowship with all creation – and to the subtle . . . conviction of solidarity that knits together the loneliness of innumerable hearts, to the solidarity . . . in illusions" (viii). The aim of any artistic work is to strike the chords of universal emotions. Ideas or theories of facts can be used against humanity, but this cannot be the case with art: for Conrad a work of art is such only if its effect is universal.

The introduction of "solidarity" brings the first part of the preface to an end.[16] After launching the piece by addressing the aesthetic dimension of his view of fiction, he has set the artist's social responsibility in the foreground. In so doing he has introduced words such as "effect," "solidarity" and "illusions," which will evolve into the key terms of his critical discourse. Now that he has made clear how the "condition of art" he aspires to is different from that notion of the artistic novel upheld by his contemporaries, he can proceed with his work's "justification." With this, he returns to the issues raised in the first sentence.

The truth an artist can render is sufficient justification for Conrad's endeavor. But, as he writes at the end of the fourth paragraph, even though "the motive then, may be held to justify the matter of the work . . . this preface, which is simply an avowal of endeavour, cannot end here – for the avowal is not yet complete" (viii–ix). The moral justification of a novel is not enough to make it universally effective. The novel requires an aesthetic conception to "aspire, however humbly, to the condition of art." Conrad's description of how an ideal craftsmanship can transform fiction into an artistic medium rounds out his "avowal of endeavour."

At the beginning of the fourth paragraph, an echo of the first line sets the initial question in the foreground again: "Fiction – if it at all aspires to be art – appeals to temperament" (ix). This qualification of the opening sentence focuses Conrad's own aesthetics of fiction. Conrad is extremely careful throughout the preface to distinguish fiction from art. Up to this point he has asserted the moral link uniting his writing and the activity of the rest of humanity by outlining a principle for all kinds of "work."[17] But in the fifth paragraph he has to explain in what way the ideal tension guiding his work has a bearing on the practice of writing. When Conrad avers that "the appeal of one temperament to all the other innumerable temperaments" (ix) alone can invest a writer's work with creative power, making his medium as effective as painting or music, he is explaining how the moral and aesthetic aspects of his artistic creed dovetail. However, an understanding of this explanation requires an interpretation of the two key terms he uses: "appeal" and "temperament."

The artist finds the terms for his individual appeal by descending "within himself"; and, as Conrad has already made clear in his discussion of his moral justification, he there discovers what he shares with his fellow men and women. Thus, the "subtle but invincible conviction of solidarity" (viii) *is* an appeal to temperament. In its reformulation in this paragraph, Conrad is explaining how it can be voiced: "Such an appeal [to other temperaments] to be effective must be an impression conveyed through the senses" (ix). The appeal fiction can make, then, requires the presence of a personal strain which filters physical impressions so as to emphasize the subjective side of experience.

In the second half of the same paragraph, Conrad illustrates how "the artistic aim when expressing itself in written words" (ix) makes its appeal. And he does so by rendering the toil necessary for the achievement of an artistic fiction. The novel's "artistic aim," Conrad writes, must "strenuously aspire" to the expressive power of other arts through a "complete, unswerving devotion" and "an unremitting never-discouraged care" (ix). Thus, just as he is about to state his aesthetics of fiction, Conrad reaffirms the bond with the active life of his fellow human beings which he had claimed in the first paragraphs of the preface. Once he has recalled the moral basis of his artistic intention, Conrad proceeds to elucidate the implications for a novelist of his answer to the question implicit in the opening sentence of the preface: how can a novel aspire to the condition of art? How can a work in prose carry, like poetry, "its justification in every line" (vii)? Conrad's answer is clear: through a "care for the shape and ring of sentences" (ix). And the reward for the novelist is nothing less than bringing "to play for an evanescent instant . . . the light of magic suggestiveness . . . over the commonplace surface of words" (ix). By juxtaposing fiction and art throughout the preface, Conrad sets in relief the ideal tension which must guide a novelist in his efforts to bring out the poetic potentialities of prose language. The aim of this quest is the creation of a suggestively impressionistic language, which alone can give universal effectiveness to the novelist's writing.

The famous "to make you *see*" declaration in the paragraph which follows the symbolist manifesto further clarifies how Conrad intends to create this suggestively impressionistic language.[18] At the beginning of the fifth paragraph, Conrad refers back to the "avowal of endeavour" which had launched the discussion of his aesthetic convictions in the fourth paragraph. By bringing together the two underlying themes of the preface, Conrad defines the "care for the shape and ring of sentences" as "that creative task" which is "the only justification for the worker in prose" (ix). Thus, when he adds, a few lines below, that "My task . . . is, by the power of the written word to make you hear, to make you feel – it is, before all, to make you *see*" (x), it is the sentence's position in the overall argument that determines the emphasis Conrad is giving to his avowed task. At the core of Conrad's artistic intention is his reliance on the suggestive power of language. His aim may very well be to make his reader see, but it will be only "by the power of the written word" that he will be able to realize his intention.[19]

Once he elucidates his own aesthetics of fiction, Conrad brings the entirety of the preceding discussion to bear on his definition of the writer's task. In the first paragraph he has described art as "a single-minded attempt to render the highest kind of justice to the visible universe, by bringing to light the truth, manifold and one, underlying its every aspect" (vii). He then writes that the writer will find the terms for his appeal within himself, "if he be deserving and fortunate" (viii). Having found these terms, he will be able to speak to "the conviction of solidarity" (viii). Subsequently, he specifies what he means in the first sentence by "condition of art": fiction must "aspire to the plasticity of sculpture, to the colour of painting, and to the magic suggestiveness of music" (ix). Finally, he has explained how he will make his appeal through the senses, as all art does: through a suggestively impressionistic language.

All these terms recur in the description of his task in paragraph seven. "In a single-minded attempt of that kind," he writes, "if one be deserving and fortunate, one may perchance . . . awaken in the hearts of the beholders that feeling of unavoidable solidarity . . . which binds men to each other and all mankind to the visible world" (x). And even more revealing is how he reformulates the notions of "appeal" and "temperament" in this definition. His task is to hold up a "fragment" rescued "from the remorseless rush of time . . . before all eyes in the light of a sincere mood." It is to "show its vibration, its colour, its form" (just as music, painting and sculpture would do) (x). His task will be to use the universal effectiveness of an artistic prose to transform memory into an appeal made by "one temperament to all the other innumerable temperaments" (ix). In the light of this formulation, his experiments in form and language in the early Marlow tales appear as attempts to put into practice the artistic ideal set forth in the preface.

The definition of his task marks the end of Conrad's aesthetic "justification." In the "coda" he addresses again the moral motivation of his work, as he had done at the beginning of the preface. There is still one point, however, that he is compelled to make before bringing his literary manifesto to an end: "It is evident that he who, rightly or wrongly, holds by the convictions expressed above cannot be faithful to any one of the temporary formulas of his craft" (x). In his own literary theory he attempts to cultivate and maintain the "enduring part" of these formulas, "the truth which each only imperfectly veils" (x). Realism, romanticism and naturalism, nonetheless, will inevitably abandon him "to the stammerings of his conscience and to the outspoken consciousness of the difficulties of his work" (xi). And when that moment comes, he must create his own critical language. Conrad's critical discourse does indeed convey "stammerings" of deeply felt but untimely convictions and an "outspoken" sense of craftsmanship.

Following his rejection of "temporary formulas," the text moves quite abruptly to a bucolic scene in which "we watch the motions of a labourer in a distant field" (xi). Conrad has been extremely careful in interweaving his twofold argument up to this point, but something is wrong, obviously, in the logical transition between these two paragraphs. However, this gap can be explained by recalling that in the original version of the preface there was an entire paragraph between the last statement of Conrad's aesthetic of fiction and the parabolical digression launching the "coda." Edward Garnett convinced Conrad that he had to delete that paragraph, and, as a result, his appeal in the preface is incomplete. The effect which Conrad was striving for in writing the preface can be recovered only by reinserting this omitted passage.

It is not surprising that Conrad chose not to restore the original text in later versions of the preface. Why should he have tested again the effectiveness of an appeal which had failed on his literary mentor, the person he took to be a sympathetic embodiment of the public? The letter which accompanied the preface's manuscript marks the beginning of the piece's negative reception. In this letter (to Edward Garnett; August 24, 1897), Conrad sounds at once anxious and enthusiastic. He wants to know Garnett's opinion about the chances he has of getting the preface printed. He needs Garnett's advice, as he writes, because he himself has "no more judgment of what is fitting in the way of literature than a cow"; "let me hear the decree soon to ease my mind," he adds; "I shall not draw one breath till your Sublime Highness has spoken to the least of his slaves" (*CL* I, 375). Garnett's decree, when it came, must have been quite a blow for Conrad. Garnett, as Ian Watt notes, did "not seem to have been enthusiastic about the Preface."[20] In particular, he objected to one paragraph, which he urged Conrad to take out because he found it was "too apologetic."[21]

Garnett must have been unhesitating in picking out what seemed obtrusive in the text since Conrad, only four days after sending the original draft, writes again to his friend acknowledging the advice to suppress the "apologetic" paragraph. Garnett's reaction was too immediate, too instinctive: in the paragraph he must have found reflected what he disliked in the preface as a whole. As Najder observes, "Garnett, who had his own complexes, did not regard this fragment as a courageous *credo* proclaiming the worth of one's own creation, but as a timid defence; finally Conrad gave up and the fragment was omitted."[22] Before giving up, however, Conrad tried to defend the paragraph he was asked to take out.

In his August 28, 1897, letter (*CL* I, 377–378) Conrad tried to explain why the paragraph is central to his argument. His tone is much more guarded than in the letter he had written four days before. He begins by thanking Garnett for his sympathy and his wisdom, which "surpasses the sagacity of the most venomous serpents." He remarks, then, that "As You may imagine I do not care a fraction of a damn for the passage you have struck out – that is, the personal part." But as a matter of fact he is not unaffected by

Garnett's criticism, for he immediately suggests that "the 8 lines at the end of the par[agraph] struck out conveying the opinion that in 'art alone there is a meaning in endeavour as apart from success' should be worked in somehow." Conrad is trying to strike a deal with Garnett. He cannot reject his advice. How could he defend the value of his theoretical statements by vindicating the relevance of the "personal part" of that statement? In any case, he warns his friend, "whether Your wisdom lets me keep [the eight lines] in or not I tell You plainly – fangs or no fangs – that there is the saving truth – the truth that saves most of us from eternal damnation." But, evidently, Garnett remained unconvinced, and Conrad left "the infamous taint" out of the preface.

The "personal" paragraph (to Garnett, September 27, 1897; CL I, 385) begins with the author asking what his audience will make of the aesthetic program that has grown out of his presentation of a simple sea tale: "It may seem strange if not downright suspicious that so much should be said in introduction to the unimportant tale of the sea which follows."[23] His rejection of all theories of art in the preceding paragraph has wound up the exposition of his artistic aim. He now draws back and queries whether what he has said up to this point "may also appear the height of conceit or folly since every word of the preface may be brought in judgment against the work it is meant to introduce." Actually, the ideas Conrad sets forth in the preface are the outcome of the reflection on the novelist's craft forced on him by the writing of The Nigger. He is dissembling here at the beginning of his "personal par[agraph]" because he is trying to link his aesthetic program to his sea tale. Unfortunately, the two sentences state too strongly the author's doubts, and his rhetorical ruse does not come off. When, in the sentence that follows, he wraps up the devices which supposedly were to launch the transition from the earlier paragraphs, the effect is confusing.

Conrad meets the doubts he has rehearsed himself with an appeal to his audience. Certainly, somebody could extrapolate from the preface a standard of evaluation which is too high for The Nigger. But a preface, as Conrad states, "if anything – is spoken in perfect good faith, as one speaks to friends, and in the hope that the unprovoked confidence shall be treated with scrupulous fairness." What this appeal to his readers' solidarity is leading to becomes immediately clear: "And, after all, everyone desires to be understood; We all with mutual indulgence give way to the pressing need of explaining ourselves." Conrad's chest-baring is so direct that these words seem to have been jotted down on impulse. But this denouement of the anxieties which urged him to write the preface is not a naive outburst of feeling. Conrad had already introduced a personal note when, a few lines above, he suggested that the artist's "conscience" and his "consciousness of the difficulties of his work" alone can guide the writer in his efforts. At this point, after having pointed out that his discussion is relevant to the reading of *The Nigger*, he explains why his own "good faith" *is* the standard for the evaluation of his fiction.

Once Conrad has carried out his transition, by qualifying his theoretical position as a morally committed literary intention, the discussion reaches the core of his "personal" pronouncement: that "saving truth" (*CL* I, 378) which he tried to preserve in the face of Garnett's criticism. After having compared the writer with "the bricklayer" and such jugglers with words as "the politician, the prophet, the fool" (thus hinting at the potential dangers of his profession), Conrad cautions himself against possible objections. "It is true," he writes, "that the disclosure of the aim otherwise than by the effective effort towards it is a confession of weakness." Conrad may be voicing extremely personal concerns in the rarefied atmosphere of literary theory, but he is not a simpleton. If he breaks the conventional distinction between preface and tale, literary criticism and fiction, it is because he wants to make the latter more effective by alerting the reader to the moral tension that he has injected into his work. In art, he adds, "such an avowal is not so fatal as it would be elsewhere. For in art alone of all the enterprises of men there is meaning in endeavor disassociated from success[,] and merit – if any merit there be – is not wholly centered in achievement but may be faintly discerned in the aim." Conrad has projected himself into the preface to say precisely this, to make explicit what his "faintly discerned" aim was in *The Nigger*.

Conrad's "personal" paragraph, then, contains a crucial tactical move in his elucidation of the principles underlying his writing. He divests the ideas he has been exposing up to this point of their hallowed abstractness by explaining which narrative and linguistic choices were dictated by his artistic consciousness. The effect he will try to convey through these choices is the moral frame of reference of artistic formulas which would be meaningless if writing did not constantly test in the artist's conscience the validity of these theories. By projecting himself into the discussion of his artistic ideal of fiction, Conrad is drawing the reader's attention to a particular aspect of the "unimportant tale . . . which follows": the language and narrative structure of the sea tale are the outcome of his effort to shape his work according to his artistic aim. The statement of this aim in the preface, then, can provide the reader with an evaluative standard for the tale.

With Conrad's "personal" paragraph back in its original place, the preface's overall direction becomes clearer. As he approaches the conclusion, the notion of "aim" moves toward the center of his argument. Before the end, however, he must stress that the value of a work of fiction is primarily conferred by the aim which directs the author's "effective effort." Otherwise, writing turns out to be a more or less successful manipulation of words. This is why he is now trying to take his self-justification beyond a purely aesthetic evaluation. There must be a way to share with readers the motivations directing the writer's search for a particular effect. He must find a novel form in which the fiction's effect communicates the writer's aim as well. Once Conrad develops a narrative structure capable of articulating a critical discourse in his tales, he will be in a position to integrate a discussion of his motivations into the "effective effort" sustaining and guiding his narrative and linguistic choices.

Read in the light of the omitted "personal" paragraph, the similitude linking "a labourer in a distant field" with "the workman of art" acquires its full meaning. This parabolical digression is actually the point of departure for Conrad's explanation of the meaning of the whole piece. In the last section of the preface, his moral and aesthetic issues are brought together in the discussion of the "aim of art" (xi). If, as he writes, in watching the labourer's movement we were "told the purpose of his exertions," we would "look with a more real interest at his efforts," and even "bring ourselves to forgive his failure" – if we are "in a brotherly frame of mind." He then refocuses the simile, along with the optical illusion, and he points out that "so it is with the workman of art." In this case, though, the difficulty does not lie in the distance which makes the exertions unintelligible. The problem is that "the aim of art" is "obscured by mists." The purpose of the preface, therefore, is to elucidate this aim, which, "like life itself, is inspiring" and "difficult." And, referring back to the distinction between the artist and scientists and thinkers he had made in the opening of the preface, he warns the reader that this aim cannot be rationally conveyed. "It is not in the clear logic of a triumphant conclusion; it is not in the unveiling of one of those heartless secrets which are called the Laws of Nature" (xi–xii). The aim of the "workman in art," instead, is to appeal to the sense of solidarity which links him to "the hands busy about the work of the earth," by revealing within "the surrounding vision of form and colour . . . a moment of vision, a sigh, a smile" (xii).

WORK

After Conrad found a parallel figurative discourse in the 1897 preface which enabled him to bring together his moral and aesthetic concerns, he used the tropes of WORK, IDEALISM and FIDELITY to enunciate the principles which underlie the belief system he had made out of his different experiences. For Conrad writing fiction *had* to be a work, a craft, just like sailing, if he was to draw inspiration from the continuity of his lives, a condition which alone could allow him to render faithfully his memories.

He directly relates his writing to the active life of men by affirming that writing is an action and that the novelist's craft is in no way superior to other kinds of WORK.[24] The implications that his respect for the everyday occupations of his readers has for Conrad's notion of craft are made clear in "Books" (1905), where he states that "literary creation being only one of the legitimate forms of human activity has no value but on the condition of not excluding the fullest recognition of all the more distinct forms of action" (*NLL*, 7).[25] In "A Glance at Two Books" (1904), instead, he explains why writing is an action by criticizing the novelist who does not have a "clear conception of his craft." "The national English novelist," he writes, "seldom regards his work – the exercise of his Art – as an achievement of active life by which he will produce certain definite effects upon the emotions of his readers . . . He does not go about building up his book with a precise intention and a steady mind" (*LE*, 132). The conviction which separates Conrad's from an elitist conception of art is no less strong than that rejection of a sentimental lack of interest in the formal aspects of writing.

The suggestive potentialities of WORK are revealed when Conrad uses the trope not as an abstraction but to discuss the crafts of his two lives, as a sailor and a writer. When he does so, sailing becomes a metaphor for writing. This metaphor is the central rhetorical pattern of Conrad's critical discourse. And it underlies his use of Marlow to voice his own concerns about writing in "Heart of Darkness" and *Lord Jim*, in which Conrad's own struggles with his medium are ingrained in his narrator's probing the disquieting truths brought to the surface by events undermining the ideal standard of conduct.[26] The writing/sailing discursive configuration also appears in his letters and non-fictional writings. Writing to A. T. Quiller Couch on December 22, 1897, for example, he remarks: "Writing in a solitude almost as great as that of the ship at sea the great living crowd outside is somehow forgotten; just as on a long, long passage the existence of continents peopled by men seems to pass out of the domain of facts" (*CL* I, 430). And in a letter to Angèle Zagòrska, he describes the writer's condition as "cette galère – where we are navigating whilst using pens by way of oars – on an ocean of ink – pour n'arriver nulle part, hélas!" (December 18, 1898; *CL* II, 132). In the preface to *The Shorter Tales of Joseph Conrad*, he casts his revisitation of his first tales, his "paper boats," in an extended nautical metaphor. It is in *A Personal Record* and *The Mirror of the Sea*, however, that the metaphor develops into a sustained figurative structure.

In the "Familiar Preface" to *A Personal Record* (1912) Conrad writes that "these memories put down without any regard for established conventions have not been thrown off without system and purpose" (*PR*, xxi). Commentators have searched *A Personal Record* for confirmation of biographical interpretations of Conrad's fiction; but they have missed both purpose and system.[27] Albert Guerard is exceptional in recognizing that *A Personal Record* "is a true work of art," one of Conrad's "most deliberately constructed books."[28] Jacques Berthoud as well has concentrated on the implications of the text's elaborateness rather than its autobiographical accuracy. Berthoud reaches the conclusion that the Conradian "record" is "devoted in its entirety to an effort of self-discovery" quite distinct from that of an autobiography, and cites the structure of *A Personal Record* and Conrad's rejection of "confessions" such as Jean-Jacques Rousseau's, to illuminate the rationale underlying the text: "It is not only merely a 'record' but a 'personal' one. It represents not simply a life, but a life understood. And in its concern to explore the parallels between Conrad the seaman and Conrad the writer, it gradually formulates a view of the relationship between life and art."[29] Conrad's memory of events from his past, rather than the events themselves, is the basis of the narration in *A Personal Record*. The difference between this piece and those fictional tales based on events from Conrad's past, such as "Youth" or "The Shadow Line," does not lie in their respective degrees of biographical accuracy, but in the manner of their telling.[30] The particular rhetorical structure which organizes Conrad's reminiscences is a one-dimensional version of the critical discourse he articulates in the multilevels of fictional language.

The hope guiding Conrad's recollections is that "from the reading of these pages there may emerge at last the vision of a personality," the figure "behind the books so fundamentally dissimilar as, for instance, 'Almayer's Folly' and 'The Secret Agent,' and yet a coherent, justifiable personality both *in its origin and in its action*" (*PR*, xxi; emphasis added). In *A Personal Record*, one finds a revisitation of the events, influences and personal allegiances embedded in the personality behind the fictional worlds of Conrad's tales. In the events of the author's past life (the personality's "origin and . . . action"), so Conrad hopes, the reader will find the key to the ideal continuity connecting all his tales.

The same concern with continuity, as it turns out, underlies the "system" which organizes the piece. The "immediate aim" of the memories (as distinguished from their "hope") is "to give the record of personal memories by presenting faithfully the feelings and sensations connected with the writing of my first book and with my first contact with the sea. In the purposely mingled resonance of this double strain a friend here and there will perhaps detect a subtle accord" (*PR*, xxi). Indeed, the subtlety of the interplay between writing and sailing is not lost when its resonance is traced back to the fictional and non-fictional works in which Conrad uses the "double strain" metaphorically to render or dramatize his fidelity to the "feelings and sensations" of his earlier experiences. In *A Personal Record*, Conrad directs his readers' attention toward the origin of the particular subjective point of view that filtered those experiences and shaped his first literary works – which is to say, the effect on him of the events that shaped his commitment to authorship.

When Conrad sat down to write *Almayer's Folly*, it was not so much the act of a simple-minded seaman sailing into the *terra incognita* of letters, as a homecoming, a recovery of that intellectual inheritance kept alive during the lonely years at sea by his reading and the correspondence with his maternal uncle, Tadeusz Bobrowski.[31] Many of the views expressed in Bobrowski's letters to his nephew are reflected in Conrad's fiction. As Avrom Fleishman points out, Bobrowski "advocates stoic patience, hard work, and the renunciation of egotism. These values, designed to correct his Polish tradition, are the source of Conrad's own guiding principles."[32] The young man receiving these letters at the other end of the world built up his subjective response to the experience he was living around the principles inherited from and later inculcated by his uncle. When Conrad used his memories to construct fictional worlds, past events were filtered through those principles and ideas which guided him while experiencing them.

In *The Mirror of the Sea* (1906), the writing/sailing metaphor does not inform the entire structure of the work; but Conrad employs it to compare the ideal and practical aspects of the two crafts whenever he is trying to express that which, in his life at sea, is still significant for him as an artist. For a reader approaching *The Mirror of the Sea* expecting recollections of adventures at sea or sweeping descriptions of exotic lands, it may be puzzling to find, instead, that the sea enters into the narrative mostly as a reflection of life aboard ships. The collection of articles is in no way nostalgic. Conrad is paying a tribute of love to the sailing ships of his youth, but the tense and elegant prose never becomes sentimental. Rather, his taut control over the writing gives the impression that the author is probing themes still vital for him. The work is not a mnemonic feat, a movement backward along the waves of reminiscence. The past is tightly embedded in the present world view of the mature novelist. At the heart of his revisitation of sea life is the "wonder" which still "troubleth me . . . gretly," as Boethius' words record in *The Mirror*'s epigraph. Why does his past at sea remain so significant for him?

The author's persona in *The Mirror of the Sea* underlines the writer's interpretation of this mystery; and the focus of Conrad's writing de-emphasizes the actuality of the setting and the men that he recalls. The much-commented-upon trope of anthropomorphization, for instance, illustrates how little Conrad was interested in an impressionistic description of the winds in "Rulers of East and West."[33] Similarly, in "The Character of the Foe," Conrad's memory of a violent gale off the Horn is connected more with the words of the boatswain than with the fury of the wind: "after all, a gale of wind, the thing of mighty sound, is inarticulate. It is a man who, in chance phrase, interprets the elemental passion of his enemy" (*MoS*, 78). Conrad seems to delight in the freedom the purely rhetorical discourse provides him, abandoning himself to the rhythm of the long sentences, the measure of which came naturally to him only when he wrote about the sea.[34] As a result of this quintessentially rhetorical mode of expression, the author's critical discourse illuminates, in *The Mirror*, the potentiality for the expression of his concern about art which the sea always had for him.

In two chapters of *The Mirror of the Sea*, "The Fine Art" and "Emblems of Hope," Conrad clearly turns his reminiscences into reflections on his art. The similitude Conrad sets up in "The Fine Art" pivots on the moral basis which must underlie the craftsmanship of any kind of art. In his discussion about the racing-yacht skippers, Conrad remarks that the "genuine masters of their craft . . . have thought of nothing but of doing their very best by the vessel under their charge. To forget one's self, to surrender all personal feeling in the service of that fine art, is the only way for a seaman to the faithful discharge of his trust" (*MoS*, 29–30). This attitude toward the "fine art" of sailing is closely related to the "Credo of the artist" he formulated in his June 20, 1913, letter to Francis Warrington Dawson. According to this credo, only through a "self-forgetful sacrifice to that remorseless fidelity to the truth of his own sensations," can a novelist successfully accomplish his task.[35]

The centrality of Conrad's metaphorical portrait of the "genuine masters of their craft" is confirmed by the close relation between the seaman's attitude toward the "fine art" of sailing and the moral assumptions which ground the preface to *The Nigger of the "Narcissus."* The artist's concern with technical problems, as Conrad expresses it in the earlier piece, is first of all an attempt to voice most effectively – that is, most faithfully – his appeal to "other innumerable temperaments" (*NoN*, ix). In the preface to *The Nigger*, Conrad explicitly establishes the condition which allows fiction to transcend conventional expectations. The famous "to make you *see*" statement of the writer's task is, in fact, meant to be an "answer to those who in the fulness of a wisdom which looks for immediate profit, demand ... to be edified, consoled, amused" (*NoN*, ix–x). Conrad's comments on a skipper's "showy perform-ance," in "The Fine Art," recalls one of the objects of his criticism in the 1897 preface: "Through a touch of self-seeking that modest artist of solid merit became untrue to his temperament. It was not with him art for art's sake: it was art for his own sake" (*MoS*, 34).[36]

The comparison between technical and literary language in "Emblems of Hope" is a further instance of how Conrad's sea experiences provided materials for his reflection on his artistic craft. The comparison follows a tirade against what Conrad calls "the degradation of the sea language in the daily press of this country" (*MoS*, 13). When a journalist refers to the act of letting go an anchor with the expression "to cast" an anchor, he is not simply using the wrong word. He is misrepresenting the action: a "lands-man must imagine the act of anchoring as a process of throwing something overboard, whereas the anchor ... is not thrown over, but simply allowed to fall" (*MoS*, 14). To use the journalist's expression is to "take a liberty with technical language" – a crime, this, "against the clearness, precision, and beauty of perfected speech" (*MoS*, 13).

Conrad's notion of sea tradition also stands behind his descrip-tion of technical language, "an instrument," as he writes, "wrought into perfection by ages of experience, a flawless thing for its purpose" (*MoS*, 13), just like an anchor. The seaman's language is absolutely denotative of direct experience. Conrad recalls the chief mate's duty of "getting the anchor"; it was he who had to control "the growth of the cable," a technical expression which again brings Conrad to pause: "the growth of the cable – a sailor's phrase which has all the force, precision, and imagery of technical language that, created by simple men with keen eyes for the real aspect of the things they see in their trade, achieves the just expres-sion seizing upon the essential, which is the ambition of the artist in words" (*MoS*, 20–21).

Nautical language is a perfect instrument for the seaman's purpose – keeping the ship afloat – because it conveys the essential of "the things they see in their trade." Thus, when Conrad asserts his own ambition as an "artist in words" in the preface to *The Nigger of the "Narcissus"* ("to find ... in the facts of life what of each is fundamental, what is enduring and essential" [*NoN*, vii]), he is launching an inquiry into the representational capability of literary language. But the first lesson Conrad learned when, in the words of "A Familiar Preface" to *A Personal Record*, he carried his "notion of good service" from his "earlier into [his] later existence" (*PR*, xvii), was that the purpose which motivates an author cannot count on the reassuring tradition of seamanship. An absolutely accurate language is possible only within a limited world view, and is therefore incapable of bringing about a universality of effect. The suggestively impressionistic language he posited in the 1897 preface could not be a realistic representation of facts.

The key difference between technical and literary language is the notion of "purpose." When Conrad became a writer, the creation of a particular effect on his readers became the purpose of his works, and his artistic conscience was the only "ideal standard of conduct" he could expect. Conrad never overcame his doubts about the effectiveness of his language. Still, in 1922, he turns an article supposedly on "the nature of Notices to Mariners" into an examination of "some of my old feelings and impressions which, strictly professional as they were, have yet contributed in the end towards the existence of a certain amount of literature; or at any rate of pages of prose" (*LE*, 39). The Notices to Mariners were instructions and information concerning navigation in a certain area, which were posted in sea ports around the world. There is "no mystification," Conrad notes, "in the language of truth contained in the Notices to Mariners": one does not expect from them "suggestion but information of an ideal accuracy." In fact, "that prose has only one ideal to attain, to hold on to: the ideal of perfect accuracy." The reason why this prose can be so accurate is that the Notices are addressed "to a special public, limited to a very definite special subject, having no connection with the intellectual culture of mankind" (*LE*, 40). When Conrad finally stepped ashore, he had to learn how to write prose "unprovided with Notices to Authors," and, he recalls, "the pains I took with it only my Maker knows!" This is why, throughout his career, he never felt confident about his medium. "I never learned to trust it. I can't trust it to this day" (*LE*, 43).[37]

Conrad's use of the sea in his fiction acquires its full meaning only in the light of the rhetorical pattern based on the notion of an "ideal standard of conduct" which underlies his articles on nautical matters. This pattern is concisely set out in "The Dover Patrol" (1921): "All ideals are built on the ground of solid achievement, which ... creates in the course of time a certain tradition, or, in other words, a standard of conduct" (*LE*, 58). In turn, this very standard "makes the most improbable achievement possible, by augmenting the power of endurance and of self-sacrifice amongst men who look to the past for their lessons and for their inspiration" (*LE*, 58). This cyclic pattern, evolved partly from history and partly from legend, is what makes sea life symbolic of Conrad's vision of humanity. It is because he chose deliberately to become a sailor that he has been able to abstract from his experiences at sea a confirmation of his beliefs, which are rooted in his cultural background.

As he writes in "Tradition" (1918), "It is perhaps because I have not been born to the inheritance of [the English Merchant Service] tradition, which has yet fashioned the fundamental part of my character in my young days, that I am so consciously aware of it" (*NLL*, 196). According to Paul Bruss, on "the basis of this comment it is easy to infer that the traditions of the Merchant Service had a profound effect on the young Conrad precisely because they replaced the aristocratic traditions of his family."[38] As a matter of fact, Conrad is vindicating that continuity with his inherited values which he has gained by assigning an ideal meaning to his work.

Even in "Tradition," Conrad makes explicit the underlying rhetorical pattern when he states that a particularly valorous deed performed at sea during the First World War is a "testimony to the continuity of the old tradition of the sea, which made by the work of men has in its turn created for them their simple ideal of conduct" (*NLL*, 201). But when he describes the ideal in his own words, it does not seem quite that simple. Instead, he uses a number of key terms current in his critical discourse to respond to Leonardo da Vinci's dictum that "Work is the law ... without action the spirit of men turns to a dead thing":

From the hard work of men are born the sympathetic consciousness of a common destiny, the fidelity to right practice which makes great craftsmen, the sense of right conduct which we may call honour, the devotion to our calling and the idealism which is not a misty, winged angel without eyes, but a divine figure of terrestrial aspect with a clear glance and with its feet resting firmly on the earth on which it was born. (*NLL*, 194)

What is ostensibly an article in defense of the Merchant Service's heroism during the war reveals something altogether different when read in the light of the critical discourse.

Conrad uses "ideal standard of conduct" to discuss in his non-fictional writings issues already addressed, figuratively, in his fiction. "Well Done" (1918), in particular, illustrates the relevance that his critical tropes can have for an interpretation of *Lord Jim*. A reading of this article uncovers a sub-text for the various interpretations of Jim recollected by Marlow. Conrad starts with an explanation of how a tradition is built up and gradually becomes a standard of conduct: "It may be that the noblest tradition is but the offspring of material conditions ... But once it has been born it becomes a spirit ... it remains an immortal ruler invested with the power of honour and shame" (*NLL*, 183).

The suggestions become even more definite when Conrad goes on to distinguish between courage and fidelity, adventure and work. Each British sailor "began by being young in his time when all risk has a glamour." But Conrad condemns the "mere love of adventure" because it "lays a man under no obligation of faithfulness to an idea and even to his own self ... courage in itself is not an ideal" (*NLL*, 189). Instead, the conscious understanding of "the nature of their work" has enabled seamen to face the risks of their daily work. This intuitive understanding, Conrad writes, "is the common fate of mankind, whose most positive achievements are born from dreams and visions followed loyally to an unknown destination" (*NLL*, 190). "To follow the dream" is Stein's exhortation, the way to survive in the "destructive element" (*LJ*, 214–215). But in "Well Done," Conrad gives a different explanation: "For the great mass of mankind the only saving grace that is needed is steady fidelity to what is nearest to hand and heart in the short moment of each human effort" (*NLL*, 190–191). Jim's jump is a betrayal of that fidelity; it is not an act of cowardice. The sea captain recognizes the young man's struggle to remain faithful to his ideal, and is willing to face the disturbing reflections which Jim's case brings to the surface.

IDEALISM

It is a telling indication of the organic quality of Conrad's thought that he conflates WORK, his most idiosyncratic and unliterary trope, and IDEALISM to stress the ideal aspect of his craft and to remind his readers of the eminently practical nature of his artistic enterprise. These two complementary expressions of his paradoxical view of fiction underlie his repeated vindications of the "ideal standard of work" which guided his writing.

In particular, he made use of WORK and IDEALISM to defend his own art against one of the most damaging critiques he ever received. William Blackwood, the publisher of *Maga*, told Conrad in an interview that he was a loss to the firm. Immediately after this encounter, Conrad wrote his famous *apologia pro arte sua*, in which he defends the value of his work by defining it as "a calm conception of a definite ideal ... pursued with pain and labour" (to William Blackwood, May 31, 1902; *CL* II, 416). This is the letter in which he most strongly insists on his control over his art. "I am not writing 'in the air,'" he avers, and his work "is not the haphazard business of a mere temperament. There is in it as much intelligent action guided by a deliberate view of the effect to be attained as in any business enterprise" (*CL* II, 417). This vehement letter illustrates how deeply ingrained the tropes of Conrad's personal critical language are in his mind. Under the stress produced by his burning humiliation, he makes use of "action" and "business," two figures drawn from the trope of WORK, to point out that his concern with EFFECT is at the core of his artistic ideal.

The author's self-defense acquires a particular significance when he uses IDEALISM to explain why his "ideal standard of work" involves an effort to control the unconscious part of his writing. Thus, when he elaborates, in the 1924 preface to *The Shorter Tales of Joseph Conrad*, on his desire for a practical effect from his tales as well as an artistic standard of writing, he is in fact opening up a number of insights into his view of the creative process. He uses here the paradoxical juxtaposition implicit in his conviction that idealism is practical to describe the role which his artistic intention has in the creation of his works. While editing his short tales, Conrad notes, he came to the realization that his original artistic aim in writing them now appeared illusory: "The deep, complex (and at times even contradictory) feelings which make up the very essence of an author's attitude to his own creation are real enough, yet they may be, often are, but shapes of cherished illusions" (*LE*, 138). He will try, nonetheless, to express these feelings, prompted by an "ineradicable suspicion that . . . our very illusions must have a practical meaning." Conrad is using the word "illusion" here in much the same way as he does in his fiction (where he uses "illusion" to convey the various meanings IDEALISM has in his essays). In *Lord Jim*, in particular, as Daniel W. Ross points out, drawing on examples of the word's usage in Freud, Nietzsche and Ernest Becker, Conrad's "saving illusion" is "less a lie against fact than a form of truth that transcends the bare factuality of existence."[39] And indeed in that novel, the author had already played on the paradox implicit in IDEALISM by dramatizing his interpretation of his own writing in the "practical remedy" Marlow and Stein offer Jim: Patusan or the world of romance in which Jim's illusions are to become real.

Conrad then proceeds, in the same preface, to explain why illusions are practical: "Are they not as characteristic of an individual as his opinions, for instance, or the features of his face? In fact, being less controllable they must be even more dangerously revelatory" (*LE*, 138). Applying this insight to his own work, Conrad observes that the original "grouping" of the stories he is editing for *The Shorter Tales* "was never the result of a preconceived plan. It 'just happened.' " Such things in one's work, he comments, "seem impressive and valuable because they spring from sources profounder than the logic of a deliberate theory suggested by acquiring learning, let us say, or by lessons drawn by analysed practice" (*LE*, 140). This issue touches the origin of Conrad's struggle for self-expression:

And no one need quarrel for such a view with an artist for whom self-expression must, by definition, be the principal object, if not the only *raison d'être*, of his existence. He will naturally take for his own, for better or worse, all the characteristics of his work; since all of them, intended or not intended, make up the individuality of his self-expression. (*LE*, 140–141)

Conrad again confirms that the language of consciousness and that of unconsciousness (the "intended" and "not intended" aspects of his writing) are interrelated when he posits two complementary "moments" in the process of the artist's self-expression. There are "moments," he writes, "when what a man most values in his work – I mean even a man of action – is precisely the part the general mystery of things plays in its shaping: the discovery of those qualities that have 'just happened' in that obscure region where honest success or honourable failure is unconsciously elaborated." At the same time, however, "there are moments too when one's idealism (for idealism is practical and sane and the enemy of things that 'just happen' and suchlike mysteries) prompts one to take up a different, more precise view of one's achievement – whatever it may be" (*LE*, 141). Whatever the outcome of his writing may be, there is a segment of his fictional language in which he has expressed his intended effect. The individuality of the artist's "self-expression" is, then, the result of an interaction between self-conscious craftsmanship and "what has got itself written."[40]

IDEALISM and WORK are again conflated when Conrad refutes the way critics have classified his work as either realistic or romantic. In words which have a particular meaning for him, he writes, in the Author's Note to *Within the Tides*, that if "the sober hue of hard work and exacting calls of duty ... of my active life ... appeal strongly to me even in retrospect it is, I suppose, because the romantic feeling of reality was in me an inborn faculty" (*WtT*, v). This oxymoron, "romantic feeling of reality," may very well be a stroke of irony on Conrad's part. Yet even if he is using it as a send-up of the critics' classifications of his fiction, he is extremely serious in using his critical discourse to vindicate his own attitude toward his work. A romantic feeling of reality, he continues,

in itself may be a curse but when disciplined by a sense of personal responsibility and a recognition of the hard facts of existence shared with the rest of mankind becomes but a point of view from which the very shadows of life appear endowed with an internal glow. And such romanticism is not a sin. It is none the worse for the knowledge of truth. It only tries to make the best of it, hard as it may be; and in this hardness discovers a certain aspect of beauty. (*WtT*, v–vi)

The suppleness and cogency with which Conrad uses the figures of "solidarity" and "work" to bring out the far-reaching moral and aesthetic implications of his reference to "personal responsibility" and "aspect of beauty" are enough to transform the phrase "internal glow" into a critical term.

It is necessary to resist, however, the temptation to take such a phrase as "romantic realism" for a literary formula – after all Conrad found that even James Fenimore Cooper could achieve an effect of poetic realism: "The road to legitimate realism is through poetical feeling, and he possesses that – only it is expressed in the leisurely manner of his time" ("Tales of the Sea," *NLL*, 56). There certainly is a touch of playfulness in the way he uses the paradoxes inherent in the trope of IDEALISM to deflate conventional distinctions between "realism" and "romanticism" – as if the matter really were not serious enough. Such is the case when he half-mockingly warns Arnold Bennett (March 10, 1902): "You just stop short of being absolutely real because you are faithful to your dogmas of realism. Now realism in art will never approach reality" (*CL* II, 390). Or when, in his letter to Sir Sidney Colvin (March 18, 1917), he claims that the contrasting labels "romantic" and "realist" are equally misleading because they altogether miss the effect he was aiming for: "*en vérité c'est les valeurs idéales des faits et gestes humains qui se sont imposés à mon activité artistique.* Whatever dramatic and narrative gifts I may have are always, instinctively, used with that object – to get at, to bring forth *les valeurs idéales*" (*LL* II, 185).[41] "Absolutely real" and "'ideal' value of things," then, seem to be interchangeable qualifiers for the same artistic aim: putting to use all the tools at one's disposal to reveal the human truth which the artist's conscience finds in facts – even if, according to critics, these tools are borrowed from different schools.

FIDELITY

A commitment to FIDELITY guides the extraordinary integration of moral and aesthetic convictions which shapes Conrad's view of fiction. FIDELITY is one of those ideas which are simple in that they impose inescapable responsibilities. And Conrad uses FIDELITY to reaffirm that he will not disregard the heaviest of his responsibilities: "garder ma pensée intacte comme dernier hommage de fidelité à une cause qui est perdue" (to Cunninghame Graham, February 8, 1899; *CL* II, 160). As it is defined in Conrad's use of FIDELITY, memory is not only a re-creation of past events. It is the only way for the writer to keep in touch with those he cannot write about because the remembrance of them is too painful. Instead, he will keep alive their memory by connecting his work with his intellectual and cultural inheritance.

The moral overtones of this trope, perhaps the least unfamiliar of Conrad's personal critical terms, develop several of the themes found in the other tropes. In the writer's effort to live up to his vision of art, his commitment to FIDELITY acquires the significance of scrupulousness in self-expression. Conrad makes explicit this connotation with the well-known phrase, "fidelity to one's sensations." In this particular phrase, FIDELITY conveys a number of implicit and explicit references to the other four tropes of Conrad's critical discourse.

Conrad's best-known statement of the importance he gave to FIDELITY occurs in the "Familiar Preface" to *A Personal Record*: "Those who read me know my conviction that the world, the temporal world, rests on a few very simple ideas; so simple that they must be as old as the hills. It rests notably, among others, on the idea of Fidelity" (*PR*, xix). The notion of Conrad's "simplicity" has been encouraged by Conrad's selection of "Fidelity" among other "simple ideas." As a matter of fact, Conrad's explanation makes clear what he means by "simple": "I have not been revolutionary in my writings. The revolutionary spirit is mighty convenient in this, that it frees one from all scruples as regards ideas" (*PR*, xix). In devising original narrative techniques and building his fictional worlds, Conrad has eschewed an egotistical drive to set up hard-surfaced, glittering intellectual systems. Acts of intellectual "resignation" (*PR*, xix), prompted by a recognition of the exacting power of his "scruples," shaped Conrad's "simple ideas" – each scruple being a reminder of his commitment to FIDELITY, each act of resignation revealing the moral value of the memories deposited in his personal experience.[42]

Commentators have not reflected enough on the significance of "resignation" as the context for the "simple ideas" passage. As a matter of fact, Conrad's vindication of "Fidelity" in the "Familiar Preface" comes as a climax to the claim that what counts is not the artist's subjective motivation, but the "manner" of presenting life in art. The artist must maintain an attitude of "resignation open-eyed, conscious and informed by love," he warns, if his "aim is to reach the very fount of laughter and tears" (*PR*, xix). Thus, "resignation" in Conrad's critical language stands for an acceptance of the paradoxical nature of human life.

The implications of "resignation" are further clarified in "Henry James: An Appreciation" (1905). Conrad's tribute to the "great artist and faithful historian" (*NLL*, 19) is indicative of how Conrad used these tributes to writers he respected to express his own idea of what fiction ought to be. He is actually writing about an ideal conception of his own work. In this particular article, Conrad uses "warlike images" (*NLL*, 15) to describe the humanity scrutinized by James. This unusual view of James' fictional world highlights the distinctive heroic quality of both the American master and his characters, their "power of renunciation" (*NLL*, 16). James' struggle for creation is compared to a battle because the artist is engaged in re-enacting that "relentless warfare" to which "the duality of man's nature" has reduced "the life-history of the earth" (*NLL*, 15).

An author's special sensibility is revealed by the particular renunciation he is willing to make. He is reaching "the utmost limit of [his] power" when he selects the subjects and characters of his tales. James' art is qualified, then, by his being "the historian of fine consciences." A "fine conscience," Conrad writes, is different from a "not fine" one, in that the latter is "less troubled by the nice discrimination of shades of conduct." Furthermore, a "fine conscience is more concerned with essentials" (*NLL*, 17). It is Marlow who, in Conrad's fiction, questions the implication of people's adherence to ideal standards of conduct and so reaches down to the essentials of the story told. Clearly, there are similarities in the "acts of renunciation" underlying the works of James and Conrad.

The tribute to James gives Conrad an opportunity to reflect as well on the differences separating himself from the master historian of fine consciences. A man, Conrad remarks, "has to sacrifice his gods to his passions or his passions to his gods" (*NLL*, 16). James' acts of renunciation are guided by the sacrifice of his "passions to his gods"; his aesthetic selection of "the reality of forms and sensations" (*NLL*, 15) enables him to create fictional worlds in which "ugliness has but little place" (*NLL*, 17). Conrad's, on the other hand, is a moral selection. His are not acts of renunciation of what could blur that "nice discrimination of shades of conduct" at the core of James' art. His are acts of "resignation" such as those vindicated in the "Familiar Preface" to *A Personal Record*.

Fidelity to one's sensations defines the path a writer must follow in order to steer clear of trying to resolve the irreconcilable dualities constituting reality – only to substitute for them an "ethical view of the universe [which] involves us at last in so many cruel and absurd contradictions" (*PR*, 92). The writer must instead focus on the precise rendering of his impressions in order to communicate the moral value of his experience. The intellectual renunciations prompted by the moral "scruples" delimiting his "simple ideas" (*PR*, xix) are not indicative of an anti-intellectual posture; rather, they are the means for a more effective expression of the artist's appeal. Is not the very "aim of creation . . . spectacular," after all? "Those visions, delicious or poignant, are a moral end in themselves" (*PR*, 92), especially when their re-creation tinges them with the author's "sensations."

Conrad uses both FIDELITY and the notion of "resignation" in the definition of fiction he sets forth in a letter to *The New York Times Saturday Book Review* (August 2, 1901). Fiction, he states, "at the point of development at which it has arrived, demands from the writer a spirit of scrupulous abnegation," if his aim is to render life's "irreconcilable antagonisms" (*CL* II, 348). Acknowledgment of these contradictions is "the only fundamental truth of fiction"; and, Conrad adds, its "recognition must be critical in its nature, inasmuch that in its character it may be joyous, it may be sad; it may be angry with revolt, or submissive in resignation. The mood does not matter. It is only the writer's self-forgetful fidelity to his sensations that matters" (*CL* II, 349).

The phrase "fidelity to [the artist's] sensations" acquires more positive aesthetic valences when Conrad uses it to suggest the impossibility of conveying the subjective side of memories and sensuous impressions without verbal and visual precision. In a later instance of the recurring phrase, Conrad recalls, in the Author's Note to *Within the Tides*, the difficulty of working with exotic subject matters: "the mere fact of dealing with matters outside the general run of everyday experience laid me under the obligation of a more scrupulous fidelity to the truth of my own sensations" (*WtT*, vi). A few years earlier, in a letter to Francis Warrington Dawson (June 20, 1913), he qualifies the phrase in the same way he had done in his 1901 letter to *The New York Times*: "Suffering is as an attribute [,] almost a condition of greatness, of devotion, of an altogether self-forgetful sacrifice to that remorseless fidelity to the truth of his own sensations at whatever cost of pain and contumely which for me is the whole Credo of the artist."[43]

Only by dedicating himself to an ideal which exacts utmost fidelity "to the truth of his own sensations" can a novelist create in the reader the kind of response which proves the effectiveness of his work's appeal – just as "in the faithful discharge of his trust" as artist he must strive after "that full possession of [himself] which is the first condition of good service ... [which he had] carried ... from [his] earlier into [his] later existence" (*PR*, xvii). The two statements only seem to contradict each other. They actually express the complexity of Conrad's integrated concept of fidelity: the precise rendition of past experiences requires self-forgetful fidelity; but at the same time, for the remembering conscience to trace and set forth the value of those experiences, the artist must preserve full control of the writing. This is the view of the creative process which Conrad was to outline in the 1924 preface to the *Shorter Tales*, the only difference being that in the later piece "intended" and "not intended" serve to distinguish the conscious from the unconscious parts of his fiction.

One of the most touching scenes in *A Personal Record* puts into tragic relief that line of intellectual continuity Conrad tried to fashion in his artistic production. In the Author's Note, Conrad recalls an episode that impressed him "more intimately" (*PR*, viii) than his father's funeral: the burning of his father's manuscripts, which the ailing man had ordered a few days before he died. "His aspect," Conrad recollects, "was to me not so much that of a man desperately ill, as mortally weary – a vanquished man. That act of destruction affected me profoundly by its air of surrender." Conrad viewed this act as a capitulation to an enemy worse than death, to the crushing claims of history over any hope of expressing one's illusions and dreams. Najder questions the accuracy of Conrad's account, since several of Apollo Korzeniowski's manuscripts are preserved in the Jagiellonian Library in Cracow.[44] The fact that Conrad may have made up the whole scene, though, can only confirm its symbolical meaning. Whether or not that burning occurred, Conrad chose to emphasize his father's defeat as a writer. Conrad voiced Apollo Korzeniowski's ideals by selecting as themes for his own works the experiences which had brought to the surface those traits of character that had allowed him to survive his family's shipwreck. Conrad's formative years at sea and in the Malayan Archipelago, sustained more by his uncle's moral guidance than by his father's self-sacrifice, proved more useful for the creation of his fictional worlds.

Conrad's efforts to convey the emotional and intellectual content of his past had a stimulating effect on his concern for the formal aspects of his writings, by directing his efforts toward a form capable of bringing his memory to react with his reader's personal experiences. "And what is a novel," he asks in *A Personal Record*, "if not a conviction of our fellow-men's existence strong enough to take upon itself a form of imagined life clearer than reality and whose accumulated verisimilitude of selected episodes puts to shame the pride of documentary history" (*PR*, 15). Conrad landed in the realm of fiction, passing through lands forgotten by history to reach the immortal sea untouched by human events. In these experiences he found material for fictional worlds in which the inevitable defeat of any illusion could be transformed into a moral victory by being set against an unconcerned universe rather than being dwarfed by the claims of the winners.

In his 1905 article on Henry James, Conrad elaborates on the difference between novels, which can preserve human experience by endowing it with "the reality of forms," and history. "Fiction," he writes,

is history, human history, or it is nothing. But it is also more than that; it stands on firmer ground, being based on the reality of forms and the observation of social phenomena, whereas history is based on documents, and the reading of print and handwriting – on second-hand impression. Thus fiction is nearer truth. But let that pass ... a novelist is a historian, the preserver, the keeper, the expounder of human experience. (*NLL*, 17)

In the same essay, Conrad suggests how a novelist can attain this form of truth: it "is rescue work, this snatching of vanishing phases of turbulence, disguised in fair words, out of the native obscurity into a light where the struggling forms may be seen, seized upon, endowed with the only possible form of permanence in this world of relative values – the permanence of memory" (*NLL*, 13).

How come, then, Conrad's belief in solidarity did not lead him to write about Poland, the "Country of Remembrances" (to Wincenty

Lutosławski, June 9, 1897; *CL* I, 359)? Conrad suggests an answer to this question in *A Personal Record*, when he writes that "One's literary life must turn frequently for sustenance to memories and seek discourse with the shades, unless one has made up one's mind to write only in order to reprove mankind for what it is, or praise it for what it is not, or – generally – to teach it how to behave" (*PR*, xv). Conrad's artistic ideal centered on a search for a form capable of achieving a representation of the universality of human experience. But the way to that form ran counter to the vindication of his personal sufferings. Conrad chose not to transform the "shades" coming to him from his Polish past into fictional characters; and yet they figured in his creative process, providing that sense of continuity in his several lives – as heir to a lost cause, as seaman, and as author. "Living with memories is a cruel business," he once wrote to Cunninghame Graham, who had lost his wife the year before; "I – who have a double life one of them peopled only by shadows growing more precious as the years pass – know what that is" (October 7, 1907; *CL* III, 491). It was only in his fictional worlds that Conrad found a verbal structure in which the struggle to realize an aesthetic aim allowed him to express implicitly his fidelity to the unvoiced side of his memory: the most important, the least communicable, his Polish past.

EFFECT

Conrad's awareness of "*Le public introuvable*" (to Galsworthy, November 1, 1910; *LL* II, 121) is often painful, because it acknowledges his estrangement from his English public. At the same time, however, this very distance forced him to clarify the problems that writing poses, in general, for individual self-expression. During one of the worst crises in Conrad's relationship with his audience, following the publication of *The Secret Agent*, he tried to explain his position on these matters in a number of illuminating letters.

In a letter to Galsworthy (January 6, 1908), Conrad voices his disappointment at the failure of his most recent novel to find a sympathetic public: "The *Secret Agent* may be pronounced by now an honourable failure. It brought me neither love nor promise of literary success. I own that I am cast down. I suppose I am a fool to have expected anything else. I suppose there is something in me that is unsympathetic to the general public . . . Foreignness I suppose" (*LL* II, 65). The subject and manner of telling of the first novel he set in London did not produce the "sensation" he had expected (to Pinker, July 30, 1907; *CL* III, 459). On the contrary, several reviewers zeroed in on the "Slavonic . . . note" in Conrad's fiction.[45] As Najder notes, the "reception of *The Secret Agent* crystallized what Conrad had long feared – that he would be classified as a curio, a writer interesting by virtue of his unique experiences and background."[46]

Commenting on this delicate moment in Conrad's life, Najder raises a number of interesting questions regarding Conrad's attitude toward his English audience. He points out that the author "contrasted himself with Kipling, the exemplar of a '*national* writer' who 'speaks of *his compatriots*' – while he, Conrad, wrote '*for them*,' that is, for the English." But Najder dismisses the relevance of this comparison because it is made "in a letter to a Frenchman."[47] The Frenchman, however, was Henry-Durand Davray, the translator of "Karain" and *The Secret Agent*, and Conrad's comparison between himself and Kipling follows by a few weeks the January 6 letter to Galsworthy. The comparison represents one of Conrad's early attempts after the failure of *The Secret Agent* to come to terms with the blow to his belief in the value of his art. As a matter of fact, Conrad's letter to Davray investigates the difficulties his alienness posed for the effectiveness of his fictional language.

For Conrad, Kipling's case exemplified the theoretical implications of his own lack of familiarity with his audience. The English language is a means which Kipling relies on to speak "de *ses compatriots*." He can tell a story about other Englishmen without needing to worry too much about his medium, because he can rely, unconsciously, on verbal and mental associations he shares with them. Kipling is familiar with both his subject and his audience, whereas Conrad could not depend on such a relationship. Conrad's formative experiences had been alien to those of his English readers; and so he could never really count on knowing what associations his words would have for them. He was consequently forced to concentrate on a medium which could reach out to "*them*." All of Conrad's efforts were directed toward establishing an intimacy based on an assumed universality of experience, that fellowship beyond linguistic barriers abridged in his formulation of the "invincible conviction of solidarity" (*NoN*, viii).

The substance of the comparison with Kipling reveals Conrad's awareness of the far-reaching implications of the problems which his particular English can pose for a translator:

Mais n'oubliez pas que la chose est écrite pour les Anglais – au point de vue de l'effet à produire sur un lecteur anglais. C'est toujours mon but. Voilà pourquoi je suis tellement un écrivain anglais se prêtant peu à la traduction. Un écrivain national comme Kipling par exemple se traduit facilement. Son intérêt est dans le sujet, l'intérêt de mon oeuvre est dans l'effet qu'elle produit.[48]

A French translator can fruitfully apply his knowledge of the English mind to faithfully render Kipling's treatment of his compatriots. In this case, the fictional language reveals the subject. Whereas, to understand the subject of Conrad's tales, the translator has to take into account the cultural distance separating the writer from his public. And translation appears even more impossible, given that the effect Conrad aims at depends on a careful choice of words, sentence patterns and rhythms.

In a second letter to Davray (February 3, 1908), Conrad points out the tensions in his fiction's language: what characterizes his work is a "goût pour l'analyse des sentiments simples avec un tour de phrase qui frappe – les Anglais. Notez bien que je ne dis pas *qui plaît*. Je crois que je ne plais à personne ici."[49] His language is intended to arouse his English readers. And this is what it does, especially in the Marlow tales, where Conrad uses the internal narrator to attract the reader's attention to the implications which the character's memories can have for them. In *Under Western Eyes*, the author will leave that to a teacher of language, and he will dissimulate his criticisms of the English audience by directing his irony toward the Swiss "divine democracy" (*UWE*, 306).

Conrad, then, still refers in 1908 to the two strategies followed in the early Marlow tales and "Karain" to describe his way of overcoming his estrangement from his English public. He had aimed, without repudiating his own identity, at creating a suggestively impressionistic language to communicate with his readers. At the same time, he had devised a narrative frame to transform into as many stimulations the distortions inevitably produced by communicating through a fictional medium. Thus, his "effect" consists largely of means to alert his readers and startle them out of their familiar way of perceiving and reading. Conrad's comments on the difficulties in establishing a communication with his English readers help locate the implications of his concern for EFFECT in a wider theoretical context. The distinction he makes between himself and Kipling explains very well Conrad's condition as one of the "poets unhoused and wanderers across language," as George Steiner describes Nabokov and other twentieth-century deracinated writers.[50]

The effect Conrad was trying to achieve could not count on a set of common fundamental structures – among which is a common language – that could provide a referential system based on unconsciously absorbed physical and mental sensations. The most elaborate case of a narrative technique that works on such a referential system is, of course, Marcel Proust's *À la recherche du temps perdu*, in which the verbal suggestiveness of common everyday French words prompts intense associations within the narrator's memory. The verbal power of such an associative mode is based on a shared linguistic community. Proust could count on a sympathetic public response to his private associations. English words had very special associations for Conrad, except, perhaps, for nautical terms, as Donald W. Rude points out.[51] Conrad himself comments on his condition with an arresting phrase he uses in a letter he wrote to Arthur Symons, a few months after his letters to Davray. "I have been quarrying my English out of a black night, working like a coal miner in his pit. For fourteen years now I have been living as if in a cave without echoes" (August 29, 1908; *LL* II, 84).

Conrad was so self-conscious about the remoteness and alienness of his past "formative impressions" that he doubted his very children could ever understand their father. In a particularly intense passage, Conrad explains in *A Personal Record* why he must pass on the "public record of these formative impressions." His revisitation of his earlier memories is not "the whim of an uneasy egotism." As a matter of fact,

It is meet that something more should be left for the novelist's children than the colours and figures of his own hard-won creation. That which in their grown-up years may appear to the world about them as the most enigmatic side of their natures and perhaps must remain for ever obscure even to themselves, will be their unconscious response to the still voice of that inexorable past from which his work of fiction and their personalities are remotely derived. (*PR*, 24–25)

Never in Conrad's writings does his personal voice stand out so obtrusively. And if he sheds his natural reserve it is to vindicate what lies at the core of his personal authorial strain: his commitment to a world living only in his memory. So deeply embedded is the expression of this fidelity in his work that he cannot separate the different offspring of his personality, his sons and his works of fiction. And in directing his children's "unconscious response" to his fiction, he points out where the key of his work lies. It is not in the "colours and figures" of his tales, but in the voice he gives to an appeal coming from his past. It is in passages such as this that the efforts Conrad makes to express his view of his art in a personal critical language become evident – and exact the reader's interest and respect.

The tropes of WORK, IDEALISM and FIDELITY define the moral commitment which transformed Conrad's personal appeal into a form of writing. From the very first, however, what was an enunciation of abstract ideals became the specific concern generating the trope of EFFECT: how was he to ensure the desired response in his readers? The preface to *The Nigger* gives the earliest answer: fiction must be "the appeal of one temperament to all the other innumerable temperaments" (*NoN*, ix). To articulate this appeal, he relied on "the power of the written word to make [the reader] hear . . . feel . . . *see*" (*NoN*, x). However, the limited success of his works, and his difficulties in putting his ideal into practice in the act of writing, forced Conrad to define with greater precision the concept of "innumerable temperaments," by elaborating a new notion of how to reach out to his public. Nonetheless, the various combinations of narrative structure and fictional language he devised to attain his artistic purpose do not bespeak a change in the ideal underlying his craft. Rather, the writer tried to increase the effectiveness of the means at his disposal. Thus, rather than counting on a suggestively impressionistic language, Conrad started to test, after *Lord Jim*, the power of those combinations to affect readers.

The outcome of this testing was the sense of craftsmanship Conrad emphasizes in his later years. His letter of July 14, 1923, to Richard Curle is remarkable in this respect. Conrad there connects his most innovative techniques with his concern for the creation of a certain effect on readers. The very concerns he voices in his letters to Davray resurface in the letter to Curle, though cast now in a personal figurative language. The later rationalization of the different impulses, reflections and experiments which went into his various combinations of narrative structure and fictional language proves to be central for an understanding of how the continuity of the tropes of WORK, IDEALISM and FIDELITY is organically related to the transformations prompted by the concerns Conrad abridges in the trope of EFFECT.

The letter to Curle is extremely important because it contains Conrad's comments on his friend's review of the Uniform Edition published by Dent that same year. Conrad makes it clear that, for him, this is an opportunity "to get freed from that infernal tail of ships and that obsession of my sea life" (*LL* II, 316). Prompted by the awareness that "the nature of my writing runs the risk of being obscured by the nature of my material," Conrad offers here his most explicit rebuttal of the way contemporary critics approached his art. This is possibly why this letter is the most forthright exposition of Conrad's view of his art since the preface to *The Nigger of the "Narcissus."*

Conrad's remarks are "extracted" from him by a "consideration" of Curle's article (*LL* II, 317). Conrad is particularly annoyed by Curle's summaries of his prefaces, and he suggests such critical terms as Curle might use in the article he still has to write for the American edition. The summarizing inevitably fails to convey their "atmosphere" because "those pages are an intensely personal expression, much more so than all the rest of my writing, with the exception of the *Personal Record*, perhaps." He then immediately recalls a previous discussion in which he himself had used the term "historical" in connection with his books. Conrad feels he has to apologize, because he was actually thinking of an article in which a critic had "concluded that my fiction was not historical of course but had an authentic quality of development and style which in its ultimate effect resembled historical perspective" (*LL* II, 317). What is interesting in Conrad's reference to the critic's remarks is how he turns them to his account to illustrate what Curle *should* write in his review.

Conrad starts out by offering his "own impression" of what the unnamed critic[52] "really meant": that his "manner of telling, perfectly devoid of familiarity as between author and reader, aimed essentially at the intimacy of a personal communication, without any thought for other effects." It is striking that Conrad repeats the argument he had employed fifteen years before to distinguish Kipling's rapport with his readers from that "intimacy of a personal communication," which is the object of his own narrative forms. Additionally, he uses this suggestive specification of his "manner of telling" in a vindication of the means he devised, throughout his career, to make more effective that "personal communication" which is the only historical basis of his fiction: "As a matter of fact, the thought for effects is there all the same (often at the cost of mere directness of narrative), and can be detected in my unconventional grouping and perspective, which are purely temperamental and wherein almost all my 'art' consists."

It took Curle's uninspired review of the Dent Uniform Edition to force Conrad to reformulate his conviction that fiction is an appeal of one temperament to "innumerable temperaments" (*NoN*, ix). Though he still refers to his artistic intention as "temperamental," he no longer locates the artistic quality of his fiction in a "care for the shape and ring of sentences." Now his craftsmanship is concerned foremost with an "unconventional" distortion of narrative structure, even "at the cost of mere directness of narrative." Be it by suggestively impressionistic language, or by "grouping and perspective," the writer's motivation remains always the "thought for effects."

Conrad's July 14 letter to Curle is an attempt to introduce into the critical discussion of his time terms which can describe his art. And even though he is rejecting biographical criticism, his comments actually engage an entire range of critical approaches. At the end of the letter to Curle he writes:

This, I suspect, has been the difficulty the critics felt in classifying [my art] as romantic or realistic. Whereas, as a matter of fact, it is fluid, depending on grouping (sequence) which shifts, and on the changing lights giving varied effects of perspective.
It is in those matters gradually, but never completely, mastered that the history of my books really consists. (*LL* II, 317)

The "historical perspective" informing Conrad's fiction is the authorial strain produced by the writer's attempt to communicate his convictions.[53] The terms he suggests for interpreting his tales run counter to all the classifications which ultimately undermine his personal artistic quest. Instead, he tries to direct the attention of his readers toward the "practical" artistic ideal he has followed over the span of almost thirty years. Conrad continues:

Of course the plastic matter of this grouping and of those lights has its importance, since without it the actuality of that grouping and that lighting could not be made evident, any more than Marconi's electric waves could be made evident without the sending-out and receiving instruments. In other words, without mankind my art, an infinitesimal thing, could not exist. (*LL* II, 317)

Thus, Conrad's illustration of what gives value to his art ends with a communications theory. His concern for the artistic and moral problems posed by "transmitting and receiving" motivates his search for ever more effective ways to avoid the pitfalls of Victorian novels, realistic representation or didacticism. The light in which the reader sees the men and women of Conrad's tales is the effect of the author's attempt to keep open lines of communication by distorting the structure of his fictional worlds.

PRECISION

PRECISION appears most commonly in Conrad's later writings, when mastery of time, space and points of view in his fiction took the place of his reliance on the suggestiveness of figurative language. His discussion of how PRECISION must guide a novelist's craft rests on a paradox: only verbal and visual precision can bring out the symbolic value of physical reality. Thus, the implications of the concern with PRECISION kept bringing Conrad back to the ideas set to paper in the preface to the *Nigger*. Visual precision remained the first requisite for a suggestive use of prose language, while verbal precision continued as the first condition for the effective evocation of the symbolic power of words. The theoretical implications of his paradoxical use of PRECISION become apparent when he tries to recast in contemporary critical language his belief in the "power of the written word" (*NoN*, x).

References to the "power of the written word" in Conrad's nonfictional writings range from the 1897 preface to the notes the writer prepared for his trip to the United States in May 1923. When he launches this theme in 1897 he is careful to connect the notions of "impression" on the senses and "appeal" to temperament, so as to point out in what way the artist's descent into himself can uncover "the very truth" of the "visible universe" (*NoN*, vii). The way is (and remained, until the end) the novelist's fidelity to the moral commitment which must underlie his narrative and linguistic choices.

Two years later, in a letter to Sir Hugh Clifford (October 9, 1899), Conrad appears to have outlined a reading model based on the non-representational "power of the written word":

words, groups of words, words standing alone, are symbols of life, have the power in their sound or their aspect to present the very thing you wish to hold up before the mental vision of your readers. The things "as they are" exist in words; therefore words should be handled with care lest the picture, the image of truth abiding in facts should become distorted – or blurred. (*CL* II, 200)

Conrad highlights here the care a writer must take in his handling of words if he is to use their symbolic power to bring out "the image of truth abiding in facts." This truth, though, has nothing to do with seeing: Conrad is aiming at the reader's "mental vision."

Conrad makes plain in his letter to Clifford that his non-representational model is concerned first of all with the moral valence of the ideal language he is trying to create. He adds that "the *whole* of the truth lies in the presentation; therefore the expression should be studied in the interest of veracity. This is the only morality of *art* apart from *subject*" (*CL* II, 200). In later letters, however, Conrad's references to his belief in "the power of the written word" are not accompanied by an effort to explain what he actually means. Ian Watt points out two particularly ornate utterances. The first appears in a letter to Ford Madox Ford (November 12, 1898): "how fine it could be . . . if the idea had a substance and words a magic power, if the invisible could be snared into a shape";[54] and the second, in a 1911 letter to an Italian admirer, Carlo Placci, where Conrad asserts his "ineradicable conviction that it is in the living word *que l'on saisit le mieux la forme du rêve*."[55] But it would be misleading to associate Conrad's continuous questioning of the power of words with the fuzzy, wistful notions expressed in these two letters. Conrad's use of the 1897 formulation of these convictions in the 1923 notes for the American trip dispels this false impression.

Conrad claims in the notes that his natural gift is a "fidelity to the evocative power of the written word," and that the written word has "a strange power both in its shape and in its sound of suggestion," which the theater and the cinema lack.[56] These claims are so strikingly resonant of the 1897 preface that he could give the impression of an aging writer going back to the earlier piece as he prepares his speech. But that impression is mistaken, because Conrad in 1923 is still reacting imaginatively to his earlier convictions, still elaborating on the figures expressive of his critical discourse. In his comparison between cinema and literature, Conrad defines the power of words with an unprecedented surface precision. "The human voice," he writes,

> as well as the written word has this strange quality that it awakens a varied response, like a sort of echo which instead of repeating the sentences would go on *developing and commenting* [*on*] *the idea*, and [it is] in that power of the word and to that property of the human mind in his readers that an artist must trust for his effects, for his success, for his very life, I mean for his artistic life.[57] (Emphasis added.)

What had been, in 1897, a belief in the poetic potentialities of prose became, in the 1923 notes, a consciousness of the intellectual echo which the sound of words could raise in the reader's mind. Rather than surmising the suggestive power of particular words, Conrad in 1923 traces the unsubstantial waves of the sense of a word as it is developed and commented on by a reader. This significant evolution illuminates the synthesis Conrad had reached in his later years. His continuous probing of the central tenets of his art finally brought together his youthful ideal and his awareness of the overruling importance that finding means to affect the "reader's mind" had for his intended effect.

By trying to ascribe Conrad's "care" for words to one or another school, commentators have missed Conrad's personal use of one of the central tenets of contemporary symbolist poetry and prose. Even though Conrad himself was aware of the proximity of his position to that of other thinkers on fiction, their formulas and theories must have lacked any concrete meaning for him when set against the hard toil of his pursuit of that "ideal standard of conduct" he had set up for the craftsman in words. His letter to Barrett H. Clark (May 4, 1918) is notable for the efforts its author makes to cast his view of symbolism in terms related to traditional critical language. This letter has drawn considerable attention because here he vindicates the continuity implicit in the evolution of his art and comes close to elucidating his view on symbolism. The two themes are introduced to answer two different questions posed by Clark and are usually dealt with separately. An underlying argument in defense of his personal integrity, however, connects his two answers. Awareness of this argument advances an understanding of the hardly repressed hostility toward the "critics" which runs through the whole letter.

At the beginning, Conrad asserts his fidelity to his convictions in answer to those critics who have "found fault with me for not being constantly myself." On the contrary, he maintains, "I am always myself. I am a man of formed character" (*LL* II, 204). He goes on to explain what he means by a work of art being symbolic, by stating, at first, "a general proposition: that a work of art is very seldom limited to one exclusive meaning and not necessarily tending to a definite conclusion. And this for the reason that the nearer it approaches art, the more it acquires a symbolic character" (*LL* II, 205). Conrad is aware that his view of art could be taken as an allegiance to "the Symbolist School of poets or prose writers." And he denies it, not because he refutes their tenets – theirs "is only a literary proceeding against which I have nothing to say" – but because he is "concerned here with something much larger." Conrad does not pause to spell out exactly what he means by "something much larger." Instead, he proceeds to enlarge on how "the symbolic conception of a work" can make "a triple appeal covering the whole field of life." His only reference to the symbolists seems to turn into a missed opportunity. And then, suddenly, he shifts from "symbolism" to a discussion of PRECISION: "I don't think you will quarrel with me on the ground of lack of precision; for as to precision of images and analysis my artistic conscience is at rest. I have given there all the truth that is in me; and all that the critics may say can make my honesty neither more nor less." The confrontation with the critics which had launched the discussion on symbolism surfaces again, but this time Conrad is speaking of his own art.

Conrad had started the letter by asserting his freedom to change "methods of composition" while remaining faithful to certain "conclusions [which] remain immovably fixed in my mind" (*LL* II, 204). He then moved on to address the issue of symbolism in art, only to return to a vindication of his "honesty"; and PRECISION is, certainly, the strongest vindication of the standard his artistic conscience has tried to live up to. Conrad at this point can wrap up the initial defense of his character: "But as to 'final effect' my conscience has nothing to do with that. It is the critic's affair to bring to its contemplation his own honesty, his sensibility and intelligence" (*LL* II, 205). Thus, once he has affirmed his personal integrity, Conrad turns his *argumentum ad hominem* against the critics. Will they engage in a reading which involves them personally? He himself did not have much patience with readings based on preconceptions or facile classifications. As he remarks in "Books" (1905), "more than one kind of intellectual cowardice hides behind the literary formulas" (*NLL*, 8).

The polemical vein in the letter to Barrett H. Clark confirms how difficult it was for Conrad to translate his convictions into critical language. Probing the possible meanings of that "something much larger" which he claims to be interested in does not lead to an understanding of his use of symbols. But his whole critical discourse is an attempt to elucidate those meanings. Throughout thirty years of prose writing he tried to point out that those immovable "conclusions" guiding his use of symbols were at the same time moral and aesthetic in character. His critical discourse itself is an attempt to create a theoretical language capable of expressing that "something much larger" which escapes classification. If this attempt has been unsuccessful, Conrad still has a right to claim that the critic must interrogate "his own honesty, his sensibility and intelligence" to discern in the texts what the writer is striving to express.

What is most startling in Conrad's May 4, 1918, letter to Clark is the naturalness with which the writer introduces PRECISION to vindicate the seriousness of his use of symbols. This sudden shift brings to the surface the central argument in the trope of PRECISION: the implications of his concern with precision, which guided the development of his sense of craftsmanship, kept bringing Conrad back to the ideas he set forth in the preface to *The Nigger*. Visual precision remained the first requisite for a suggestive use of prose language, while verbal precision remained the *sine qua non* for the rendering of the symbolic power of words. Conrad remarks on the necessity of finding a synthesis between suggestiveness and precision in a letter to Mrs. E. L. Sanderson (September [1910]). "In letters," he warns Mrs. Sanderson, "suggestiveness itself, – a great quality – must be obtained by precise expression" (*LL* II, 118). The most complex and far-reaching treatment of this issue is, however, the preface Conrad wrote for Ada Galsworthy's Maupassant translation (*Yvette and Other Stories*, 1904). Here, Conrad gives an unexpected twist to his discussion of how to achieve suggestiveness through visual and verbal precision.

The appeal in the preface to *The Nigger* for a "magic suggestiveness" which could breathe new life "over the commonplace surface of words" (*NoN*, ix) has been traced as a derivative of Flaubert's plea for "the right word." Why, then, does Conrad write in his 1904 preface to Ada Galsworthy's translation that "Maupassant, of whom it has been said that he is the master of the *mot juste*, has never been a dealer in words" (*NLL*, 28)? Obviously, something has happened between 1897 and 1904 that has refocused Conrad's sense of what the lesson from Flaubert and Maupassant had actually been. Conrad's evaluation of Maupassant's art in the 1904 preface can free the analysis of their relationship from later views of Maupassant as a writer ever in search of *"le mot juste."*

Maupassant's greatness is due to "the austerity of his talent," which is revealed by the way he "refrains from setting his cleverness against the eloquence of the facts ... [A]ll his high qualities appear inherent in the very things of which he speaks, as if they had been altogether independent of his presentation. Facts, and again facts are his unique concern" (*NLL*, 27). Conrad is making use of a rhetorical ruse he often adopts to justify himself, in order to defend Maupassant's austere fidelity to facts: he questions the readers' ability to understand the effectiveness of the writer's art. Maupassant's "simple and clear exposition of vital facts" did not earn him "the vast applause of the crowd." Just as "worthless glass beads strung on a thread have charmed at all times our brothers the unsophisticated savages of the islands," as Conrad ironically observes, "Words alone strung upon a convention have fascinated us" (*NLL*, 27–28). But Maupassant's "wares have been, not glass beads, but polished gems" (*NLL*, 28). How does Maupassant's austere concern with facts alone translate into a word-polishing art? This is the question implicit in Conrad's twofold recognition of the writer's greatness; and he finds the answer in the kind of precision which gives to Maupassant's words their particular power.

Conrad elucidates this point when he compares the early drafts of Maupassant's tales with their definitive versions. He recognizes the "unwearied endeavour" of Maupassant's craftsmanship in the way he improved "the true shape and detail" of his tales rather than their "diction." Nothing indeed is wrong in the early drafts' "expression"; it is "the conception which is at fault. The subjects have not yet been adequately seen." Conrad finds in Maupassant's revisions that the French writer's "vision by a more scrupulous, prolonged and devoted attention to the aspects of the visible world discovered at last the right words as if miraculously impressed for him upon the face of things and events" (*NLL*, 28). If the French writer does find the *mot juste*, it is only through a more precise rendering of "the visible universe" (*NoN*, vii). "His facts," he explains, "are so perfectly rendered that, like the actualities of life itself, they demand from the reader the faculty of observation which is rare, the power of appreciation which is generally wanting in most of us who are guided mainly by empty phrases requiring no effort, demanding from us no qualities except a vague susceptibility to emotion" (*NLL*, 27).

This is a far cry from the 1897 preface's aesthetic of fiction, which postulated that only through a "care for the shape and ring of sentences" can a novelist's medium acquire the status of art and thereby "reach the secret spring of responsive emotions" (*NoN*, ix). This change cannot be explained by positing a shift in Conrad's allegiances: there are too many traces of Maupassant's influence in the 1897 preface. More likely, the evolution of the artistic standard which motivated his commitment to authorship entailed a shift in the means he relied on to create a response in his readers. Conrad wrote the piece on Maupassant in May, 1904, while he was working on *Nostromo*, the novel which marks his return to the Flaubertian narrator of *Almayer's Folly*. Thus, the reasons for this shift are to be found in the transformation of Conrad's artistic purpose in these crucial years.

The analysis of the critical discourse of his 1897–1900 "paper boats" in the following chapters will provide a context for this shift. However, the examination of the PRECISION and EFFECT tropes already suggests what the reading of these tales will confirm. As a result of his probing of his medium's limits in his "paper boats," Conrad came to rely for the effectiveness of his writing in his later fiction more on time shifts, ironic narration and changing points of view than on a suggestively impressionistic language. It was in the distortions created by his "grouping (sequence)" and "changing lights" (*LL* II, 317) that Conrad found an alternative way of achieving PRECISION. Once he realized that he could not depend on his rhetorical self-projection in his fiction for a direct communication with his readers, he realized that it was impossible to make his "grown-up child's dreams" come true. This conclusion allowed him to wed his skeptical world view to his artistic convictions. The result was the paradoxical vein which runs at the center of his critical discourse. Fiction itself is paradoxical, and Conrad ceaselessly draws the reader's attention to the fact that the novelist is in a unique position to dramatize the truth of the irreconcilable dualities constituting reality. The paradoxes characterizing both the ambiguous semantic structure of Conrad's tales and his contradictory statements about his art are the most eloquent indication of the organic quality of his thinking.

CHAPTER 2

Working on language and structure: alternative strategies in The Nigger of the "Narcissus," "Karain" and "Youth"

Ford Madox Ford, in his preface to the posthumously published fragment of *The Sisters*, writes that Conrad stopped work on the unfinished story as a result of Garnett's suggestion that he try a more congenial (and commercially viable) sea story.[1] Conrad acknowledges his literary mentor's intervention in a March 23, 1896, letter (*CL* I, 268):

> you have driven home the conviction and I *shall* write the sea-story – at once (12 months). It will be on the lines indicated to you ... I am looking for a sensational title ... I suggest
>
> THE RESCUER
> A Tale of Narrow Waters

However, Conrad simply could not bring himself to write this tale, and *The Rescuer* was only completed twenty years later, with the title *The Rescue*. There was something in the tale which proved to be too irksome for him at that early stage in his career.

Why was it that Conrad could not write this love story at sea, set in the oriental surroundings he had evoked in his Malayan tales? Moser's answer – Conrad's inability to portray the passion between Lingard and Beatrix, the female heroine in the first draft[2] – has satisfied many commentators, who have used Moser's readings of passages portraying love themes in Conrad's novels to demonstrate the author's lack of control over his own writing and the "decline" of his creative power. In fact, it was precisely the first, tentative attempts to meet the ideal standard Conrad was setting up for his fiction which hindered the completion of *The Rescuer*.

Conrad himself gives Garnett an explanation of the basic untruthfulness he found in the writing of the love story set in the

South Seas, right after completing the first part: "Is the writing utter bosh? I had some hazy idea that in the first part I would present to the reader the impression of the sea – the ship – the seamen. But I doubt having conveyed anything but the picture of my own folly. – I doubt the sincerity of my own impressions" (June 10, 1896; *CL* I, 287). Garnett could not possibly understand what the sea meant for Conrad. Understandably, from his own point of view, the experiences of a sea captain could provide materials to add color to a popular story. Instead, the actual writing set off in Conrad a reflection on his "impressions" of his sea life which could be dealt with only by bringing into focus his subjective response to those experiences. The tale in *The Rescuer* was going one way and the actualization of that "hazy idea" – to be formulated in later years as the artist's "fidelity to the truth of his own sensations" – another. Conrad pursued the latter direction, and out of that "hazy idea" came *The Nigger of the "Narcissus."*[3]

In later years, Conrad used words which recall both the June 10, 1896, letter to Garnett and the "fidelity to the truth of my sensations" formula to explain what the actual writing of his sea story had meant for him. In the 1914 note "To My Readers in America," he avers that *The Nigger* "is the book by which, not as a novelist perhaps, but as an artist striving for the utmost sincerity of expression, I am willing to stand or fall."[4] What he had learned about fiction while he was writing *The Nigger* became his own standard of evaluation of his work. It is this standard that he will apply in the preface when he distinguishes between novelist and artist. In the same 1914 note, he describes the 1897 preface as the turning point of his artistic self-awareness. "After writing the last words of [*The Nigger*] . . . I understood that I had done with the sea, and that henceforth I had to be a writer. And almost without laying down the pen I wrote a preface, trying to express the spirit in which I was entering on the task of my new life."[5] The novel's completion, Conrad claims in his later reconstruction, led to a change of attitude to his craft.[6] He wrote the preface to communicate the hopes, fears and intuitions which accompanied this change.

In his first deep-sea tale Conrad had found the right tone for his fictional language and had begun to orchestrate different voices and points of view. He also went to the extent of using phrases from Maupassant to adjust the elegance of his expression to the clarity of his vision.[7] And, of even greater importance, each solution to a technical problem, each step toward an even greater effectiveness of his language resulted in an increased fidelity to the memories of his life at sea. As a result, for the first time the *déraciné* Polish aristocrat could use his fiction to appeal to his audience's instinctive recognition of a common set of values. The "spirit" he voices in the preface is not a narcissistic deciphering of his Muse's oracular calling. Conrad's "spirit" is rather a newly discovered confidence in his medium's power to convey his personal appeal to his English readers. The self-assurance which Conrad gained from the completion of *The Nigger* reflects the connection between the craftsman's sense of accomplishment and the man's enthusiasm for having found the means of realizing an ideal continuity between his old and his new life.

The Nigger of the "Narcissus"

Conrad's "striving for the utmost sincerity of expression" in his recollections of the sea initiates his quest for more effective means of expression. As Frederick Karl notes, Conrad's first sea story represents his initial attempt "to comment through a construct and not through a patchwork of discourse."[8] It is the quest for a truthful rendition of the complexity of his impressions that leads the writer to set up an interplay of different points of view which will eventually develop into the frame narrative of the Marlow tales. In the transitional form of *The Nigger*, language and narrative form illustrate different aspects of his discussion of the themes underlying his creative recollections. If the formal structure of the novel is centered upon the community of seamen, the sea is the central element of its language.

The sea allows Conrad's language to develop its natural cadence and verbal richness. Sentences in *The Nigger* have a greater suppleness, their length appearing more natural because of the enveloping effect of the different natural elements they portray. In its frequent, persistent connotations of "mysterious," "immortal" and "immense," the sea is the central verbal device for descriptions, ironical juxtapositions, and authorial commentary. Paragraphs acquire their proper functions with the inverted closure, a device that consists of descriptive passages closed by a reference to practical matters or nautical details, or accounts of events and actions closed by a reference to the sea or the wind. These techniques and verbal usages effectively convey the impression of the constant presence of the sea and its relevance to the men on board.

The novel's language certainly shows that the writer has found a more personal form of expression in the language depicting life on a sailing ship. At the same time, the sea provides him with a symbolical setting in which he can discuss the problematical quality of language. This setting's effectiveness for this purpose appears clearly in the scene which follows the climax of the story. The captain is facing his crew after the attempted mutiny, and he asks them to voice their grievances. But the sailors realize that they are unable to express their thoughts. The first person narrator describes them a few hours later, in the afternoon:

> Very little was said. The problem of life seemed too voluminous for the narrow limits of human speech, and by common consent it was abandoned to the great sea that had from the beginning enfolded it in its immense grip; to the sea that knew all, and would in time infallibly unveil to each the wisdom hidden in all the errors, the certitude that lurks in doubts, the realm of safety and peace beyond the frontiers of sorrow and fear. (*NoN*, 138)

The life of each individual crew member acquires its significance not through a self-seeking activity, but through an acceptance of a traditional code which links each with his fellows in an elemental struggle with nature. This particular acceptance of the sea code is a "common consent" to substitute the sea for common speech as a mode of reference to a life larger than the ordered society of a sailing ship.

The sea, therefore, even as it enriches the novelist's language, ultimately appears as the limit between the sayable and the unsayable. This is the radical contradiction which generates the gallery of first person narrators, of which Marlow is the best-known representative. The "children of the sea" are unconcerned with the profound meaning of the sea surrounding their ship. Like Singleton, who prophesies that Jimmy Wait will die the moment land comes in sight ("The sea will have her own" [130]), they accept its mysterious ways. Marlow, instead, is driven by his own imaginative and probing consciousness to test to the utmost limit the code uniting the men on board, by trying to behold the sea's depth and immensity. This probing, dramatized in so many of the later captains, from "Heart of Darkness" to "The Shadow Line," is represented more effectively through a first person narrative.[9] The conflict of points of view which characterizes *The Nigger* is intended, then, as an assertion of the sea code's value and its successful testing in the minds, not of thinly fictionalized crypto-writers but of actual seamen.

The Nigger's transitional nature is confirmed when attention is shifted from the novel's language to the narrative structure. The effort to render the impression of sea life bears as a first fruit a first person narrator who, after an introductory chapter told by an impersonal narrator, acts as speaker for the crew of the *Narcissus*. Throughout the tale the first person narrator maintains a particular stance, speaking as a collective "us," until the end, when he emerges as an individual to address a formal appeal to his fellow seamen.

The much-commented-upon lack of consistency in the handling of point of view in *The Nigger* is partly an effect of Conrad's need to preserve a direct channel of communication with the reader. Thus, one finds pieces of introspection in which the impersonal narrator directly refers to the first mate's or the cook's thoughts, or descriptive passages in which the author speaks of – or for – the sea.[10] Both kinds of break undermine the authority of the crew's speaker as narrator.[11] It is the crew's intrinsic inability to translate the presence of the sea into common speech that compels the omniscient narrator to fill in the inevitable gaps in the tale. But the thoughts of certain characters are indispensable for tying up the loose ends of the story, by emphasizing the limitations of the first person narrator and setting him in the ironic perspective which orders the contrasting points of view.[12]

The critical strictures regarding this lack of narrative consistency are more concerned with a theory of the novel than the effectiveness of Conrad's shifts in points of view.[13] The treatment of the story is far more impressive here than in Conrad's first two novels. The conflict of points of view in the sea tale does not produce a dissonant effect. On the contrary. The symphony of speeches, dialects, whispers and secret thoughts lends a choral quality to the voices of the ship's community.[14] Conrad's orchestration succeeds in combining the atmosphere of the forecastle with the presence of the sea in its dual role of antagonist and protagonist.

It is the ironic perspective in which Conrad sets the first person narrator's account that brings order to the contrasting points of view. At the core of *The Nigger*'s ironic structure is a nautical decision: the captain's order not to cut the masts, which the men – from whom the narrator is not detached – see as sheer indifference to their fate. As two anonymous sailors put it: " 'if the blamed sticks had been cut out of her she would be running along on her bottom now like any decent ship, an' giv' us all a chance,' said some one, with a sigh. – 'The old man wouldn't have it . . . much he cares for us,' whispered another." The first mate's retort focuses on how the sea code deals with the sailors' fears: " 'Care for you!' exclaimed Mr. Baker, angrily. 'Why should he care for you? . . . We are here to take care of the ship' " (79). The story's subsequent unraveling thoroughly acquits the skipper from the seamen's charge of unfairness: the decision eventually proves to save the ship. Once the wind shifts, the *Narcissus* stays its course. Without the masts it would have drifted toward the South Pole.[15]

The crew's fundamental attitude of unquestioning acceptance of the sea puts their respect for the captain in a different light: he is their link with the sea. The men's acceptance of the sea code is the most eloquent act they can perform within the limits of their mute "common consent." They can relate to the sea only as a body of men; and, in the larger frame of significance which their struggle with the sea gives to their lives, the principle of authority that saves the ship becomes the medium through which they can express their own individuality.

The Nigger of the "Narcissus" is the only sea tale in which Conrad uses a crew member as narrator. The choice is appropriate for the rendition of his own impressions of life aboard a sailing ship, and it is active in the implicit authorial comment about the captain's authority. But this choice has implications which illuminate Conrad's subsequent use of the sea in his fiction. The sea in *The Nigger* is a fierce antagonist of her crew. Against its overwhelming power, the men can set but the force of an ancient tradition ingrained in their instincts and a unifying symbol – the ship.[16] These two factors, sea code and love for the ship, allow the men to keep functioning, while preserving their relation with the sea itself. They are "the children of the sea" whose struggle with the elements is set in the natural world. In the impersonal narrator's words:

The true peace of God begins at any spot a thousand miles from the nearest land; and when He sends there the messengers of His might it is not in terrible wrath against crime, presumption, and folly, but paternally, to chasten simple hearts – ignorant hearts that know nothing of life, and beat undisturbed by envy or greed. (31)

The choice of a crew member as first person narrator in Conrad's first deep-sea tale is surely consistent with the "common consent" uniting the men in their relation with the sea. There is no attempt in *The Nigger* to unveil the secrets of the sea. "The brotherhood of the sea" (30) is presented as a covenant between a mythical sea and a group of numb men who do not ask the kind of questions Marlow will try to answer.

But using a crew member as center of consciousness limited Conrad's probing of the range of resonances of the human tragedy reflected in the mirror of the sea. After *The Nigger*, he would always select officers – at first, aging officers – to be the internal narrators of his sea tales. The captain is, above all, the link between the men and the sea, but he is also the only one aboard ship who is aware of the ambiguities existing within the "ideal standard of conduct" on which his authority rests.

The cadence and the impressionistic suggestiveness with which *The Nigger of the "Narcissus"* signals the introduction of the sea theme will become Marlow's language. It would be a mistake, however, to believe that Marlow descends directly from *The Nigger*'s first person narrator. Marlow is instead the outcome of the problems Conrad started to grapple with during the actual writing of *The Nigger*, and which had their first articulation in the preface set to paper a few months later. At the same time, out of the formal experiments that characterize *The Nigger*, a different device will take shape in the Marlow tales, and the interplay in contrasting points of view becomes the narrative frame structure.[17]

"Karain"

The deceptive simplicity of "Karain" and its exotic subject matter have led several commentators to disregard the story altogether. Frederick Karl goes so far as to say that "Karain" "did not engage Conrad intellectually."[18] This view is contradicted by the comments Conrad makes in the 1919 Author's Note to *Tales of Unrest*.

The insights which he provides in his revisitation suggest just how important was the position he assigned to this tale in the context of his decision to become an author.

When, twenty-two years after writing "Karain," Conrad tried to explain what he had been striving for in the story, he found that reading the tale produced in himself "the effect of something seen through a pair of glasses from a rather advantageous position." The visual simile is developed as Conrad adds that in the story he had "not gone back to the Archipelago." He had "only turned for another look at it." At the time he was "absorbed by the distant view, so absorbed that [he] didn't notice then that the *motif* of the story is almost identical with the *motif* of The Lagoon" (*TU*, vii). Here, again, Conrad's comments on his own art, far from being casual, focus on the central issues behind his writing. Oddly enough, in the Author's Note, Conrad does not discuss the single stories in a chronological sequence. He first writes about his third story, "The Lagoon," then about the second, "An Outpost of Progress," and lastly about the first complete tale he ever wrote, "The Idiots."[19] This confusion could be explained by appealing to Conrad's defective memory (in this same Author's Note, he refers to "Karain," his fourth short story, as his third). However, such an explanation contrasts with the use Conrad makes of what turns out to be a chronological reorganization – that is, the setting up of an explicit juxtaposition of "The Idiots" with "Karain."

The opposition pivots on *The Nigger of the "Narcissus,"* which Conrad had begun in June 1896 in Brittany (where he had just finished "The Idiots" [May 24, 1896]) and completed on February 19, 1897, when he had probably already started "Karain."[20] Conrad is interested in connecting the three works in order to outline his artistic evolution launched by the writing of *The Nigger*. He writes:

> The Idiots is such an obviously derivative piece of work that it is impossible for me to say anything about it here. The suggestion of it was not mental but visual: the actual idiots. It was after an interval of long groping amongst vague impulses and hesitations which ended in the production of The Nigger that I turned to my third short story in the order of time, the first in this volume: Karain: A Memory. (vii)

The shift which in Conrad's view determined the evolution from

"The Idiots" to "Karain" was largely the outcome of that "groping amongst vague impulses and hesitations" which went into the writing of *The Nigger*. Thus, the clarity Conrad gained while he was writing his first sea story produced a double result: in the preface to *The Nigger*, particular emphasis is given to a symbolic use of language, while in the Malayan story Conrad appears to be more concerned with the effect he can achieve by ordering conflicting points of view into a narrative frame. Conrad's narrative solutions and his reflections on his art in that crucial period were proceeding along parallel lines.

The visual similes in the 1919 Author's Note convey Conrad's recognition of "Karain"'s position in his work. It had been an improvement over "The Idiots," the suggestion for which "was not mental but visual" (vii). "Karain"'s visual quality, instead, is mental, to the extent that the author was so absorbed by the possibility offered by the narrative technique – that is, "the distant view" – that the motif itself became minor. The narrative frame in "Karain," then, can be seen as a revealing development in Conrad's reflections on the art of the novel which started with the writing of *The Nigger* and would lead to the later works with an omniscient narrator.

Conrad did not immediately evolve a more comprehensive "distant view," but chose instead to transform the first person narrator of *The Nigger* into a personally involved storyteller. At this stage, Conrad was trying to synthesize alternative strategies, applying the ideal view of fiction he had set forth in the preface to *The Nigger* to his actual narrative choices. The outcome of this synthesis can be seen only if the development of his work is considered not as an evolution toward a more "mature" style, but rather as an accretive process passing through metamorphoses rather than breaches.

"The Return," which Conrad began a few weeks before "Karain,"[21] clearly suggests why the writer could not transpose into a Flaubertian narrative form the conclusions he had reached in *The Nigger*. Both stories were written while he was working on the preface to *The Nigger*. And the treatment of the subject in "The Return" could certainly seem more cognate with the stance adopted in the preface – or at least with the position dominant in the artistic circles from which Conrad drew models for expression of his *symboliste* ideas. "The Return" is a story rich in *décadent* clichés, explicit in its exposure of English middle-class conventions, and self-conscious in its insertion of the poet figure, with its disturbing "Thorns and Arabesques" corollary. Conrad's critique of his Philistine audience is common to the narrative frame of "Karain" and the Marlow tales, but the tone and form in these tales are very different from those in "The Return."

The ironic tone of "The Return" only stresses that which makes Conrad's later trenchant handling of men and women in *The Secret Agent* so effective. In the 1897 tale, he is not yet able to convey the Dickensian sympathy throbbing in the ironic descriptions of characters such as Mr. Verloc or Inspector Heat. Ultimately, the ironic narrator in the earlier story is not truly objective. Conrad cannot yet handle impersonal narration and create, at the same time, a fictional world in which complexities of language and structure express an objective ambiguity. "The Return" is also interesting in that its language differs radically from the Conradese of the early Malayan stories. The comparatively concise language of "The Return" is neither precise nor suggestive. Evidently, the cosmopolitan setting did not evoke the kind of response which Conrad associated with the convoluted language of certain descriptions in *Almayer's Folly* or "The Lagoon."

"The Return" is not a proper expression of the ideals set forth in the preface to *The Nigger*: it seems only a parody of the artist's vision as outlined there. It is in "Karain," instead, that vision and language come together for the first time in a narrative form effectively adjusted to the organization of the structural tension latent in *The Nigger*. In later years, Conrad called "Karain" "the very first short story" he had ever written.[22] Certainly, the Conradian novella in its characteristic form begins with this tale. Here the author sets to work an internal consciousness which originates the multilevel structure of meaning characteristic of the Marlow tales. In "Karain," the elements which will go into the later elaborate structure are identifiable. But already this early application of the narrative frame anticipates how Conrad will use this device. Semantic ambiguity in the two narrators' suggestion of different levels of reading contradicts – or at least makes less relevant – the explicit story.

At the beginning of "Karain," Conrad offers the reader a number of hints as to the possible idiosyncrasies and biases which will condition the narrator's interpretation/distortion of the events he relates. The reader is told that the anonymous narrator is a mem-

ber of a class of persons who have lived dangerously and now share
the same sidewalk with him. A slight detachment is suggested,
nonetheless, when the narrator refers to the "befogged respect-
ability" of the newspapers in which he finds "the intelligence of
various native risings in the Eastern Archipelago" (3). The news
brings to mind his own experiences. He can see scenes from his past
in the reports coming from that part of the world. His memory
interacts with the reader's everyday life because it enlarges the
limited vision of other, distant worlds. "Karain"'s narrator will
take upon himself King Henry IV's admonition – "Be it thy course
to busy giddy minds with foreign quarrels" – which Conrad chose
as an epigraph for *Tales of Unrest*.

The narrator's enlarged vision, however, is disconnected from
the common perception of reality. His very past sets him apart from
his audience. His basic idiosyncrasy is an unresolved contradiction
between Western disbelief and Eastern illusion, and his narrative is
an enactment of this open dilemma. The two cultures are juxtaposed in the Jubilee sixpence scene which brings the whole narration to a climax. On a structural level, however, the effect of the
narrator's split sensitivity is far more subtle: he refrains from relating a fiction within a fiction, ostensibly isolating Karain's own
narrative.

The frame narrative in "Heart of Darkness" is distinguished
from the internal narrator who has personally undergone the
experience he is relating. The frame narrator in "Karain" is,
instead, also the person who has been changed by his experience in
the Archipelago. The basic difference lies in the authority assigned
to the narrators in the two frame structures. In "Heart of Darkness," Marlow's authority is derived from his having lived through
the experience he is relating, and his narrative can consequently
articulate in part a fictional form of a paradoxical statement. In
"Karain," the frame narrator does not have the authority to
integrate the voice of the Other into his story, and he must therefore distinguish it structurally from his own point of view.
"Karain"'s narrative does not conflate experience and testimony,
but distinguishes – in the writing as well – between narrator and
protagonist.

The vividness of Karain's presence in the story is symbolic of the
narrator's romantic past. His impressionistic descriptions of the
Malay chief, it follows, are consistent with his own persona. The

impressionistic suggestiveness of his story, however, does not necessarily make him a reliable witness. Conrad illustrates the narrator's attitude toward Karain in the first paragraphs, through a number of allusions to the Malay's theatricality.[23] Karain's first gesture is a "theatrical sweep" (4). Later, the narrator comments, he "presented himself essentially as an actor," and his land "was the stage where, dressed splendidly for his part, he strutted, incomparably dignified" (6). As the narrator recalls, "Day after day he appeared before us incomparably faithful to the illusions of the stage, and at sunset the night descended upon him quickly, like a falling curtain" (9). In his article "Conrad's 'Karain' and *Lord Jim*," Bruce Johnson writes that Conrad "continually reminds us that Karain is on a stage."[24] As a matter of fact, the theatrical references tell us more about the frame narrator than about Karain. The former's insistence upon the dramatic quality of Karain's performance of his duties reveals his own uncomprehending view of Malayan life and his inability to recognize its reality. The theater motif thus refocuses the narrator's initial characterization, undermining that faculty of vision he had claimed in the beginning.

The narrator himself questions the actuality of a power that requires such theatrical appearances. Thus, for example, when he notes that "It was almost impossible to remember who he was – only a petty chief of a conveniently isolated corner of Mindanao" (7), the historical specification is aimed at belittling Karain's self-importance. By so doing, the narrator stresses what he takes to be the illusory quality of Karain's power. But the momentary detachment of the "objective" view seen through Western eyes is balanced by an insight into the actual value of Karain's illusory power: his "quality was to appear clothed in the illusion of unavoidable success" (7). Karain's adoption of a stage-like appearance is necessary to keep his people united.

At the beginning of Chapter II, a shift occurs in Karain's characterization. The narrator recalls that "it was at night that he talked openly, forgetting the exactions of his stage" (10). Behind the public façade there is a living human being, real inasmuch as he talks "openly." Karain comes to life as a character by talking, by breaking through the narrator's enveloping tale. The structure of the short story gradually develops a fictional reality distinct from that of the reader and the frame narrator. But Conrad, as yet, does not allow the voice of the Other to affect the whole structure of his fiction.

The distance between the narrator and his audience is established by his personal memories of the Eastern Archipelago. The vividness of these memories gives him the power of vision which makes him a storyteller. But the linguistic and structural difference in "Karain" between the white man's narrative and the Malay's story is explicit. Later, in "Heart of Darkness," Conrad expands the fictional segment from Karain's eleven-page-long story to Marlow's tormented experience; and the frame narrator's function is reduced to recording the responses prompted by the amazing tale taking form aboard the *Nellie*.

But Conrad is already grappling with the issues he will address more explicitly in the African tale. The discursive form he uses to state the difficulties in establishing a communication between two radically different cultures suggests that he is moving in that direction. The writer's concerns surface when he reaches the point at which he transforms Karain from character to narrator to launch his narrative. The crucial passage which signals the shift from the frame narrator's account to Karain's tale foreshadows the more elaborate delineation of a critical discourse in "Heart of Darkness" and *Lord Jim*.

Toward the end of Chapter III, Karain has just made his sudden entry into the schooner's cabin. He is running from an invisible enemy, and the white men keep on questioning him about "what" is frightening him. Karain exclaims "Oh! the strength of unbelievers!" (24) who cannot see "who" is after him. The narrator reads into his look the power which the incomprehensible jumble of materials the whites rely on for their lives must have in Karain's eyes. The narrator, nonetheless, is aware that the unbelievers' strength has a price: "the strong life of white men . . . rolls on irresistible and hard on the edge of outer darkness" (26). The two men face each other from different worlds.

Awareness of an "outer darkness" is the distinctive trait which characterizes the group of men identified as "us" at the beginning of the tale. The disturbing inheritance which these men continue to carry with them during their lives among their more sedate countrymen ultimately confers on the narrator his authority and provides him with the clarity of vision to see through an otherwise opaque East. The narrator has not been able to render these memories in a tale; he lets them speak for themselves, in the words of Karain. Conrad does not have him interpret the Malay's story, and after the internal tale is over, the frame narrator will appear as an actor in the drama taking place in the short story.

The way in which Conrad sets up the juxtaposition of tale with frame narrative in "Karain" anticipates the care he will take in foregrounding the critical discourse in the Marlow tales. At first, Karain is presented essentially as an actor and can talk openly only at night. But when the Malay is transformed into a narrator ("We expected him to speak. The necessity within him tore at his lips" [26]), the frame narrator becomes aware of his reality. And he immediately questions the prejudice "that a native will not speak to a white man." In denying this commonplace, he makes an extremely telling distinction between the white man coming as a "master . . . to teach or to rule," and the "wanderer" who "asks for nothing and accepts all things." In the latter case, "words are spoken that take no account of race or colour. One heart speaks – another one listens" (26). This is precisely what is happening aboard the schooner, and the magical quality of this encounter gives Karain's story-within-the-story a living reality. The narrator has qualified himself since the beginning as a "wanderer," and this is why he is in a position to relate the words spoken by the Malay. The truthfulness of his account depends on the kind of person he is.

"He spoke at last," begins the next paragraph, and the narrator comments: "It is impossible to convey the effect of his story. It is undying, it is but a memory, and its vividness cannot be made clear to another mind" (26). This is Conrad speaking, and in this first example of a narrator's direct address to his imaginary audience, one finds definite verbal anticipations of Marlow's brooding reflections. "Effect" is the concern of the novelist, not of the storyteller, and it is one of the fundamental tropes of Conrad's critical discourse. It is only natural that Conrad's disguise should wear thin in this climactic passage of his orchestration of languages and points of view. Read in the context of Conrad's overruling concern with EFFECT, the narrator's doubts reveal that at the time Conrad wrote "Karain" the concept of the radical incommunicability of subjective experience was already well established in his view of fiction.

A rhetorical commentary in which Conrad invests an internal narrator with his own concerns accompanies "Karain"'s conclusion. After Karain's tragic tale ends, the narrator seems to see him for the first time. And he expresses this revelation in words made significant by the tale's context and their association with Conrad's critical discourse. "I looked at that man, loyal to a vision, betrayed by his dream, spurned by his illusion" (40). Karain is no longer an actor. He has become, through his actualization as a storyteller, the embodiment of all illusions:

looking at his rigid figure, I thought of his wanderings, of that obscure Odyssey of revenge, of all the men that wander amongst illusions; of the illusions as restless as men; of the illusions faithful, faithless; of the illusions that give joy, that give sorrow, that give pain, that give peace; of the invincible illusions that can make life and death appear serene, inspiring, tormented, or ignoble. (40)

Thus, Conrad evokes the tropes of FIDELITY and IDEALISM the first time he uses an internal narrator to integrate critical discourse and fictional language. Awareness of the ideas he casts in these tropes helps solve the paradox of someone becoming real once he embodies all illusions. This paradox is not the result of some inner conflict which the writer was unable to solve either emotionally or rationally. On the contrary. It is the radical of the tension underlying his struggle with the novel form in the 1897–1900 period. He could not reconcile himself with the sense of unreality inherent in writing. In "Karain," the first occurrence of the narrative frame indicates the course he will take in order to overcome the limitations of the novel: the discursive line he wanted to open to his readers.

Conrad has given to the frame narrator's account a form which illustrates how Karain's reality has remained paradoxical for him, even after his return to Britain. In looking back to his youth, the frame narrator refers, figuratively, to both the meaning of his memories and the commitment which binds him to their enduring lesson. This puzzlement has become part of the narrator's life, and he cannot dismiss the power of illusion. He comes to represent an ideal reader who is willing to make fiction part of his own life, to accept the implications of an intellectual encounter with an alien reality.

"Karain"'s narrator has witnessed the effect an illusion can have on a man, but he cannot articulate the meaning of that experience. He is caught in the middle when, at the end of the story, he watches Karain and the Malays leave the schooner for the last time. Karain lifts his arms and points to "the infallible charm" – the Jubilee sixpence; his men stare "very much puzzled and impressed," and the narrator can only conjecture: "I wondered what they thought; what he thought; . . . what the reader thinks" (52). Conrad needs an internal narrator who can voice both experience and testimony. In order to achieve this, he has to develop a technique that can express in one narrative voice those functions divided into two different segments in "Karain." Marlow will be able to bring this about by throwing the gauntlet down before his public, pointing out their own imperfections.

"Youth"

The unsolved dilemma which still conditioned the frame narrator in "Karain" was, in a way, an extremely autobiographical theme for Conrad. He was dramatizing the alienness of his memories from the culture of his audience. In so doing, he makes a first attempt to establish a communication which takes into account the distant voices, the unsolvable paradoxes, the writer's coming to terms with the limits of points of view. With the introduction of Marlow's inquiring consciousness, the "fictional" segment – expressive of an alien point of view – is no longer separated from the narrator's memory, and the two segments present in "Karain" are moulded into a tale in which story and commentary counterpoint different interpretations of the same event.

In the Malay tale, however, the narrative frame highlights clashing points of view. The same will be true of "Heart of Darkness" and *Lord Jim*. In these tales, Conrad addresses issues which he knows will be extremely disquieting for his Western readers. This is not the case in "Youth," where the frame narrator assures Marlow of the sympathy and solidarity he can count on when handling a theme such as youth. In his first Marlow tale Conrad is trying to use autobiography and "the bond of the sea" to overcome his sense of separation from his audience.

The frame narrator in "Youth" stresses uniquely his agreement and sympathy with Marlow. In the opening paragraphs of the short story, he qualifies himself and the whole narrative in a couple of passing remarks. The way the story is told "could have occurred nowhere but in England" (Y, 3). Familiarity with the sea is taken for granted by Marlow throughout the tale: "We were flying light, and you may imagine how bad it was when I tell you we had smashed bulwarks and a flooded deck" (6). Moreover, the narrator's acquaintance with Marlow is slight – he has never seen his name written – but they are all united by the "bond of the sea, and also the fellowship of the craft" (3). He then all but disappears, to return in the last paragraph to answer Marlow's final appeal: "and, tell me, wasn't that the best time, that time when we were young at sea ... ?" (42). His answer, "And we all nodded at him," is accompanied by a description of the old men, worn out, and nostalgic for their lost youth and illusions. Conrad probably never achieved such a perfect ending. All the different narrative elements come together and there is a real aesthetic pleasure in the way the whole matter is brought to rest.

However, the agreement between narrative frame and story is, in a sense, a Pyrrhic victory. Conrad had selected for "Youth" a theme which would meet the largest possible approval from the public: a nostalgic song for lost youth, a wistful regret for the passing of time. So important is this for Marlow that he addresses his audience as old men: "She was tired – that old ship. Her youth was where mine is – where yours is – you fellows who listen to this yarn" (17). And in a way he is right: the narrative's effectiveness depends ultimately on the readers/listeners sharing the common fate of growing old.

In relating how he experienced his adventures as a young second mate aboard the *Judea*, the mature Marlow offers a commentary on the events and the behavior of his younger self. This interjected duality is fully expressed in the form given to the account of the *Judea*'s ordeal, seen through the eyes of the young Marlow and told by the old captain. Rhetoric and impressionistic narrative express two distinguishable attitudes of the same character. But what makes this tale unique in Conrad is that eventually these two points of view are brought together in the story's happy ending. The ease with which Conrad shifts from a description to his comment is unique:

I remember sixteen hours on end with a mouth dry as a cinder and a steering-oar over the stern to keep my first command head on to a breaking sea. I did not know how good a man I was till then. I remember the drawn faces, the dejected figures of my two men, *and I remember my youth* and the feeling that will never come back any more ... the triumphant conviction of strength, the heat of life in the handful of dust, the glow in the heart that with every year grows dim, grows cold, grows small, and expires – and expires, too soon, too soon – before life itself. (36–37; emphasis added)

Marlow comments on this passage: "And this is how I see the East." When Conrad describes the young Marlow's arrival in port and his first physical contact with the East, he reaffirms, "But for me all the East is contained in that vision of my youth. It is all in that moment when I opened my young eyes on it" (42). The old Marlow then establishes an equation between romantic vision and memory, thus making a selection of his memories which his audience's approval confirms.

Although the mature Marlow in "Youth" manages to conflate his narrative with the point of view of the younger self, a distinction can be made between their respective narrative authority. The young Marlow's way of "seeing" his adventure is ironically undermined by the old captain. The story is full of references to the young Marlow's idealization of all his experiences, in particular his romantic reading of the *Judea*'s motto, "Do or Die." Far from appearing prosaic, these words seem extremely inspiring to the young Marlow: "I remember it took my fancy immensely. There was a touch of romance in it" (5). During a storm the ship "seemed to me to throw up, like an appeal, like a defiance, like a cry to the clouds without mercy" its motto (12). But when the ship sinks, the old Marlow points out how "the unconsumed stern was the last to sink; but the paint had gone, had cracked, had peeled off and there were no letters, there was no word, no stubborn device that was like her soul, to flash at the rising sun her creed and her name" (35).

There is a definite ironic streak, then, in the old Marlow's recollection of his former impressions, made even more obvious by the fact that his audience is made up of seamen. The young Marlow is a bad reader, and his elderly counterpart does not miss any chance to point out the contrast between his own narrative authority and that of his younger self. In the tale, Conrad is not mocking his own idealized view of the sea; at the time of his voyage aboard the *Palestine* he had already lost his youthful enthusiasm. In "Initiation," one of the articles included in *The Mirror of the Sea*, Conrad recalls the Danish barque episode which signaled his final detachment from a romantic view of the sea (*MoS*, 128–148). The fact that the episode related in "Initiation" took place before the voyage aboard the *Palestine*, which Conrad recreated in "Youth,"[25] further undermines the reliability of the young Marlow's impressionistic account.

Marlow and the narrative frame create a number of different points of view which, while making one single interpretation extremely problematical, notably enrich the textual language. The structure may well obscure the tale's meaning, but the narrative authority that determines which language is more accurate in portraying the events is unquestionable: Marlow's reflections provide the perspective for all the voices and images and the past moments of his personality which form his narrative. In "Youth," the perspective created by the conflation of rhetoric and story clearly indicates that the mature Marlow's ironic commentary has a greater narrative authority than the young Marlow's impressionistic account. If the latter's point of view were not contained within the old man's voice of experience, the vividness of the story could not, by itself, bring forth the detachment and involvement needed to express the individual and universal experience of growing old. The young Marlow is basically the necessary counterpoint of experience.

The Marlow technique was used only once, in "Youth," as a device to establish direct communication between author and audience. The two narrations interwoven throughout the short story cannot be separated; the centrality of their interrelation is sanctioned by the frame narrator's final assent. When this assent is no longer sought – in "Heart of Darkness" and *Lord Jim* – the rhetoric/story conflation evolves into radical opposition between fictional rendition and communication, and the Marlow technique then becomes a device for investigating areas of consciousness in which lack of communication is expressive of resistance to unwelcome truths. When Marlow probes the listeners' response in "Heart of Darkness," he will not try to use his rhetorical interruptions of the story to connect his narration with a positive view easily accepted by his audience. Instead, his commentary will activate a nervous tension sustained by his own direct challenging of their beliefs. By so doing, Conrad draws the reader's attention toward those uncomfortable insights he had acquired by living and, in particular, writing about, the experience narrated. The characteristic ambiguity of any reading of "Heart of Darkness" and *Lord Jim* is determined, basically, by a conflict between fictional story and rhetorical commentary in which the latter constantly questions the validity of the former by challenging its reality. It will be in these works that the critical discourse in Conrad's fictional language will acquire its proper "realistic" function: namely, the articulation of an extra-fictional communication between author and reader.

CHAPTER 3

The mirror effect in "Heart of Darkness"

"Heart of Darkness" is the furthest point in Conrad's attempt to communicate his intended effect through a suggestive language paralleled by an extra-fictional communication. In carrying out this effort, he used the narrative strategies he had been defining through "Karain" and "Youth" for an explicit discussion of his interpretation of his own writing. And, in effect, he uses for the first time in "Heart of Darkness" the frame narrator's involvement and Marlow's commentary to probe the theoretical assumptions underlying the possibility of communicating past subjective experience.

An interpretation of the critical discourse which directs the readers' attention to the difficulties the writer had in re-creating his subjective experience helps clarify how Conrad gave shape to the suggestively impressionistic language he had first envisaged in the preface to *The Nigger of the "Narcissus."* The effectiveness of the tale's language is the result of a narrative strategy based on the interweaving of two languages. Through an impressionistic account, Conrad makes the readers "hear . . . feel and . . . see" (*NoN*, x) scenes and characters from the past. On the other hand, through Marlow's commentary, Conrad strives after a different kind of accuracy: that precision which he calls, in his non-fictional writings, "fidelity to the truth of my own sensations."

In the tale's critical discourse, Conrad casts the latter, overriding, concern in terms which he later explains in his Author's Note to *Typhoon and Other Stories.* In this 1919 reflection, he first states that all the stories in the collection "were written with a conscientious regard for the truth of my own sensations" (*T*, vii). He then defends his intention in writing "Falk" by remarking that "in most of my writings I insist not on the events but on their effect upon the persons in the tale" (*T*, vii). Marlow makes this concern explicit in "Heart of Darkness" when he warns his audience, "I don't want to bother you much with what happened to me personally." But they must know the events of the story "to understand the effect of it" on him (*Y*, 51). The way Conrad chose to convey this effect was a juxtaposition between a *story* of "what happened" to Marlow and a *tale* of the effect that those events had on him.

The conflictive effect apparent in "Heart of Darkness" follows from Conrad's struggle with the theoretical issues raised by the writing of the story. This very effect, ironically enough, has given rise to most of the tale's adverse criticism. Those commentators who set the narrative's impressionism against Marlow's "mixing himself up with the narrative"[1] cannot forgive Conrad for holding back the reader with hazy problems in a work otherwise so successful in its visual, "realistic" representations. F. R. Leavis, for example, bases his reading of "Heart of Darkness" on the contrast of its most realistic impressionistic descriptions with Marlow's rhetorical interruptions and Conrad's "adjectival insistence upon inexpressible and incomprehensible mystery."[2] In *The Great Tradition*, Leavis springs at Marlow's comments, "I've been . . . repeating the phrases we pronounced – but what's the good? They were common everyday words" (144), with a sort of saturnine élan: "What's the good, indeed? If he cannot through the concrete presentment of incident, setting and image invest the words with the terrific something that, by themselves, they fail to convey, then no amount of adjectival and ejaculatory emphasis will do it."[3] The problem with this critical approach is that Marlow's interruptions are meant to question the very possibility of "investing the words" through concrete details. The impressionistic language cannot be read without its "adjectival and ejaculatory" gloss.

The aim of Marlow's narrative, embedded as it is in the narrative frame, has nothing to do with an impressionistic effect achieved through realistic details. The *story*'s impressionistic portrayal acquires its proper significance only when reflected within the "rhetorical" portion of the narrative. The mirror effect thus outlined envisages a basic paradox: the most "realistic" passages in "Heart of Darkness" are not the physical descriptions but Marlow's rhetorical addresses to the audience: these dramatize the transformation of such descriptions into a tale of his memories.[4] In these moments Marlow defines himself – and is defined by the frame narrator/listener – as a figure outside fiction whose function is to probe and emphasize the actuality of his act of telling.

Conrad plays on the illusory quality of an impressionistic re-creation of memory to discuss the question which orders the tale's critical discourse: how to write (and read) a story? The way in which he articulates this question is the clearest example of how the critical discourse works in the early Marlow tales. Two pieces of writing can help recognize the terms in which Conrad casts this question and trace his tentative answer: the tale's 1917 Author's Note and a letter he wrote to Cunninghame Graham after the appearance of the tale's first installment.[5]

Conrad warns his friend in his February 8, 1899, letter that he may still be disappointed by the next two installments: "So far the note struck chimes in with your convictions – mais après?" In the next installments, he writes, "the idea is so wrapped up in second-ary notions that You – even You! – may miss it. And also You must remember that I don't start with an abstract notion. I start with definite images and as their rendering is true some little effect is produced" (*CL* II, 157–158). This passage has received a great amount of critical attention, especially for Conrad's claim that his method posits first a concrete image, and only later an idea, or "abstract notion."[6] Though the visual precision of Conrad's tales fully justifies this claim, the interpretation of the passage is incom-plete if one does not take into account the fact that Conrad employs four terms to indicate the conceptual element in his creativity: "idea," "secondary notions," "abstract notion" and, later in the same letter, "right intention." Furthermore, by concentrating on how Conrad starts writing, one misses the whole emphasis of the paragraph, which is concerned primarily with the problem of EFFECT, the ultimate aim of his craftsmanship.

Conrad's misgivings are not of a stylistic nature. If he is caution-ing his friend it is not because he doubts whether he has found the *mot juste*. The "truth" of his rendering of images has to do with the inability to solve the moral and theoretical problems posited by his vision. Conrad's fictions at their best steer clear of any didacticism or propaganda – the only cases in which an artist starts with an "abstract notion." Every literary image necessarily contains an "idea" given by the writer's subjective experience of the objective world. Inevitably, in trying to render that image, its "truth" – to continue with Conrad's terminology – is determined by the parallel rendition of the visual details and the "secondary notions" which, far from being abstract, represent the guiding principles by which to act. (For example, the final "choice of nightmare" which leads Marlow to remain faithful to Kurtz's memory, as well as his appraisal of the cannibals' "restraint," are both "secondary notions.") In writing to Cunninghame Graham, Conrad is expressing his concern that the effect of his work may be lost when his convictions are different from those of his readers.

As long as Cunninghame Graham finds confirmation of his own ideas in the piece, he will like it, whether or not he agrees with the writer's convictions. But what will he think of the "idea" when Conrad's uncomfortable "secondary notions" will set in the foreground a difference from rather than a similarity with his own convictions? "There is an après," Conrad again forewarns his friend, but "I think that if you look a little into the episodes you will find in them the right intention though I fear nothing that is practically effective" (*CL* II, 158). Conrad's exhortation reflects what Marlow tries to do in the tale. His fellow agnostic Scottish friend is quite the opposite from the listeners aboard the *Nellie*, and Conrad knows he will find a sympathetic reader in the Socialist aristocrat when he denounces the horrors of imperialism. But the tale's development will not have a practical, propagandist effect. The inevitable conflict between artistic effect and practical effectiveness is not solved in "Heart of Darkness" – to the point that today his "secondary notions" are considered imperialistic and racist.[7]

Eighteen years later, in the Author's Note to *Youth: A Narrative; and Two Other Stories*, Conrad explains how he had tried to force Cunninghame Graham and the other readers to "look a little into the episodes." He compares at first "Youth" and "Heart of Darkness." The earlier tale "is a feat of memory. It is a record of experience; but that experience, in its facts, in its inwardness and in its outward colouring, begins and ends in myself" (x–xi). In effect, Conrad in "Youth" had used an impressionistic language to recreate the glamorous appearance that the events of the story had for the young Marlow. In "Heart of Darkness," instead, experience is "pushed a little . . . beyond the actual facts of the case for the perfectly legitimate, I believe, purpose of bringing it home to the minds and bosoms of the readers." In the African tale, "it was no longer a matter of sincere colouring. It was like another art altogether." So much so that Conrad resorts to an aural metaphor to describe how he tried to surcharge the effect of the tale's "colouring": "That sombre theme had to be given a sinister resonance, a tonality of its own, a continued vibration that, I hoped, would hang in the air and dwell on the ear after the last note had been struck" (xi).

This striking description reveals the theoretical overtones of the language Conrad was striving for in writing "Heart of Darkness." The mirror effect between impressionistic language and the re-creation of subjective experience dramatizes in the text the difficulty of translating the memory of visual and aural sensations into words. Conrad made a radical choice to overcome this difficulty: he would rely on verbal suggestions rather than the realism of visual impressions to convey the effect which the Congo experience had on Marlow. This choice is made explicit in a reading model outlined in a passage set at the climax of the tale's critical discourse. And it is also evident in the shifts from "seeing" to "hearing" in the tale's imagery as Marlow approaches Kurtz. These shifts effectively integrate the tale's imagery with its thematic structure. Once the intellectual drama created by Conrad's narrative strategy is uncovered, the writer's paradoxical statement – realistic narrative is illusionary, whereas trying to establish a direct line of communication with the readers is concrete – appears to give unity to the text.

I

The exchange between Marlow and the would-be-listener/frame narrator in the tale's opening provides the key for a reading of the different linguistic levels sketched by the narrative frame. The frame narrator has a double function in the first pages. His most explicit function includes the describing of the setting (the way he stresses the "bond of the sea"), introducing the characters, and reminding the reader that he is the same narrative voice of "Youth": "Between us there was, as I have already said somewhere, the bond of the sea" (45). His second, more important function, begins when he launches into a rhapsodic hymn to the "spirit of the past" which the Thames evokes in a seaman. In this long passage he expresses views which were certainly also Conrad's, such as the actuality of the memories which form the tradition of the British navy "for a man who has, as the phrase goes, 'followed the sea' with reverence and affection" (47). Conrad did indeed write, in "Legends" (1924), the essay he was working on when he died, that legends "are a form of memory . . . a fine form of imaginative recognition of the past" (*LE*, 44). In "Tradition" (1918), he points out that it is "perhaps because I have not been born to the inheritance of [the Merchant Service] tradition . . . that I am so consciously aware of it" (*NLL*, 196). Understandably, then, some commentators have identified the frame narrator with Conrad himself.[8] This identification, however, hinders a proper reading of Conrad's handling of the voice, of that irony which allows him to mingle those platitudes Marlow will later attack with insights inserted in the narration.[9] When the frame narrator embroiders on the instinctive feelings arising from the sunset on the river, the legends become banners of civilization. At this point the frame narrator voices a kind of language which Marlow will later attack, a language which is part of the narrative frame, while the frame narrator's first reflections, we learn by contrast, were silent.

When Marlow first speaks it is immediately clear that he is pursuing a completely different thought. He has been thinking that "this also . . . has been one of the dark places of the earth" (48). And when he recalls the light which "came out of this river since," he stops to address the frame narrator, "you say Knights?" (49), thus questioning the narrator's reference to "all the men of whom the nation is proud, from Sir Francis Drake to Sir John Franklin, knights all, titled and untitled – the great knights-errant of the sea" (47). Conrad is clearly having Marlow question the frame narrator's generalization about how they all "looked at the venerable stream," differentiating the internal narrator's outlook from the one of his audience, and setting up that ironic perspective which characterizes the conflict between the wandering seaman and his listeners.[10]

As the frame narrator's reliability is being undermined, his role changes again. Conrad uses his comments on what Marlow is saying to point out the way in which Marlow tells a story. Conrad maps out this strategy in the first pages through a series of duets and "asides" in which the critical discourse makes clear from the very beginning that in this tale the telling of the story is extremely problematical. The passages in which the tale's critical discourse is first made explicit are the frame narrator's famous disquisition about "the meaning of an episode" for Marlow, and the latter's own reminder that his first concern is with "the effect of [an experience] on me." The two passages cast light on one another, illuminating the implications of the narrative's dual quality.

Marlow is described, at first, in opposition to other seamen. He is a wanderer, they are "sedentary": their minds "are of the stay-at-home order" and their yarns "have a direct simplicity, the whole meaning of which lies within the shell of a cracked nut." Marlow spins yarns like any other seaman, but his stories – like his mind – are "not typical." For him, the frame narrator explains, "the meaning of an episode was not inside like a kernel but outside, enveloping the tale which brought it out only as a glow brings out a haze, in the likeness of one of these misty halos that sometimes are made visible by the spectral illumination of moonshine" (48). The only way of obtaining a "meaning" would be to crack the tale's nutshell and thus extract the meaning one wants to find. The frame narrator is cautioning the readers about such a procedure; and he does so by focusing attention on the tale itself rather than the story.

Critical commentaries on this passage have usually centered attention on the physical juxtaposition of "inside" and "outside," as if "episode" were the pivot on which Conrad's distinction balances.[11] As a matter of fact, the pivotal term is "tale." The episode's meaning is brought out by the tale, "as a glow brings out a haze." The telling, rather than the event itself, generates meaning.[12] The "spectral illumination of moonshine" would then seem to stand for the inner vision which elaborates past experiences into memory and linguistic rendition, while the tale is the account of both an event and its effect on the writer. The frame narrator is drawing the reader's attention to the duality of Marlow's story. He warns his readers that they must not concentrate on Marlow's account of the events in which he is protagonist, but rather on the distortions which the re-creation of his subjective experience produces on the narrative. The "meaning" of the episode lies in the traces of how he experienced those events.

Another duet between Marlow and the frame narrator a few pages later further clarifies the mirror quality of "Heart of Darkness"'s language. Marlow begins his narrative, and the listeners resign themselves, as the frame narrator remarks, to "hear about one of Marlow's inconclusive experiences" (51) – inconclusive, certainly, since only haze would come out of the cracked nutshell. Before starting, however, Marlow warns his audience that

"I don't want to bother you much with what happened to me personally." The frame narrator comments: "showing in this remark the weakness of many tellers of tales who seem so often unaware of what their audience would best like to hear." In this "aside" the frame narrator's didactic function appears in its clearest form. Conrad underlines the tension the Marlow figure exercises on his audience's expectations by using the narrator to point out the different challenges brought to a conventional reading of the story.

Marlow then explains that he will have to "bother" his audience with the events of the story so that they can "understand the effect of it on me." This passage, in elucidating the terms of the *story–tale* juxtaposition suggested in the "misty halos" passage, brings to an end Conrad's discussion of the narrative strategy underlying Marlow's yarn. He then introduces the story proper, always emphasizing the perspective he has established on the respective importance of events and effect. In order "to understand the effect of it on me," Marlow offers his listeners a précis of the whole story, accompanied by a statement of its significance for him:

to understand the effect of it on me you ought to know how I got out there, what I saw, how I went up that river to the place where I first met the poor chap. It was the farthest point of navigation and the culminating point of my experience. It seemed somehow to throw a kind of light on everything about me – and into my thoughts. It was sombre enough, too – and pitiful – not extraordinary in any way – not very clear either. No, not very clear. And yet it seemed to throw a kind of light. (51)

The technique at work in this passage reminds one of the Greek tragedies in which an actor appeared at the opening to tell the story. The motifs are similarly anticipated in "Heart of Darkness": the self-knowledge he has acquired during the voyage, the light–darkness opposition, the "poor chap" he will meet. Marlow's description of Kurtz as that "poor chap," in particular, suggests that by the time he begins his storytelling he has recovered from his African "nightmare." Its evocation, however, will bring back the shock waves of his encounter with Kurtz in the wilderness.

Once Marlow's story begins, his function as a figure stressing the actuality of his act of telling becomes apparent. He is more than a character: he is the actualization of the "story" in linguistic terms.[13]

In narrative terms, he originates changes in rhythm, by looking at, or thinking about, different events and feelings. In effect, his narration in "Heart of Darkness" is made of a series of vignettes and descriptions of persons he meets, causing variations of rhythm within the same paragraph when he shifts from impressionistic descriptions to commentary. Even the ironic juxtaposition technique (which in later works will be achieved through authorial changes of point of view) is presented as an apparently unreflecting redirection of Marlow's attention.

Marlow performs his role as narrative device through his accounts of "what [he] saw" (51). By so doing, he brings into play irony, thematic juxtapositions and shifts in tone and pace. This quality of his narrative gives him a particular role in articulating the thematic imagery which grounds the story's symbolic structure: the interplay between light and darkness. Isolated from its context, this interplay could appear to generate only a multitude of paradoxes. However, viewed within the transformation of the sensory references in Marlow's description of his voyage, it comes to be part of a more comprehensive discourse. Later in his narrative, the mirror effect will reveal how he will evolve from his role as eye witness. In trying to relate the wilderness' appeal, Marlow will start to mistrust his eyes and will increasingly rely on his hearing.

Marlow first sees Africa from a French steamer: "I watched the coast. Watching a coast as it slips by the ship is like thinking about an enigma. There it is before you . . . always mute with an air of whispering, Come and find out" (60). His view of the "almost featureless" continent is closely associated with the absurdity of the white men's activity, and he feels that his condition keeps him "away from the truth of things, within the toil of a mournful and senseless delusion." A sound comes as a relief: "The voice of the surf heard now and then was a positive pleasure, like the speech of a brother. It was something natural, that had its reason, that had a meaning." This is Marlow the seaman speaking, and this impulse is extended to the sight of the natives vigorously paddling their boats: they "gave one a momentary contact with reality." The energy of these men "was as natural and true as the surf along their coast. They were a great comfort to look at. For a time I would feel I belonged still to a world of straightforward facts" (61). His recognition of their reality does not allow him to solve the enigma of the mysterious coast, but helps him distinguish himself from the colonialists.

In "Heart of Darkness," a "positive" sound or sight is often followed by a "negative" one. This pattern, constantly repeated, eventually forms a corollary to the seeing–hearing motif: the opposition between the sounds of civilization and the sounds – or silence – of the wilderness. This connotation of the dominant imagery motif suggests to what extent Marlow's rendition of what he has seen or heard depends on the text's rhetorical organization and its critical discourse. This pattern is at work again in the episode of the "incomprehensible" French man-of-war, "firing into a continent." A man-of-war is a perfectly known entity from Marlow's culture, while the African continent is an enigma. The appearance of the former in this setting is unnatural; the sounds which accompany its sight, ludicrous: "Pop, would go one of the six-inch guns; a small flame would dart and vanish, a little white smoke would disappear, a tiny projectile would give a feeble screech – and nothing happened." A remark Marlow hears aboard the steamer, made by somebody "assuring me earnestly there was a camp of natives – he called them enemies!" (62), further sets the French ship's shelling within European culture: the definition "enemies" would justify the aggression, but in fact it makes it even more absurd.[14]

It is this cultural conflict which creates the difficulties Marlow has in relating his experiences. That the black men working on their paddles are "natural and true" does not lead him to find a way of understanding or describing them. The "meaning" that he is unable to grasp is constantly there, before his eyes, and yet it is utterly obscured. It is as "natural" as the voice of the surf, "something natural, that had its reason, that had a meaning." But he is forced within the limits of the language of those who label the natives as "enemies" or "criminals."[15]

The way in which the tale's rhetorical organization proceeds in parallel with the sequence of the story's episodes reveals the steps by which Conrad undermines the white men's language – and, consequently, many of the ideological presuppositions which ground his audience's response. Right after the French battleship episode, Marlow reaches the Congo's estuary and from there continues aboard a small steamer up river to the Company's station. As Marlow walked toward the station, he recalls, a "heavy and dull detonation shook the ground, a puff of smoke came out of the cliff, and that was all." One is reminded of the ship, of course, and Marlow duly points it out: "Another report from the cliff made me think suddenly of that ship of war I had seen firing into a continent. It was the same kind of ominous voice." Conrad further stresses, in a strikingly impressionistic scene, the way in which Marlow's sudden thought reflects earlier episodes. The blastings occur while a group of chained black men pass next to him: "Six black men advanced . . . erect and slow . . . I could see every rib, the joints of their limbs were like knots in a rope." Marlow's description of the chain-gang is often anthologized for the vividness of its impressionistic details. Its larger effect, though, is lost if one misses how explicitly Marlow's comment connects it with his earlier juxtaposition of the free black men with the French ship: "these men could by no stretch of imagination be called enemies. They were called criminals, and the outraged law, like the bursting shells, had come to them, an insoluble mystery from the sea" (64). But, then, the discourse which Conrad articulates through Marlow's rhetorical interruptions has interesting political overtones. Whereas the impressionistic narrative describes the effects of imperialism, Marlow's reflections point out its cause: the will to power of European culture. Thus, the tale's mirror effect illuminates a resistance to unwelcome insights in the scathing rejections of the internal narrator's commentary.

Marlow's connecting function sets in relief the continuity of different images and situations, referring them to the tale's fundamental themes. His mental associations or abrupt shifts of attention make these connections possible, drawing the readers' attention to the way in which the tale's progress brings together critical discourse and realistic narration. At times, Marlow's thoughts acquire a proleptic quality. But since his tale is the expression of a reminiscence, these prophetic anticipations represent moments in the telling in which, *post hoc*, he detects illustrative presagements of what is yet to come. A clear example of these anticipations, which are revelatory of the organic integrity of tale and story, occurs as Marlow is turning away from the path to avoid the chain-gang. He is shocked by this particularly repulsive form of violence: "these were strong, lusty, red-eyed devils, that swayed and drove men –

men, I tell you" (65). He then checks his inflamed burst of eloquence and pauses in his storytelling to note:

But as I stood on this hillside, I foresaw that in the blinding sunshine of that land I would become acquainted with a flabby, pretending, weak-eyed devil of a rapacious and pitiless folly. How insidious he could be, too, I was only to find out several months later and a thousand miles farther. For a moment I stood appalled, as though by a warning. (65)

These proleptic visions and connecting associations sustain the "continued vibration" Conrad refers to in his Author's Note.

Marlow at this point enters the "grove of death." In this scene as well, references to the legalistic justification of the blacks' exploitation stress the horror inspired by the nightmare he portrays. The men dying in the shade had been "Brought from all the recesses of the coast in all the legality of time contracts, lost in uncongenial surroundings, fed on unfamiliar food" (66). This information is part of that discourse which at times emerges in Marlow's exchanges with his audience, and at other times appears in the fictional language to emphasize particular themes in the narrative structure. In the "grove of death" episode Marlow's descriptive details of the black workers resonate with the (non)sense of the law/shells coming to them mysteriously from the sea. The idea of "legality of time contracts" could appear simply ironic if Marlow in the preceding pages had not made vividly clear the tragic association of violence and ideology.

The *story–tale*'s mirror effect casts the sinister light of the "grove of death" scene on Marlow's encounter with the Company station's chief accountant. The "bit of white worsted" (67) round the neck of an agonizing black is recollected a few paragraphs later by the immaculate appearance of the chief accountant. It is from him that Marlow first hears Kurtz's name, along with a number of hints which will acquire their significance only later. The accountant's special thematic function is to underline the horror of the "grove of death." As he works in his office he breaks out: "When one has got to make correct entries, one comes to hate those savages – hate them to the death." Perhaps he is writing down some legal "time contracts." But just in case someone may miss the point, Marlow, on leaving the office, notes that the accountant, "bent over his books, was making correct entries of perfectly correct transactions; and fifty feet below the doorstep I could see the still tree-tops of the grove of death" (70). Connections within the text are made, as usual, through the evocation of the particular effect the scene had on Marlow.

The contrast between the common humanity Marlow recognizes with the natives and the absurdity of the whites' presence is radicalized during the two-hundred-mile tramp to the Company's Central Station. This is his first contact with the wilderness. But the landscape is not yet the absolute Other he will face while he is approaching Kurtz's Inner Station. The traces of the white colonists have covered the entire forest with a hallucinatory grimness. Again, Marlow uses a sound to convey his recognition of his solidarity with the blacks. At night he hears "far-off drums . . . a sound weird, appealing, suggestive, and wild – and perhaps with as profound a meaning as the sound of bells in a Christian country" (71). As he proceeds on his journey, however, he introduces a motif which will later allow him to convey a sense of the presence of wilderness itself, its silence. Wilderness persists, in daylight, as silence. The silence motif starts as a notation of the positive or "natural" presence of the wilderness as distinct from the white men's "fantastic invasion" (76).[16] It will then become the salient feature of the descriptions as well, until it will come to appear as the dominant note in the tale's "continued vibration."

The description of the Central Station and the traders whom Marlow calls "a lot of faithless pilgrims" enriches the conflict between the sounds of civilization and the silence of the wilderness with a destructive vehemence unequaled in Conrad's writing. A new word is added to the ideological repertoire characterizing the conquest: "The word 'ivory' rang in the air, was whispered, was sighed. You would think they were praying to it . . . By Jove! I've never seen anything so unreal in my life" (76). No detail could be more effective than the evocation of an uncanny silence, throbbing with life, surrounding the ivory-worshiping camp: "through the faint sounds of that lamentable courtyard, the silence of the land went home to one's very heart – its mystery, its greatness, the amazing reality of its concealed life" (80). Nowhere is this reality more apparent than in Marlow's efforts to express the effect of what he saw:

The great wall of vegetation, an exuberant and entangled mass of trunks, branches, leaves, boughs, festoons, motionless in the moonlight, was like a rioting invasion of soundless life, a rolling wave of plants, piled up, crested, ready to topple over the creek, to sweep every little man of us out of his little existence. And it moved not. (86)

Those repetitions piled one on top of the other render the impossibility of organizing into a rational picture the vitality of the wilderness. There is something in that vitality which speaks, but the human mind is unable to understand it.

Marlow's perception, from the beginning of his adventure – that the effectiveness of the white man's language in this alien world was based only on its violence – opened the possibility of distinguishing himself from the greedy pilgrims. But it also exposed him to the appeal of the wilderness. At this point no piece of writing or speech purporting to carry a rational, civilized "message" can help him. He must extract from the menacing silence surrounding him something to help him understand what he is both seeing and feeling. This something can be expressed only by Kurtz.

On the first night in the camp, a preposterous figure introduces Kurtz into the narrative. A brickmaker who makes no bricks, he is a telling representative of how "work" is being done in the Central Station. Actually, the brickmaker is the Station manager's spy, and he is trying to learn something about the connections between Marlow and Kurtz. In this dialogue, words torn from the enclosing silence begin to free Kurtz's figure from the haze surrounding his name. The brickmaker, speaking about him, begins to "declaim suddenly," portraying him as "the guidance of the cause intrusted to us by Europe." But these qualities are a hindrance: according to the brickmaker, Kurtz, the "emissary of pity, and science, and progress," is a member of an opposed faction, the "gang of virtue" (79); and he is convinced that Marlow, too, was sent by the same group.

Marlow does not contradict the brickmaker because he hopes this lie can help Kurtz. This is Marlow's first positive gesture in favor of Kurtz, and its justification leads to the climax of the tale's critical discourse. Why does Marlow lie for Kurtz? The argument set up in the long scene with the brickmaker, "this papier-maché Mephistopheles" (81), emphasizes the abstract quality of the attraction Marlow feels for Kurtz, who is associated at first with the question of the jungle's stillness: "I wondered whether the stillness on the face of the immensity looking at us two were meant as an appeal or as a menace." A series of questions follow, under the appalling shadow of the wilderness. "I felt," Marlow continues, "how big, how confoundedly big, was that thing that couldn't talk, and perhaps was deaf as well." He is utterly lost in the heart of the forest. "I could see a little ivory coming out from there, and I had heard Mr. Kurtz was in there. I had heard enough about it, too – God knows! Yet somehow it didn't bring any image with it – no more than if I had been told an angel or a fiend was in there" (81). Will Marlow's tale "bring any image" of Kurtz out of the wilderness? Will he see "an angel or a fiend"; will he hear "an appeal or . . . a menace"? This is the principal narrative problem of Marlow's voyage toward Kurtz.

The relevance of Marlow's not having seen Kurtz at this point is central for the narrative strategy underlying the voyage toward Kurtz, which becomes apparent when Conrad sets the narrative frame's function in the foreground in this passage in order to emphasize the theoretical issues he will be tackling in the tale. Marlow explains his white lie with the notion that "it somehow would be of help to that Kurtz whom at the time I did not see – you understand." What should his listeners understand? He widens the scope of "seeing" apparently to explain what he means: "He was just a word for me. I did not see the man in the name any more than you do. Do you see him? Do you see the story? Do you see anything?" (82). In having Marlow voice this appeal – which is a far more troubled formulation of Conrad's 1897 definition of his task: "to make you hear, to make you feel – it is, before all, to make you *see*" (*NoN*, x) – the author is dramatizing his own doubts about being able to communicate with his readers.

The meta-narrative quality of the passage is confirmed by the narrator's comparing the re-creation of his past to a dream. "It seems to me," Marlow tells his listeners, "I am trying to tell you a dream – making a vain attempt, because no relation of a dream can convey the dream-sensation" (82).[17] This is not simply another of Conrad's frequent revisitations of the Calderonian "la vida es sueño." The central word in Marlow's appeal to his listeners is not "dream," but "dream-sensation." Conrad elaborates on this distinction in the paragraph which follows: "No, it is impossible; it is impossible to convey the life-sensation of any given epoch of one's existence – that which makes its truth, its meaning – its subtle and penetrating essence. It is impossible. We live, as we dream – alone" (82). The questions Marlow is raising are of central importance for an understanding of the conflicts arising from the difficulties Conrad found in expressing the conscious and unconscious mnemonic materials he worked into his fiction.[18] The analysis of the trope of FIDELITY has shown that a commitment to voicing an appeal coming from his past guided his work. But nowhere in his canon does Conrad link the issue of memory with writing as explicitly as he does in "Heart of Darkness." Marlow's skeptical "it is impossible to convey the life-sensation of any given epoch of one's existence" is an explicit formulation of Conrad's difficulties in translating into words his "fidelity to the truth of [his] sensations." This formulation sets in the foreground the theoretical dimension of the narrative strategy underlying the *tale–story*'s mirror effect: the "life-sensation" that Marlow is struggling to express is nothing else than the "effect" on him (51).

Jeremy Hawthorn, in *Joseph Conrad: Language and Fictional Self-Consciousness* (1979), reads Marlow's words as a reflection on the "*isolation* of writing that induces a dream-like feeling of unreality for the novelist."[19] He then uses a remark Conrad made in his introduction to Thomas Beer's study of Stephen Crane – "life is but a dream – especially for those of us who have never kept a diary or possessed a notebook in our lives" (*LE*, 93) – to point out when writing is not a dream. For Conrad, he concludes, it "seems clear that what was *not* a dream ... was collective, physical work to achieve a common goal."[20] A reading which takes into account the parallelism of the "dream-" and the "life-sensation" paragraphs invites a different interpretation of the interesting cross-reading suggested by Hawthorn. In his introduction, Conrad is saying that one's life seen only through memory appears as a dream. But then, in writing, the dream-like quality of memory undergoes a transformation. A writer, in re-creating materials from his past feels as if he were reliving a dream; and in writing he finds a way of recovering a sense of the reality of the sensations his former self experienced. Writing, therefore, is not equated to relating a dream: it is an extremely concrete act. What is problematical is the communication of that "life-sensation" which in one's past represents the essence of subjective experience.

The passage launched by Marlow's "It seems to me I am trying to tell you a dream" (82) is Conrad's most direct discussion of that difficult relationship with his audience which in his non-fictional writings he addresses through the trope of EFFECT. It provides therefore a key to understanding the difficulties he was trying to surmount through the narrative frame structure. Conrad's childhood experience had been totally alien to that of his English readers: he could never really count on an identification between his linguistic associations and those of his audience. His use of his personal memories leads to a sequence of irreconcilable dualities. On the one hand, his memory was all that was left of his community; and integrating the expression of his memories was a commitment to that community. On the other hand, his reminiscences had to be translated into English words to be expressed in a communicable form. The aesthetics of fiction he enunciated in 1897 represents the clearest indication of the solution he attempted: he would try to achieve the "condition of art" (*NoN*, vii) in order to create a literary language which could transcend his alienness from his audience without repudiating his own cultural identity.

In the paragraph following the "life-sensation" passage, Conrad reverts to using an "aside" of the frame narrator to share his doubts and hopes with his readers. After the frame narrator has interjected – "He paused again as if reflecting" – Marlow picks up the "seeing" theme which had launched his meditations: "Of course in this you fellows see more than I could then. You see me, whom you know . . ." The frame narrator introduces at this point in the narrative his longest remark. He recalls, at first, that "It had become so pitch dark that we listeners could hardly see one another" (83). Why does the listener comment that aboard the yawl they could not see one another in response to Marlow's "You see me" appeal? The apparently rambling digression suddenly tightens:

It had become so pitch dark that we listeners could hardly see one another. For a long time already he, sitting apart, had been no more to us than a voice. There was not a word from anybody. The others might have been asleep, but I was awake. I listened, I listened on the watch for the sentence, for the word, that would give me the clue to the faint uneasiness inspired by this narrative that seemed to shape itself without human lips in the heavy night-air of the river. (83)

Here, the frame narrator brings out, as if he were a litmus paper, the intellectual and emotional effect the author is seeking. His "uneasiness" is proof that the tale is undermining the placid security he had voiced at the beginning, and that in the increasing darkness he is losing those bearings which supported his comfortable notion of history. At this point in the narrative he has a very clear notion of what could provide him with a "clue" to the irrational feeling generated by the tale: a sentence, or a word.[21] This statement, viewed outside its textual background, loses much of its significance. Guerard, for example, commenting on this passage, notes that "there is no single word; not even the word *trance* will do."[22] But the word, the sentence, is the *tale* which the frame narrator is listening to in the darkness.

This passage confirms the role Conrad assigned to the frame narrator in the duets with Marlow in the first pages of "Heart of Darkness." He is an ideal reader aware of the mechanism of Marlow's storytelling. The frame narrator has tuned in to Marlow's tale. Marlow's effort to convey the effect on himself of his past experience is met by the frame narrator's attempt to come to terms with the "uneasiness" created by the "unspeakable" portion of the tale. In this definitive formulation of the reading model envisaged at the opening of the short story, Marlow's "you fellows see more than I could then" (83) is converted into the listener's realization that only particular words chosen by the narrator can bring out the meaning of the story, "as a glow brings out a haze" (48).[23] The "continued vibration" of the theme's "sinister resonance" (xi) echoes in the perplexed language of Marlow's revisitation of his past.

The listener's comment brings to a climax the expression of Marlow's frustration at not being able to communicate the "life-sensation" of his past experience or, at a meta-narrative level, Conrad's effort to make the reader see the essence of that dream set down in the process of writing. The context of the silent duet is Conrad's attempt to overcome the communication gap between himself and his audience by creating a suggestive language. There is in the frame narrator's words a tone of urgency on Conrad's part. At this point he has deployed all the rhetorical devices which the narrative structure put at his disposal, and he has drawn the boundaries between *tale* and *story*. As Marlow comes to terms with the limitation of his senses and intellect in their confrontation with the wilderness, the theoretical problems suggested in the "life-sensation" passage are given a spatial, physical dimension.[24] Once the voyage toward Kurtz begins, hearing and seeing become narrative elements embodied in the Marlow figure.

II

The impressionistic descriptions of what Marlow saw in Africa are mirrored by the reflections of what he felt and heard (or imagined he was hearing) in the oppressive silence of the forest.[25] Conrad uses two themes to connect his narrator's sensations during his journey up-river with the tale's underlying discourse. At first, he introduces WORK, to explain how Marlow's rational defenses react under stress. Then, as the captain gets closer to Kurtz's Inner Station, the author describes the kind of revelation his narrator anticipates from his meeting with the ivory trader. These two themes add a particular suspense to the tale: the narrator's urge to understand what he is hearing and feeling develops into a growing eagerness to listen to Kurtz. The success of his narration/re-creation depends on having the reader "see" through his tale what he heard in the heart of darkness.

On one of the last nights at the Central Station, Marlow is lying quietly on the steamer's deck. He is listening to the manager and his uncle talking about Kurtz. At one point he hears them wondering why Kurtz had suddenly returned to the deserted Inner Station instead of accompanying his ivory to the Central Station. "They were at a loss for an adequate motive." But not Marlow: "As to me, I seemed to see Kurtz for the first time. It was a distinct glimpse." He believes he can envisage the scene because he feels he sympathizes with the motive of Kurtz's behavior: "I did not know the motive. Perhaps he was just simply a fine fellow who stuck to his work for its own sake" (90). It is Marlow's imagination not his rationalization that makes him the narrative voice Conrad needs. At the same time, however, his seaman-like approach makes him the ideal witness who can put into words the effect the wilderness had on him.[26]

Throughout the navigation Marlow reacts against the passivity engendered by the powerful stillness of the jungle, by forcing himself to concentrate on his work. But the more he tries to shut out the wilderness, the more its appeal becomes invasive and his concern with his work appears to him as a holding on to a straw. His first direct contact with the jungle's silence touches him deeply:

There were moments when one's past came back to one, as it will sometimes when you have not a moment to spare to yourself; but it came in the shape of an unrestful and noisy dream, remembered with wonder amongst the overwhelming realities of this strange world of plants, and water, and silence. And this stillness of life did not in the least resemble a peace. It was the stillness of an implacable force brooding over an inscrutable intention. (93)

This last sentence has been singled out as the flattest and most superfluous instance of Conradian rhetoric. And yet every single word, starting from "stillness" (which indeed is the physical manifestation of both "force" and "intention"), carries a definite meaning. "Stillness of life" is an oxymoronic concept difficult to grasp other than as an undefined aggression poised to be set loose. The world of men, of language and time, appears as a "noisy dream" opposed to the "overwhelming realities" of this silent world.

Conrad renders the "effect" this world has on Marlow by having what he sees interact with the abstract feelings that the wilderness arouses in his imagination. Conrad is trying to reify "stillness," but this can be done only by expressing Marlow's imaginative response. Nowhere does "it" appear more vividly than when the captain remarks: "It looked at you with a vengeful aspect." Fortunately, his work helps Marlow resist the fascination of this silent mermaid song: "I got used to it afterwards; I did not see it any more; I had no time." He is responsible for the ship; and, by concentrating on "signs of hidden banks . . . [and] . . . signs of dead wood" (93), he can keep himself safe from imagination – for the time being at least.

This does not mean that in telling the tale he is unaware of what he was doing at that time:

When you have to attend to things of that sort, to the mere incidents of the surface, the reality – the reality, I tell you – fades. The inner truth is hidden – luckily, luckily. But I felt it all the same; I felt often its mysterious stillness watching me at my monkey tricks, just as it watches you fellows performing on your respective tight-ropes for – what is it? half-a-crown a tumble. (93–94)

"Try to be civil, Marlow," a listener complains, and Marlow excuses himself, adding "I forgot the heartache which makes up the rest of the price" (94). Conrad is acknowledging how the tale could affect his readers, and he provokes them through Marlow, just as he will in *Lord Jim*, where the "price" is spelled out more clearly: "I could be eloquent were I not afraid you fellows had starved your imaginations to feed your bodies" (*LJ*, 225). Marlow's awareness (during his storytelling) of the defenses he had been building against the appeal of the wilderness opens the way to an extension of his experience to his listener's life.

Marlow's own imagination is sick, and the recognition of its response to the mute appeal of the wilderness brings him to hope that Kurtz's words could make him understand, rationally, what that appeal means. The captain's disgust for the violence and greed of Europeans leaves him defenseless. The only way out for Marlow is to find the words to convert into expressions of his consciousness the sensations and impressions he is receiving in a dream-like state.

As Marlow approaches the Inner Station, Kurtz comes to appear increasingly as a "voice," and the whole sense of Marlow's quest is turned into a chance to hear Kurtz speak. This comes to Marlow as a revelation after his helmsman has been killed during an attack. He is angrily taking off his blood-soaked shoes when he is struck by a sudden realization:

I couldn't have been more disgusted if I had travelled all this way for the sole purpose of talking with Mr. Kurtz. Talking with . . . I flung one shoe overboard, and became aware that that was exactly what I had been looking forward to – a talk with Kurtz. I made the strange discovery that I had never imagined him as doing, you know, but as discoursing. (113)

He then explicitly contrasts seeing Kurtz with hearing him: "I didn't say to myself, 'Now I will never see him,' . . . but, 'now I will never hear him.' The man presented himself as a voice" (113). After establishing this expectation, Marlow places in perspective how Kurtz's "gift" makes him significant in the tale. He acknowledges that Kurtz is connected in his memory with all sorts of reprehensible actions, but "That was not the point." What is important is that he was "a gifted creature." And among his gifts "the one . . . that carried with it a sense of real presence, was his ability to talk, his words" (113). This may well seem a paradox.

Could eloquence ever constitute a "real presence"? It is indeed paradoxical, but intentionally so. Only in this way can Marlow explain why he expects Kurtz to give him the words to understand the appeal of the wilderness which he feels resounding in his imagination. Kurtz has "the gift of expression, the bewildering, the illuminating, the most exalted and the most contemptible, the pulsating stream of light, or the deceitful flow from the heart of an impenetrable darkness" (113–114). Conrad resorts to a string of paradoxes to recast the light–darkness opposition structuring the tale's imagery. He is seeking in this particular logical form a means of bringing out in a linguistic expression the irrational content which underlies his experience in Africa.

The writer uses the narrative frame as well to emphasize that he is quickening the tension of Marlow's tale. A listener interrupts the narrator while he is saying how desperate he was for having missed the chance to hear Kurtz. Marlow reacts vehemently: "Why do you sigh in this beastly way, somebody? Absurd? . . . This is the worst of trying to tell" (114). Conrad foresees that his audience will have great difficulties in following him, and he jabs at his readers, probing their mental apathy: "Here you all are, each moored with two good addresses, like a hulk with two anchors, a butcher round one corner, a policeman round another" (114). Conrad is questioning the reader's right to judge Kurtz, and by so doing he highlights the character's function in the tale's critical discourse. Further on in the tale Marlow will inform the reader that he "had turned to the wilderness really, not to Mr. Kurtz" (138); and, certainly, Kurtz's function in the tale is to "translate" into English the otherwise inaudible whisper of the wilderness. He will allow Marlow to narrate the darkness, allowing him to get as close as he can to the words which sounded out for him the echo from Kurtz's hollowness.

The problem Marlow faces is how to convey the radically inexpressible voice of the wilderness. The language he is forced to use is exposed when he tells his audience about Kurtz's "beautiful piece of writing," rich with "exotic Immensity ruled by an august Benevolence" and ending with "an exposition of a method": "Exterminate all the brutes!" (118). This chilling unmasking of the reality behind the white man's language wraps up the combined elements of the sounds-of-civilization theme. There is an implied contrast between Kurtz's report and the copy of *An Inquiry into Some Points of*

Seamanship that Marlow finds in a hut along the banks of the river. The two pieces of writing stand for different uses of language, but read in the heart of the darkness, they seem similar in showing how feeble is the language of civilization when it has to contain the insurgence of irrationality. The rules of conduct set down in the seaman's manual are primarily rational defenses Marlow opposes to the appeal of the wilderness. They give him the illusory sensation that he can still escape from the conclusions reached during his voyage. The book, he confesses, had given him "a delicious sensation of having come upon something unmistakably real" (99). As it turns out, the *Inquiry* had been left behind by the absurd Russian harlequin.

Marlow's last chance to understand what he is hearing in his imagination is that speaking to Kurtz will help him interpret the silence of the jungle. But the appearance of the Russian harlequin restores Marlow's self-control. The young enthusiast lets Marlow perceive for the first time how dangerous Kurtz is, thus preparing him for what will come next. His discovery of Kurtz's report already made clear how eloquence is only a manifestation of those sounds of civilization which come to the people and land of Africa like shells lobbed from the sea. Now, at the end of his journey, he will *see* how Kurtz has interpreted the appeal of the wilderness. The way Conrad contrives this shift in the use of the hearing–seeing theme, while preparing the solution he will give to the suspense built around Kurtz, is worth following step by step.

Marlow can see in the young Russian a practical effect of Kurtz's eloquence, and it becomes immediately clear to him that the young man's "devotion to Kurtz . . . [was] . . . the most dangerous thing in every way he had come upon so far." In the scene of the first encounter between Kurtz and the Russian there is an echo of what Marlow had waited for during the whole trip: "I suppose Kurtz wanted an audience, because on a certain occasion, when encamped in the forest, they had talked all night, or more probably Kurtz had talked." Marlow's own expectation starts waning, and when the young adventurer cries, "He made me see things – things," Marlow's last hope to have the wilderness rationalized and explained is lost. Here, in front of him, he has the living proof that the danger is amplified by Kurtz's words. As the Russian is talking, he looks around. And as he does so, he says "I don't know why, but I assure you that never, never before, did this land, this river, this jungle, the very arch of this blazing sky, appear to me so hopeless and so dark, so impenetrable to human thought, so pitiless to human weakness" (127). Marlow is learning to detach himself from the imaginary creature he had created, and in the process partly recovers his self-consciousness – along with confidence in his sight, increased by a pair of binoculars.

When he can no longer stand the story of Kurtz's exploits, Marlow breaks in with, "Why! he's mad." But the Russian replies as usual that, had Marlow "heard him talk, only two days ago," he would not have dared "hint at such a thing . . ." The suspending ellipsis emphasizes how abrupt the attention shift is this time: ". . . I had taken up my binoculars while we talked, and was looking at the shore." He is really "turning to wilderness," trying to ignore the feeling created by the Russian harlequin's account of Kurtz's behavior. It is the same impulse which had originally made him seek the famous trader. It is as if he were comparing the Russian mariner's tale to the woods: "There was no sign on the face of nature of this amazing tale that was not so much told as suggested to me in desolate exclamations, completed by shrugs, in interrupted phrases, in hints ending in deep sighs" (129). A word is a sound, and speech only a series of grimaces, at the moment of insight which comes with an awareness of the human suffering Kurtz is causing in the adoring natives. "The consciousness of there being people in that bush," he recalls, "made me uneasy." His sense of a common humanity gives Marlow the chance again to use his sight and moral perception. What he sees with his binoculars are the "symbolic . . . heads on the stakes" (130). And it is at this point, with the binoculars trained on the heads of the "rebels," that Marlow understands what he can hear from Kurtz. The trader will not be able to voice the appeal resonant in the wilderness in any noble form. He can, however, reveal the frightening basis of the appeal which the silence had held for him as he entered the heart of darkness.

Marlow recognizes in what way the wilderness has triumphed over the white man's conquest, singling out the apostle of light: "the wilderness had found him out early, and had taken on him a terrible vengeance for the fantastic invasion" (131). The chilling glimpses of the appeal he thought he had heard during the voyage find confirmation in what he surmises had happened to Kurtz: "I think [the wilderness] had whispered to him things about himself which he did not know, things of which he had no conception till he took counsel with this great solitude – and the whisper had proved irresistibly fascinating. It echoed loudly within him because he was hollow at the core . . . I put down the glass" (131). In passages such as this, tale and story are so bound together as to make Conrad's narrative strategies seem organic. There is nothing obtrusive in the superimposition of rhetorical comment on the moral act of recoiling in front of the horrible scene. It is difficult to tell if what is voiced here is Marlow's instinctive response or the reflection originated by his re-creation of the scene. What is certain, at any rate, is that a fundamentally moral judgment colors his view of how the wilderness has acted on Kurtz. Marlow is no longer imagining. Now that he *knows* that Kurtz is "hollow at the core," Marlow is able to read the wilderness' appeal as a message coming from within himself rather than from without. Inner and outer landscapes are no longer confused, for at this point in the story Marlow finds his moral bearings in the alien reality of the jungle and is able to pass judgment. Marlow's projections culminate in the "hollow at the core" passage. As of now, Marlow still has to meet Kurtz, but he no longer expects him to shed any light on the darkness that has engulfed him on the trip up the river. He now knows that whatever he will hear from Kurtz will be an echo of that same darkness – and that he is now better equipped to interpret it.

When Kurtz finally appears, Marlow's response is ironic, slightly disdainful. Marlow watches the demagogue through his binoculars, and after chafing the Russian about Kurtz's ability to "talk so well of love in general" (133) he actually sees Kurtz talking – but from a safe distance: "I could not hear a sound, but through my glasses I saw the thin arm extended commandingly, the lower jaw moving, the eyes of that apparition shining darkly far in its bony head that nodded with grotesque jerks" (133–134). As long as Marlow is beyond the reach of Kurtz's voice, his glasses – those invaluable instruments for dominating reality – will protect him. As long as he will *see* him speak rather than hear him, his imagination will be left at rest. Once Kurtz is aboard, however, Marlow falls under his spell. He is struck at first by his voice: "The volume of tone he emitted without effort, almost without the trouble of moving his lips, amazed me. A voice! a voice!" (135). The humanity of the natives has been outraged by Kurtz as much as by the other traders. Why, then, does Marlow "choose" Kurtz? He answers, "Ah! but it was something to have at least a choice of nightmares." The following pages will partly explain what this choice means. But for the moment Marlow qualifies his turning to Kurtz by specifying, "I had turned to the wilderness really, not to Mr. Kurtz, who, I was ready to admit, was as good as buried" (138). Marlow has only one way out: if he wants to be truthful both to his convictions and to what he has discovered about himself in the solitude of the jungle, he must accept the dark side of wilderness.

On his way to Africa, Marlow had described his impression of the voyage along the coast as "a weary pilgrimage amongst hints for nightmares" (62). As he narrates the story, the string of impressions will appear to Marlow as if seen in a dream. It is only after he has related his encounter with Kurtz that he comes out of the trance he had entered during the re-creation of the past and finds that those "hints for nightmares" have found confirmation. He stresses over and over again how the nightmares are brought about by his choice not to dismiss Kurtz's memory:

I did not betray Mr. Kurtz – it was ordered I should never betray him – it was written I should be loyal to the nightmare of my choice (141) . . . It is strange how I accepted this unforeseen partnership, this choice of nightmares forced upon me (147) . . . I remained to dream the nightmare out to the end, and to show my loyalty to Kurtz once more (150).

Once he is back in the "sepulchral city" he sneers at the people who seem to be hurrying "to dream their insignificant and silly dreams" (152). His own dream has opened such insights into the mere show played by his fellow men to cover their true motives that even their dreams seem untrue.

In "Heart of Darkness," "dream" describes the experience in Africa, and "nightmare" Marlow's living out the "moral shock" (141) in which his encounter with Kurtz culminated. This distinction is important for understanding how the thematic progress outlined by the critical discourse participates in the tale's rhythmic pattern. It would be difficult to explain the changes Marlow undergoes during his telling without envisaging the complex effect that the stirring of his memories has on him. Several commentators have investigated the implications of Marlow's Buddha-like characterization. Robert O. Evans, for example, suggests that "Conrad seems to wish the reader to think of Marlow at the time he is telling the story as one making a recollection in tranquillity."[27] Rather, Marlow's urge to tell the story in order to cope with the painful inheritance of his past recalls Coleridge's Ancient Mariner. The "pose of a Buddha preaching in European clothes" (50) is dropped by the time Marlow reaches the farthest point of his narration.

His first reference to Kurtz, "the poor chap" (51), suggests how much he had succeeded in removing from his consciousness the lingering recollection of the shock. Conrad's play on "dream" and "nightmare" reveals that, just as "the meaning of an episode" was "brought . . . out" for Marlow by the tale (48), the actuality of the pain – the nightmare – is brought out by the act of telling (or writing) his trance-like revisitation of the dream. The rational composure which characterizes the controlled rage, tenuously veiled by an urbane irony at the beginning of the narrative, is reflected in the long sentences, the relaxed tone he uses with his listeners. Yes, one knows that the narrator is interested in relating the effect of those experiences on him – but, one supposes, only the effect they had on him while he lived them. Once the trip up the river begins, however, and style and rhythm become tortuous, nervous, and the tale more radically different from the story, Marlow's reflections seem to take place anew, as if he were again – or for the first time – discovering the significance of episodes and scenes. While he is unraveling his memories, Marlow is also confronting the actuality of the puzzling and painful feeling his own tale is evoking. One discovers, then, that what had begun as telling a dream has become experiencing a nightmare – and the effect of it on Marlow is there, vibrating throughout the tale.

III

The figure of a frame narrator perceptive enough to synthesize Marlow's narrative technique and to understand how the tale must be read allows Conrad to discuss his own difficulties in communicating with his readers. However, at the end of "Heart of Darkness," when the critical discourse outlines the disturbing notion of a fictional tale turning into a nightmare once its content becomes real, Conrad cannot use the device of casting this notion into an appeal to Marlow's audience. In order to extricate himself from this dilemma, one which involves the basic issue of whether or not a tale can be told, Conrad has recourse to two highly ambiguous scenes to build the ending: Kurtz's final pronouncement and Marlow's interview with Kurtz's Intended.

The shifts occurring in the seeing–hearing motif emphasize the process which leads to a balancing of Marlow's imagination with his moral conviction. This balance brings to an end the expectation of what Kurtz will say. Readings which have not individuated the complex mechanism building up that expectation will inevitably find Kurtz's cry an anti-climax, a representative case of Conrad's evasiveness.[28] Actually, the pronouncement is a most appropriate way of concluding Conrad's discussion of the theoretical aspects of the tale's imagery.

Marlow's quest for an eloquent expression of the appeal he thought he had heard from the wilderness will be unfulfilled, and he will be unable to give his listeners the awaited word or sentence. The mirror quality that *tale* and *story* have in "Heart of Darkness" constitutes Conrad's final attempt to embody the chimera of suggestiveness he had first evoked in the preface to *The Nigger of the "Narcissus."* The hearing motif expresses at the same time an effort to transcend the limits of common referentiality and the ultimate acknowledgment of that dependence on visual suggestion which fictional language cannot escape.

Thus, when Marlow comes upon Kurtz, who has crawled back to the natives' campfire, he finds that it would be useless to try to express in words the effect of Kurtz's speech. As he tells his audience, "I've been telling you what we said – repeating the phrases we pronounced – but what's the good? They were common everyday words – the familiar, vague sounds exchanged on every waking day of life." All he can say is that, for him, those words had "the terrific suggestiveness" (144) of words heard in dreams or nightmares. Marlow has striven after the words to convey how he had experienced the events while living them. All he has been able to do is map the limit between the sayable and the unsayable. And, in so doing, he has brought out the nightmarish sensation which lingers in his memory.

Kurtz does not move beyond the fictional structure to make an absolute statement. His words can be perceived only through the structure constituted by thematic imagery, narrative form and the momentum which the rhythm of Marlow's narration gains at the end of the tale. It is only appropriate that Kurtz's "final burst of sincerity" (145) should be conveyed to the readers/listeners through Marlow's imagining of what Kurtz sees at the moment of his death.[29] That Conrad is playing on "seeing" is made clear at the beginning of the scene, when Marlow enters Kurtz's cabin with a candle and Kurtz complains "I am lying here in the dark waiting for death" – and Marlow notes that "The light was within a foot of his eyes" (149). It is Marlow who sees the death working on his features. He recalls: "Anything approaching the change that came over his features I have never seen before, and hope never to see again. Oh, I wasn't touched. I was fascinated. It was as though a veil had been rent. I saw on that ivory face the expression of sombre pride, of ruthless power, of craven terror – of an intense and hopeless despair." Marlow's description of what he saw, or imagined he was seeing, is enhanced by his comment: "Did he live his life again in every detail of desire, temptation, and surrender during that supreme moment of complete knowledge? He cried in a whisper at some image, at some vision – he cried out twice, a cry that was no more than a breath – 'The horror! The horror!'" (149). When Marlow is told of the death he comments that Kurtz "was a remarkable man" (151), and adds, bitterly, "The voice was gone. What else had been there?" (150). Not much, possibly, since it is his imagination which made "an affirmation, a moral victory" (151) out of Kurtz's final cry. And the resonance of that cry will reverberate in the captain's life, making it a nightmare. His narrative aboard the *Nellie* has been an attempt to unravel what he could have possibly seen in Kurtz's face while he was dying, and what he heard in the cry.

If Marlow's narrative were to break off at this point, after he has declared why he has remained loyal to Kurtz's memory ("it was a victory! That is why I have remained loyal to Kurtz to the last, and even beyond" [151]), it would be impossible to understand, retroactively, his narrative persona. How did Marlow cope with the frightening memories from Africa? In what way did he internalize his loyalty to Kurtz's phantom? And, finally, how did he manage to control his rage and emotions in order to construct a narrative from a historical comparison, through a half-playful, half-gruesome recollection, down to a disturbing piece of self-analysis? All these questions underscore the issue of the tale's "reality" – that is, how, by communicating its content, the author–narrator conveys that nightmare which is the realistic edge of the dream.

In the scene with Kurtz's Intended, which was to lock in the whole story, and make it "something quite on another plane than an anecdote of a man who went mad in the Centre of Africa" (to William Blackwood, May 31, 1902; *CL* II, 417), Conrad wraps up all the loose ends of the tale. Before his visit to the Intended, Marlow explains what he is seeking by handing her the portrait and letters Kurtz had given him. He has disposed, by then, of all of Kurtz's belongings. All that remained was "his memory and his Intended." Though Marlow is not sure of what his motives had been at the time, he does believe something: "I wanted to give that up, too, to the past, in a way – to surrender personally all that remained of him with me to that oblivion which is the last word of our common fate." As he explains, "I thought his memory was like the other memories of the dead that accumulate in every man's life – a vague impress on the brain of shadows that had fallen on it in their swift and final passage" (155). But casting off Kurtz will not be so simple.

Once Marlow arrives in front of the Intended's house, he recalls, "I had a vision of him on the stretcher, opening his mouth voraciously, as if to devour all the earth with all its mankind. He lived then before me; he lived as much as he had ever lived." The tension within the narrative becomes uncanny, throbbing like veins in the head. The vision "seemed to enter the house" (155) with Marlow, carrying all the visual and aural impressions stored in his memory. He realizes what is happening, and realizes what he must do: "It was a moment of triumph for the wilderness, an invading and vengeful rush which, it seemed to me, I would have to keep back alone for the salvation of another soul" (156). What should he tell the Intended to save her from the truth? How well could he now repeat those "common everyday words" which at night in the forest had appeared surcharged with "terrific suggestiveness" (144); now "those broken phrases came back to me, were heard again in their ominous and terrifying simplicity" (156). Perhaps he could pronounce them. But he dares not, neither to her nor to his audience. Their truth is best left inside Marlow's memory. The narrator will not share the nightmare.

Marlow's reticence with the Intended is prompted by the impact her dignified sorrow has on him. Here Marlow experiences one of those revelations which are important for his particular narrative function. He realizes how, for her, Kurtz "had died only yesterday," and this impression is rendered in visual and aural terms: "I saw her and him in the same instant of time – his death and her sorrow – I saw her sorrow in the very moment of his death. Do you understand? I saw them together – I heard them together" (157). Marlow understands that he will be loyal to her sorrow rather than to Kurtz's death. Up to that moment his death was not related to the world Marlow was able to return to: once back in Brussels he used Kurtz's memory as a shield against the superficial sanity of its citizens. The man who had died with a vision of horror "had kicked himself loose of the earth" (144) and Marlow has filtered his own experience through Kurtz's ultimate vision ("It is his extremity that I seem to have lived through" [151]). Now that he has discovered that someone has been left behind in the protected world of ideal truthfulness, and that her "despairing regret" (157) is exposed to the shock-waves of Kurtz's "eternal condemnation," he realizes that he will have to give up the precarious balance of the "choice of nightmares." The dialogue which follows dramatically illustrates the price Marlow is going to pay for the girl's sanity. If at the end he will be forced into saying a downright lie, throughout the scene the ambiguity of language creates an unbearable tension.[30] Marlow uses the nuances language offers him to hold back the whisper echoing in his head. Which Kurtz is more actual, the one in his memory or the one living on in his Intended's sorrow? Marlow has indeed stumbled "into a place of cruel and absurd mysteries not fit for a human being to behold" (157).

The Marlow who at the end of his narrative admits, "Hadn't he [Kurtz] said he wanted only justice? But I couldn't. I could not tell her. It would have been too dark – too dark altogether" (162), is an eloquent portrait of the persona who launched the narrative at the beginning. He had set out to pick at the gross security of his audience, perhaps also telling about "the poor chap" (51) he had met down there. He could not foresee that the "effect of it" on him could grow out of the telling of the tale, out of the ambiguity of that language which could have otherwise helped him once more to deflect the onslaught of the memory of the wilderness.

What should have been only a device – that is, the structure of the narrative – has become the main agent of the tale's effect. What

Conrad had sought by extending the tension produced by rhythm, rhetoric and imagery to its breaking point is achieved in "Heart of Darkness" by involving the reader in an intellectual drama without a solution. All kinds of responses have been evoked, and every time the author has taken in the reader he has given a further twist to the narrative propelling him forward with a "Do you understand?" At the end the listener will not find a clue to the tale unravelling in the darkness, but this conclusion has already been anticipated by Marlow's experience. The "uneasiness" (83) the frame narrator had hoped the tale could allay is precisely that effect of the tale's reality which must linger on after the tale is over.

CHAPTER 4

Lord Jim *(I): the narrator as interpreter*

In his Author's Note to *Lord Jim*, Conrad claims that his "first thought was of a short story, concerned only with the pilgrim ship episode; nothing more" (*LJ*, viii). After a few pages, however, he dropped the subject and forgot all about the story. Only later, he continues, did he realize that the *Patna* episode "was a good starting-point for a free and wandering tale; that it was an event, too, which could conceivably colour the whole 'sentiment of existence' in a simple and sensitive character." Those first pages provided the subject for *Lord Jim*, but "the whole was deliberately rewritten." Eloise Knapp Hay has taken Conrad's claim literally, and has suggested different reasons as to why Conrad extended beyond Marlow's inquiry the story based on the *Jeddah* case.[1] There is, however, enough evidence that Patusan was part of the original story. Alexander Janta, in his examination of the first sketch of the novel, notes that while Conrad "wrote the title of his intended story *Jim: A Sketch* and underlined it with one bold stroke . . . he already had an awareness of the entire scope of the two part story, comprising both the *Patna* episode and its consequence – Patusan."[2] The transformation of the first sketch is not the outcome of a change in the tale's subject. The novel developed beyond the limitations of the original short story when Conrad introduced Marlow after he had written "Heart of Darkness."[3] Regarding Conrad's rewriting, as John A. Palmer writes, it "is inescapable that Marlow had come as an illumination to Conrad: that the plastic possibility represented by an 'oral' narrator had freed his tale from conventional rhetorical patterns, and *enabled* it to be 'free and wandering.'"[4]

The Author's Note should not be dismissed too quickly, as it often is by Conrad's biographers.[5] Conrad's account of the novel's genesis is an accurate description of the effect he sought when he rewrote the twenty-eight pages of the first draft, and his chronology actually clarifies what happened in the pause between the first draft and the following deliberate rewriting. In writing "Heart of Darkness" he discovered the narrative frame's potentialities for conveying to his readers the universality of the "ship episode." He then organized Marlow's interpretation of Jim's case in such a way as to make the issues raised by Jim's fateful jump require the fictional stage of Patusan to "colour the whole 'sentiment of existence.'"

Though Jim's adventurous exploits in Patusan were part of the original story, critics have found that the Malayan romance marks a qualitative shift in Marlow's narrative which seriously flaws the novel.[6] However, once one acknowledges the dynamic effect that the themes underlying Marlow's inquiry into the *Patna* case have on the narrative structure, the critical allegation that the novel is split into two parts falls apart. The split, in fact, occurs within Marlow's oral narrative, which is elaborately framed by Conrad within two different narrative forms: the impersonal narration at the beginning (Chapters 1–4) and the written account that Marlow sends to the "privileged reader" (Chapters 36–45). The central section has been considered as a whole story; and as a result of this elision of the text, the shift in Marlow's narrative has appeared confusing and contradictory. A division of the text based on the three different narrative techniques, on the other hand, reveals the integrating logic of the tale's structure: Jim's enigma is contained within the coordinates established by the frame structure.[7]

The first step toward recognition of a precise strategy on Conrad's part requires an understanding of how the first and third narrative segments perform their frame function. The light which the frame segments cast on Marlow's oral narrative is more apparent, of course, at the junctures between the segments. A clear indication of what is at work beneath the narrative is given by a particular theme recurring in the chapters that close, respectively, the impersonal narration (Chapter 4) and the Patusan section (Chapter 35), and the chapter that opens Marlow's written account (Chapter 36): the theme of the radical conflict between the "language of facts" and the expression/interpretation circuit activated by Marlow's involvement in shaping Jim's fate.

The junctures between the different segments bring forth the rationale underlying the tale's narrative structure. At the end of each segment the themes embodied in Jim's figure are synthesized with the author's discourse in theoretical problems, which the following segment's narrative form appears more appropriate to solve. In particular, the two central themes of Marlow's interpretation of Jim's case – the reality/illusion opposition and the issue of the protagonist's existence – undergo a continuing reformulation in statements qualified each time by the narrational context. Ultimately, since the division in segments sets theoretical issues in the foreground, Marlow's utterances also act as nerve fibers transmitting the thought content from one segment to the other, testing it in a fictional three-dimensional drama.

The "analytic" segment of *Lord Jim*, from the beginning of Marlow's narrative up to the Stein interview, is Conrad's most sustained and explicit use of the critical discourse in his fiction. Here, he develops to their utmost limits the alternative strategies he had elaborated in the months which followed his completion of *The Nigger of the "Narcissus."* He uses Marlow's commentary to keep a direct line of communication open between author and audience. And at the same time the narrator's rhetorical interruptions draw his reader's attention to the symbolically suggestive language which Marlow articulates to interpret the mystery of Jim's personality.

Marlow's mind is at work interpreting those ideas and testing those convictions which Conrad addressed in his non-fictional writings. The tropes of WORK and FIDELITY, as well as the notion of an "ideal standard of conduct," lie at the core of Marlow's initial condemnation of Jim, and the trope of IDEALISM is used to convey the mature seaman's growing recognition of his own solidarity with the young man's illusions. And throughout his inquiry, his questioning the respective values of conflicting languages and of the reality of Jim's illusions will enable Conrad metaphorically to discuss his own struggle with his craft.

I

The persona of the first segment narrator, frequently pointing out those basic tenets of work, duty and seamanship, is the prototypical Conradian captain. His point of view embodies the fidelity to that "fixed standard of conduct" (50) which Marlow hopes he will eventually be able to vindicate. For example, in stressing why Jim could not live up to that standard, the omniscient narrator observes that Jim's experiences at sea never led him to sea-life's "only

reward . . . the perfect love of the work. This reward eluded him"
(10). Only by taking into account his persona is it possible more
fully to appreciate the unbearable tension which pervades his
omniscient narration. Seen through the eye of a seaman, the night
aboard the *Patna* in Chapter 3 (often described as portraying the
serenity of a night at sea!) is a sailor's nightmare. The ship is a
steamer "eaten up with rust worse than a condemned water-tank"
(13–14), under the responsibility of a villainous renegade and two
alcoholic engineers, one of whom "had 'got on' after a sort" after
being "kicked quietly out of his ship twenty years ago or more."
Jim, who is blind to all this (and the narrator is using here all his
power as Olympian narrator, reporting the young man's thoughts
to make his point), is "faintly amused by the scene" of the quarrel
between the drunken second-engineer and the skipper (24). As the
narrator notes, Jim "was too pleasurably languid to dislike actively
this or any other thing. The quality of these men did not matter; he
rubbed shoulders with them, but they could not touch him; he
shared the air they breathed, but he was different" (24–25).

On a second reading, the hints as to Jim's weakness set forth in
the first three chapters are almost obsessive. Only then does one
realize why they have stuck so strongly to the image one has of Jim
even later. So deep is the narrator's knowledge of the early signs of
Jim's weakness that he is able to portray in the training-ship episode the motives which made him unfit for the seacraft's work. The
silent contest between impersonal narrator and Marlow takes place
precisely on this ground: Conrad has the reader see Jim first of all
through a damning judgment made in the name of the sea code
from which Marlow himself departs in his quest. The "free and
wandering tale" (viii), in all its convolutions, then, does have at
least one forward movement. On a conceptual level, Marlow
initially shares the impersonal narrator's negative judgment, which
can also be that of the reader, but then a doubt emerges to lead him
toward an unremitting self-scrutiny.[8]

The novel opens with a physical description of Jim: "He was an
inch, perhaps two under six feet" (3). The implication of this point
of view for a reading of Jim's personality becomes apparent in the
second and third paragraphs. Jim is attributed with universal
characteristics: he "possesses Ability in the abstract" (4) and is
driven in his flight by a "keen perception of the Intolerable" (5).
The ineffable qualities of Jim's character that Marlow will gradu-

ally discover are here stated in an absolutized reading: illusory potentiality becomes abstract "Ability"; the wounds inflicted by actuality on Jim's subjectivity become morbidity toward the "Intolerable."

In the first three paragraphs the impersonal narrator gives the reader a précis of Jim's story up to the point which Marlow has reached in his knowledge of the case, when he starts his narration. (The only episode omitted, of course, is the most important one, Jim's fateful jump. But the mystery about Jim's "criminal weakness" is vital for the suspense which keeps the reader's interest alive.) In this summary of the events of the story, a reliance on physical appearance pairs off with a readily made moral condemnation. With Marlow's entrance the ambiguity of seeing and the problematic nature of telling a story will make judging impossible.

The passage from the impersonal narrator's segment to Marlow's narrative at the end of Chapter 4 is done so skillfully that the narration thus launched leaves the reader with the sensation that the tale and the Marlowian voice coincide. Once the themes and motifs Conrad uses to introduce Marlow's yarn are taken into account, however, one is in a position to set both the impersonal narrator's segment and the internal narrator's yarn in the context of the critical discourse. And, one realizes that there are significant differences in point of view between the two narrators, differences of fundamental importance for understanding the Marlow–Jim relationship.[9]

In the courtroom scene Conrad makes Marlow's function clear before having him speak – and this exactly when the suspense about what Jim has done is being set up. This is the only occasion on which the author gives a glimpse of Jim's thoughts. The magistrates have asked him "pointed questions" and he, trying "to tell honestly the truth of this experience" (28), finds himself using figurative language: "he said, speaking of the ship: 'She went over whatever it was as easy as a snake crawling over a stick.'" The impersonal narrator comments that the "illustration was good," but "the questions were aiming at facts." Jim, however, is seeking an explanation, not facts: "They wanted facts. Facts! They demanded facts from him, as if facts could explain anything!" (29).

The vividness of his painful memory could make Jim actually

relive the scene in the courtroom: "he could have reproduced like an echo the moaning of the engineer for the better information of these men who wanted facts." Jim is willing to face the shame and humiliation of the witness-box because the explanation of his act, he hopes, can reconcile himself – as well as the audience of his hypothetical heroic gestes – with the obscure motives which impelled his desertion: "After his first feeling of revolt he had come round to the view that only a meticulous precision of statement would bring out the true horror behind the appalling face of things" (30).[10] But can the precise words he is seeking express what his imagination had seen? Can the gap between objectivity and subjectivity be bridged by the language which grounds the inter-human conventions he has broken? Jim's attempt cannot be communicated:

The facts those men were so eager to know had been visible, tangible, open to the senses, occupying their place in space and time, requiring for their existence a fourteen-hundred-ton steamer and twenty-seven minutes by the watch; they made a whole that had features, shades of expression, a complicated aspect that could be remembered by the eye, and something else besides, something invisible, a directing spirit of perdition that dwelt within, like a malevolent soul in a detestable body. (30–31)

Facts are structured in a perfectly intelligible language for those who accept them as the ultimate horizon of their existence. These persons could walk through the heart of darkness without hearing any voice speaking through the sounds and sights of the wilderness. Conrad does not need to state whether or not Jim is justified in giving at least as much importance to that "something else beside" as to the facts of that night aboard the *Patna*. By sheer accumulation, in a recurring motif running throughout the tale, Jim and Marlow acknowledge the presence of "the Dark Powers" (*LJ*, 121; cf. 7, 10, 105, 109, 159, 246, 354, 405). The issue is not the (non-)existence of something beyond facts. Rather, the issue is how to test the value of one's convictions in action when "there appears on the face of facts a sinister violence of intention" (10).

Marlow will later remark on the ideal value of Jim's behavior. But already Jim's presence in the witness-box demonstrates that he is hanging on to what could save his ideal self-image from the facts of his existential shipwreck. Thus, his dramatic efforts to explain are but an attempt to establish a "truth" – that is, something he can share with his audience. But the distance between words and intention becomes too great:

He wanted to go on talking for truth's sake, perhaps for his own sake also; and while his utterance was deliberate, his mind positively flew round and round the serried circle of facts that had surged up all about him to cut him off from the rest of his kind . . . This awful activity of mind made him hesitate at times in his speech. (31)

Shortly after this passage Conrad brings Marlow into the narrative, by having Jim notice him. A few strokes suggest those qualities which will make him an ideal narrator of Jim's ordeal: he "sat apart from the others, with his face worn and clouded, but with quiet eyes that glanced straight, interested and clear" (32). This person is unconventional, experienced and troubled. Once he will start telling his story, his recollections will be accurate, sympathetic and perceptive. But this is not enough, and the narrator points out an intuition of Jim's: "This fellow . . . looks at me as though he could see somebody or something past my shoulder" (33). The unexpressed object of Jim's words – "something else besides" (31) – finds a place in the world in the "interested" glance of the stranger sitting in the courtroom. The mechanism which superintends the passage from the impersonal narration (in its extreme form of reported thought) to Marlow's yarn is basically a reflection of what Jim wishes to put into words in the captain's sympathetic response.

The central element of Marlow's characterization is that he will take over the burden of explaining Jim's character. As Ernest Bevan observes, "Marlow holds the twin aspects of Jim's story in balance: the surface fact of his violation of duty, and the depths – the implications and ambiguities – beneath that violation . . . In elucidating and pursuing Jim's history, Marlow is less a judge than an enumerator of implications."[11] A few lines after Marlow's first appearance, in fact, Jim starts to doubt "whether he would ever again speak out as long as he lived" (33). Conrad then explicitly sets up a juxtaposition of Jim's problems with language and the narrative which follows:

The sound of his own truthful statements confirmed his deliberate opinion that speech was of no use to him any longer. That man there seemed to be aware of his hopeless difficulty. Jim looked at him, then turned away resolutely, as after a final parting.

And later on, many times, in distant parts of the world, Marlow showed himself willing to remember Jim, to remember him at length, in detail and audibly. (33)

The "final parting," then, is such, first of all, on a narrational level. From now on, no omniscient narrator will relate Jim's thoughts. It will be Marlow's interpretation of the young man's utterances that will dramatize and carry on Jim's doubts about language.[12] Throughout his inquiry into the moral overtones of the *Patna* case, Marlow will unravel Jim's figurative expressions by echoing them through a suggestively impressionistic language. It is in this way that his interpretation reflects his own imaginative response to that conflict between facts and subjective experience which he detects in Jim's words.

The subtle interplay between Chapter 4 and Chapter 5, in which Marlow's narrative begins, sets in the foreground a theme which reflects Conrad's emphasis on contrasting ways of knowing and, consequently, telling a story: the difference between appearance and seeing. Through this theme, the author articulates a discourse which accompanies the shift in narrative technique associated with the problems of language and communication experienced by Jim. In the light of this discourse, Marlow's introduction can be recognized for what it is – basically, a justification of a certain narrative method and a suggestion of its theoretical implications – and the first touches of his moral self-portrait can be set in their proper context.

Marlow opens his story by wondering what it is that makes him "run up against men with soft spots, with hard spots, with hidden plague spots, by Jove! and loosens their tongues at the sight of me for their infernal confidences" (34). He then congratulates his host Charlie for the excellent dinner and jocularly rehearses the pleasantness of the evening – only to hint eventually at how "Of course there are men here and there to whom the whole of life is like an after-dinner hour with a cigar; easy, pleasant, empty, perhaps enlivened by some fable of strife to be forgotten before the end is told – before the end is told – even if there happens to be any end to it" (35). Are the readers/listeners satisfied with a distinction between their own limited experience, which is "real," and that of the "fable of strife"'s protagonist, which is fictional? Or could instead an awareness of the universality of Jim's case become terribly real for a reader willing to face "the depths of horror" (45) it evokes? For Marlow, of course, there is no "end to it" and, as he provokes his audience, he will constantly try to point out in what way the tale is unveiling the implication Jim's case has for every human being.

After this first break, Marlow again picks up the thread of his narrative and says, "My eyes met his for the first time at that inquiry" (35), a remark connected only with the impersonal narrator's focusing on Jim's last reported thought during the trial: "This fellow – ran the thought – looks at me as though he could see somebody or something past my shoulder. He had come across that man before – in the street perhaps" (33). In his own narrative, however, Marlow does not proceed to report about the scene in the courtroom, but about the first time he had seen Jim, in front of the harbor office. Why, then, does he refer to the first time their eyes met? The context of the references to seeing in this chapter is not only the thematic structure of the story and the events narrated, but a discussion about the ambiguity of "seeing" as a medium for knowing another human being.

Bearing in mind the kind of communication established between Marlow and Jim later in the courtroom, the sea captain's first impression is particularly interesting: "looking at him, knowing all he knew and a little more too, I was as angry as though I had detected him trying to get something out of me by false pretences" (40). Conrad focuses on Marlow's response to Jim's appearance – and his resistance to its appealing quality – rather than using him "to make [us] *see*." The most damning consideration Marlow makes is: "I would have trusted the deck to that youngster on the strength of a single glance, and gone to sleep with both eyes – and, by Jove! it wouldn't have been safe. There are depths of horror in that thought" (45). Thus, Marlow's first encounter with Jim brings his own projections to the surface. The crime the young man has committed clashes with what Marlow sees. The investigation of this contradiction will lead eventually to the narrator's involvement in the *Patna* affair.

The rhetorical context of the narrative makes apparent that Marlow's personal involvement coincides with Conrad's attempt to involve the reader as well. Earlier in the same chapter, Conrad has already articulated the same themes in a way which emphasizes their universal, rather than personal, relevance. Marlow's response to Jim's apparently unconcerned attitude ("I waited to see him overwhelmed, confounded, pierced through and through, squirming like an impaled beetle" [42]) leads him to a digression quite different in tone: "Nothing more awful than to watch a man who has been found out, not in a crime but in a more than criminal weakness" (42). He freezes in his own act of watching Jim and offers a disquieting distinction. One can become a criminal "in a legal sense," a condition which "the spirit may well survive" (43) and from which one is prevented by the "commonest sort of fortitude" (42). But there is also a "weakness unknown" from which "not one of us is safe" (43).

At the end of the digression Conrad returns to the "appearance" theme and then proceeds to another rhetorical tirade, which is characteristic of how he interweaves different narrative threads:

there are things – they look small enough sometimes too – by which some of us are totally and completely undone. I watched the youngster there. I liked his appearance; I knew his appearance; he came from the right place; he was one of us. He stood there for all the parentage of his kind. (43)

Jim appeals to Marlow's sympathy because his appearance accords with an "appearance" he knows. The "parentage of his kind" which he stands for surely involves "honest faith," "the instinct of courage," the "inborn ability to look temptations straight in the face," an "unthinking and blessed stiffness . . . backed by a faith invulnerable to the strength of facts, to the contagion of example, to the solicitation of ideas" (43).

Understandably, as Marlow himself notes in commenting on his tirade: "This has nothing to do with Jim, directly; only he was outwardly so typical of that good, stupid kind we like to feel marching right and left of us in life" (43–44). The ugly fact of his desertion, however, makes the whole difference: it forces Marlow to distinguish between seeing and appearance. At the end of this passage, he moves from the inflated peroration to a personal case, giving a slight twist to the appearance motif: "He was the kind of fellow you would, on the strength of his looks, leave in charge of the deck – figuratively and professionally speaking. I say I would, and I ought to know." He "knows" Jim's appearance because the young seaman reminds him of all the boys he has turned out to serve "the craft of the sea" (44). Ultimately, Marlow's comment, "I couldn't believe it. I tell you I wanted to see him squirm for the honour of the craft" (46), is the most vivid expression of how he "sees" Jim.[13]

Quite appropriately, the chapter in which the ambiguity of seeing is discussed ends with Marlow's visit to the *Patna*'s chief-engineer, the alcoholic who claims, "Only my eyes were good enough to see. I am famous for my eyesight" – and sees "Millions of pink toads" (52). The hospital visit is Marlow's first active involvement in Jim's case. Why should this story interest him? he asks rhetorically. Until that moment he has managed to strike a precarious balance between a sympathetic response to Jim's appearance and a visceral revulsion tinged with fear for the young man's "more than criminal weakness" (42). The values of seamanship provide him with the most detached and human condemnation of Jim's act. Thus, now that he is about to give free play to his curiosity, he qualifies himself again, first of all, as a seaman: "Why I longed to go grubbing into the deplorable details of an occurrence which, after all, concerned me no more than as a member of an obscure body of men held together by a community of inglorious toil and by fidelity to a certain standard of conduct, I can't explain" (50). "Community" and "fidelity" – these are words recalling Conrad's own voice.

Though Marlow's inquiry may ultimately question these absolute concepts, he is aware that they must be tested: "I have a distinct notion I wished to find something. Perhaps, unconsciously, I hoped I would find that something, some profound and redeeming cause, some merciful explanation, some convincing shadow of an excuse." At the time of his storytelling he is aware of how impossible his task was, "the laying of . . . the doubt of the sovereign power enthroned in a fixed standard of conduct" (50). He concedes that he was looking for a miracle; but, he asks, "why did I desire it so ardently?" (51). The answer is framed as a question, but it actually is, in an extremely condensed language, a first resolution of the conflict at work in this first chapter of Marlow's narrative:

Was it for my own sake that I wished to find some shadow of an excuse for that young fellow whom I had never seen before, but whose appearance alone added a touch of personal concern to the thoughts suggested by the knowledge of his weakness – made it a thing of mystery and terror – like a hint of a destructive fate ready for us all whose youth – in its day – had resembled his youth? I fear that such was the secret motive of my prying. (51)

The radical of Marlow's narrative lies in this "secret motive." His own youthful illusions come back to life in what he reads in Jim's appearance. And the disjunction between what he knows – the breaking of the sea code – and what he sees – Jim's appearance – casts a retrospective doubt on the past years of honorable work at sea.[14]

This disturbing confrontation with his own past does not lead him to substitute a sentimental for a judgmental attitude. Instead, sending a shiver down his spine, it uncovers the central problem of youthful illusion, the most cherished legacy of his life at sea. The link between Jim's appearance and the Janus-like notion of illusion, which will generate many of the paradoxes running through the tale, reappears again later in the novel. During the long talk on the verandah of the Malabar Hotel, Marlow has "a distinct glimpse" of Jim: he was a youngster "of the sort you like to imagine yourself to have been; of the sort whose appearance claims the fellowship of these illusions you had thought gone out, extinct, cold" (128).

Marlow's concern with Jim's appearance and attitude, rather than his physical characteristics, far from making him a superficial observer, characterizes him as a narrator concerned with the conceptual side of experience. His interpretation of Jim's appearance is sustained by a kind of "seeing" which Conrad contrasts with the impersonal narrator's physical description of a young man "an inch, perhaps two, under six feet" (3). Through this interpretation a first answer is given to the narrative problem posed by Jim's being at a loss for words at the end of the impersonal narrator's segment: the "fellow" looking at him "as though he could see somebody or something past my shoulder" (33) is looking at the projection of his own youthful self, and through his narrative will try to demonstrate the universality of the young man's condition.

As in "Karain," "Youth" and "Heart of Darkness," Conrad sets up *Lord Jim*'s narrative structure by starting from the problem addressed rather than from a theoretical model. In the case of Marlow's inquiry into the mystery of Jim's personality, the illustration of his "appearance" launches the frame structure. The author, however, does not re-create in the novel that parallel development of inner and outer voyage which enables Marlow in "Heart of Darkness" to describe his encounter with Kurtz as "the farthest point of navigation" (*Y*, 51). Yet, a similar nautical metaphor in *Lord Jim* brings together those problematical elements in Marlow's response to Jim's personality, both at the beginning and at the end of their acquaintance. Trying to sum up his first impression of Jim, Marlow explains:

I don't pretend I understood him. The views he let me have of himself were like those glimpses through the shifting rents in a thick fog – bits of vivid and vanishing detail, giving no connected idea of the general aspect of a country. They fed one's curiosity without satisfying it; they were no good for purposes of orientation. (76)

It is not a web of words which he is trying to unravel, but the elusive mystery of a flesh and blood human being.[15] As Marlow notes while he is about to take upon himself the responsibility of Jim's future, "It is when we try to grapple with another man's intimate need that we perceive how incomprehensible, wavering, and misty are the beings that share with us the sight of the stars and the warmth of the sun" (179–180). Until the end Jim will remain "under a cloud, inscrutable at heart" (416), and the different threads which form the narration will never lead from one point to another or toward a greater knowledge of the quest's object. All Marlow can hope to gain – and pass on to his audience – is a series of "glimpses" into Jim's personality. These glimpses, carefully orchestrated, are at the core of Jim's and Marlow's talks. They are the articulation of Marlow's recollection of Jim "at length, in detail and audibly," which had launched him as the narrator who could help Jim, after the young man had reached the conclusion "that speech was of no use to him any longer" (33).

The efforts Conrad makes to connect the "glimpses" with other themes enhance rather than solve the paradoxes of Jim's case. What Marlow describes as "glimpses" turn out to be expressions of figurative language, such as those Jim used in answering the magistrate's questions, in his attempts "to tell honestly the truth of this experience" (28). In Marlow's retelling of the trial in the second chapter of his narrative, he explains why Jim's answers were incomprehensible to the magistrate and assessors, but fundamental to his interpretation: "the questions put to him necessarily led him away from what to me, for instance, would have been the only truth worth knowing. You can't expect the constituted authorities to inquire into the state of a man's soul – or is it only of his liver?" (56–57). The official inquiry's "object was not the fundamental why, but the superficial how, of this affair" (56).[16] Marlow will carry on his psychological inquiry precisely by interpreting the figurative language which the magistrates dismiss.

During the night talk on the verandah of the Malabar Hotel, Jim is holding his head in his hands, a sign of his desperation. His story has reached the fatal moment before his jump. Marlow comments: "These were things he could not explain to the court – and not even to me; but I would have been little fitted for the reception of his confidences had I not been able at times to understand the pauses between the words" (105). Marlow is not boasting of a supernatural perceptiveness. With this comment, Conrad sets in the foreground the function he has assigned to his internal narrator. Marlow will spin a suggestively impressionistic language out of Jim's concise figurative expressions, unraveling from those glimpses that metaphoric language which, as Donald Yelton argues, characterizes *Lord Jim* and "Heart of Darkness."[17]

The narrator's efforts to reproduce the effect of Jim's words are aimed at revealing that which the language of facts cannot represent. As he recalls, Jim "related facts which I have not forgotten, but at this distance of time I couldn't recall his very words: I only remember that he managed wonderfully to convey the brooding rancour of his mind into the bare recital of events" (105). Jim's telling how a "flake of rust" peeled off the bulkhead is a first illustration of how Conrad uses the long night talk to make explicit the metaphoric language's function within the tale's semantic structure. Jim stops, suddenly, and breaks out in anguish with "What could I do – what?" (84). Marlow adds, "I can easily picture him to myself in the peopled gloom of the cavernous place ... I can see him glaring at the iron" (84–85). In other instances Marlow adopts less fluent techniques to indicate that he is elaborating on Jim's expressions, as when he is telling about the four men's first moments in the *Patna*'s boat: "The sea hissed 'like twenty thousand kettles.' That's his [Jim's] simile, not mine" (112). Again, during the re-creation of the scene in the lower deck, Jim tells Marlow that "his first impulse was to shout . . . but such an overwhelming sense of his helplessness came over him that he was not able to produce a sound." This is the "event"; but, as Marlow elaborates, "This is, I suppose, what people mean by the tongue cleaving to the roof of the mouth. 'Too dry,' was the concise expression he used in reference to this state" (85).

This technique finds its most thorough application during Marlow's account of the four castaways adrift at night. Jim's words, such as they are, would not appear particularly evocative. But they have a marked effect on the experienced seaman Marlow: "I was struck by the suggestive truth of his words. There is something peculiar in a small boat upon the wide sea . . . When your ship fails you, your whole world seems to fail you" (120–121). Marlow then continues his description of the night at sea, until he encounters another of Jim's figurative expressions: "and then he muttered something about the sunrise being of a kind that foretells a calm day." Marlow comments upon these words, in what seems at first a master's characteristically paternalistic way: "You know that sailor habit of referring to the weather in every connection" (122). As it turns out, however, this comment introduces Marlow's participation in the scene's rendering:

And on my side his few mumbled words were enough to make me see the lower limb of the sun clearing the line of the horizon, the tremble of a vast ripple running over all the visible expanse of the sea, as if the waters had shuddered, giving birth to the globe of light, while the last puff of the breeze would stir the air in a sigh of relief. (122–123)

Jim's mutter has been translated into an evocative representation.

While Marlow follows his own responses, Jim continues his grim recital, and with an abrupt, almost film-cutting, effect, his words follow Marlow's lyrical imaginary sunrise: "They sat in the stern shoulder to shoulder, with the skipper in the middle, like three dirty owls, and stared at me." Marlow is almost frightened by these words said "with an intention of hate that distilled a corrosive virtue into the commonplace words like a drop of powerful poison falling into a glass of water." But, as for Marlow, his "thoughts dwelt upon that sunrise." And all the while he continues in his earlier vein: "I could imagine under the pellucid emptiness of the sky these four men imprisoned in the solitude of the sea" (123). Jim does not indulge in a scenic description, concentrated as he is on the human drama, and Marlow's imagination is touched instead by the ominous spell the sea and the rising sun are casting on all four of them. The effect is a multilayered accretion of figurative expressions in which the power of the images is just as important as the emphasis given, in the interplay between the two characters, to the verisimilitude of Jim's figurative language.

Marlow's insistence upon the effect of that greater reality which Jim's figurative language gives to his story prepares the way for the subsequent development of the young man's reality, his "existing" in the eyes of Marlow, Stein and, perhaps, the reader. Jim's figurative expressions constitute the most radically fictional language of the whole tale, comparable to Karain's story told in Malay. Every other utterance, reflection or description constitutes a narrative frame. In avowing the reality of these expressions, Marlow is vindicating the reality of fiction as opposed to a view limited to the language of facts.

It is no mere coincidence, then, that Conrad has explicitly set up an opposition between Marlow's reading of Jim's figurative language and the nautical assessors' inability to relate such a language to facts. The problem is that, although the facts of the *Patna* affair are all perfectly known at the trial's opening, the magistrate and assessors (as well as the community they stand for) are trying to uncover a further fact which could be represented as a motive – thus extenuating the uncomfortable danger which this story evokes. The motive, however, is not a fact, and Marlow is left alone with Jim in trying to discover it. The nautical assessors' function – assessing facts within facts – is the opposite of that assigned by Shakespeare to the players in *Hamlet*: creating a drama within a drama, showing the audience the veiled truth of fiction. The court's inquiry is a "professional reading" of the facts of Jim's case, and Conrad uses Marlow to give reality to an alternative reading.

The recognition of the figurative language's reality which Conrad is stimulating in the reader further elucidates that discussion of Jim's case which Conrad had started by using his narrator to distinguish between seeing and appearing. The aim of this discussion is to amplify Jim's ordeal by soliciting in the reader both an identification with, and a condemnation of, the character. It is in the light of this narrative strategy that the "telling of the tale," as Randall Craig notes, "engages readers in the interpretive experience that is itself the subject of the tale; the teller of the tale provides readers with the model of how to participate successfully in the experience."[18] A few examples of Marlow's interpretation of Jim's words materially illustrate the different "truths" the narrator is trying to uncover as an alternative to the official inquiry.

As the two men are talking on the verandah of the hotel, Marlow describes Jim talking in extremely vivid tones: "He drew quick breaths at every few words and shot quick glances at my face, as though in his anguish he were watchful of the effect" (92–93). And yet the narrator's reflection goes in an opposite direction:

He was not speaking to me, he was only speaking before me, in a dispute with an invisible personality, an antagonistic and inseparable partner of his existence – another possessor of his soul. These were issues beyond the competency of a court of inquiry: it was a subtle and momentous quarrel as to the true essence of life, and did not want a judge. (93)

Jim had been telling about his reaction when the bulkhead seemed ready to give way. During his dramatic account he addresses Marlow vehemently: "Would you have had the courage to swing the maul for the first blow if you had seen that bulkhead? Don't say you would: you had not seen it; nobody would" (92). To whom is Jim speaking? And why does Marlow define the subject of this contest as "the true essence of life"? He gives a first answer in the ensuing digression.

Marlow's first concern is with the kind of involvement asked of him. Jim wants "an accomplice." But Marlow does not want to take sides in "a dispute impossible of decision" (93). By so doing, however, he is not shutting off Jim's disquieting question; instead, he is accepting it in its most open dimension: the young man's "quarrel" with an invisible opponent envisages a universal predicament. And Marlow intends to face it, being "fair to all the phantoms in possession – to the reputable that ha[s] its claims and to the disreputable that ha[s] its exigencies." This first formulation of Marlow's insight into the trial torturing Jim may not yet be clear to his audience: "I can't explain to you who haven't seen him and who hear his words only at second hand the mixed nature of my feelings." The "mixed feelings" can be expressed only by a paradox: "I was made to look at the convention that lurks in all truth and on the essential sincerity of falsehood." Marlow, in his attempt to explain, had indulged at first in an abstract term: "It seemed to me I was being made to comprehend the Inconceivable" – only to observe "and I know of nothing to compare with the discomfort of such a sensation." Conrad does not seek an impressionistic representation of the sights and sounds of Jim's anguish. He forces his audience to undergo the same loss of familiar landmarks that Marlow experiences in trying to reconstruct his response to Jim's words. It is only the sense of the statement that is paradoxical, not the phrasing itself: convention "lurks" in truth as if it were an untouchable or dangerous element, while falsehood is essentially sincere. Marlow "*was made to look*" (93, emphasis added) at this reversal of accepted values, and he is passing it on.

Conrad takes for granted the paradoxical nature of human experience, and his critical discourse is mainly an examination of fiction's aptness for representing this quality of the human condition. For this reason his rhetorical insertion of an indication of the role that paradox will have in the overall semantic structure at this point in *Lord Jim* is particularly important. Starting from the impossibility of communicating his "mixed" feelings, he manages, by the end of the paragraph, to state in the clearest possible way the importance Jim's case has for his audience. After having drawn attention to the moral effect of that at which he "was made to look," Marlow recasts the paradoxical statement in figurative language: "He appealed to all sides at once – to the side turned perpetually to the light of day, and to that side of us which, like the other hemisphere of the moon, exists stealthily in perpetual darkness, with only a fearful ashy light falling at times on the edge" (93). The rhetorical progress structuring this digression exploits a particular quality of figurative language: the effect of the overall image or sound-complex diffuses the meaning of the words. Thus, in this case, the provoking content of the paradoxical statement is actually brought home to each reader by the words "that side of us," even though attention is concentrated on the double image of the two faces of the moon.

Marlow brings his argument to a momentary conclusion in the next sentences. At first he recalls how he had been swayed by Jim, then he admits that the "occasion was obscure, insignificant" (93).

Nonetheless, as he goes on to say, "the mystery of his attitude got hold of me as though he had been an individual in the forefront of his kind, as if the obscure truth involved were momentous enough to affect mankind's conception of itself." Thus, the digression begun with the analysis of Marlow's own involvement ends with his first explicit statement of the universal significance of Jim's predicament.

The frame narrator interrupts Marlow's narration right after the climax reached in this rhetorical digression. With a technique he often used in "Heart of Darkness," Conrad is bringing the under-lying critical discourse to the surface by imprinting a rhetorical tension on the flow of narrative which needs to be eased before the story can be continued. These interruptions are central to a frame structure, serving to remind the reader that a certain utterance must be ascribed to a specific character whose personality provides its immediate context. In this case the interruption is used to explain why Marlow thinks that Jim's case should "affect mankind's conception of itself."

The frame narrator relates how "Marlow paused to put new life into his expiring cheroot, seemed to forget all about the story, and abruptly began again" (93–94). When Marlow picks up his narra-tive again he first excuses himself for getting interested, explains what sort of "weakness" makes him act as he does – and be a narrator of a certain kind: "My weakness consists in not having a discriminating eye for the incidental – for the externals – . . . A confounded democratic quality of vision" (94). This concern with what is universal in the human condition will allow him to recog-nize the kind of opportunities that Patusan represents for Jim and the particular form of success he will achieve there – a "quality of vision," this, which distinguishes him from those whose "minds are struck by the externals of such a success." But "to Jim's successes there were no externals" (226), as he will remark at the beginning of the Patusan section.

In his recital of contrition, Marlow also associates his "failing" with a passive attitude toward narration: he does not set his story in motion to act on his audience's conscience. It is their common indolence which invites the yarn-spinning: "it's a failing; and then comes a soft evening; a lot of men too indolent for whist – and a story . . ." At this point a second interruption underlines the fact that Marlow's words do not find a response in his immediate audience: "He paused again to wait for an encouraging remark perhaps, but nobody spoke; only the host, as if reluctantly performing a duty, murmured – 'You are so subtle, Marlow.'" Marlow's answer seals off the whole digression: "Who? I? . . . Oh, no! But *he* was; and try as I may for the success of this yarn I am missing innumerable shades – they were so fine, so difficult to render in colourless words. Because he complicated matters by being so simple, too – the simplest poor devil!" (94). He has stood out of his narrative in order to point out some of the implications of Jim's story, and, by turning back to the tale, he indicates in the language Jim himself uses the real source of the story's subtlety. He can then resume his rendering of the story through Jim's words, which now have a sharper edge. Marlow himself is only fathoming the range of his response, and the audience's interpretative faculty must be directed instead toward Jim's words, the core of the tale's fictional language.

Another example of the function Marlow's commentary has in articulating a reading of Jim's personality occurs in the scene on the eve of the sentencing. Marlow is offering Jim money to get away before being humiliated in court the next day. It was Brierly who had originally proposed the plan to Marlow, who had refused indignantly. But now he is beginning to feel the strain of exposure to the moral tension building up in Jim's story. At the beginning of his tale he had confessed: "Was it for my own sake that I wished to find some shadow of an excuse for that young fellow?" (51). Now, one hundred pages later, Marlow has to admit that, "If he had not enlisted my sympathies he had done better for himself – he had gone to the very fount and origin of that sentiment, he had reached the secret sensibility of my egoism" (152). Marlow's moral self-portrait in the first chapter of his narrative had prepared the reader for an unsparing test of certain judgmental automatisms. Has the reader been affected by the underlying tension? Marlow does not pretend to explain why he wishes the guilty Jim to escape: "I don't think I could; but if you haven't got a sort of notion by this time, then I must have been very obscure in my narrative, or you too sleepy to seize upon the sense of my words. I don't defend my morality" (152). Marlow then addresses his audience in the form characteristic of his emerging role in the critical discourse, by offering two reasons for his candid confession: "I am concealing nothing from you, because were I to do so my action would appear more unintelligible than any man's action has the right to be, and – in the second place – to-morrow you shall forget my sincerity along with the other lessons of the past" (152–153). In passages such as this, Marlow's independent existence as a character is seriously questioned. Some of Marlow's utterances may have been used by Conrad to express his own ideas, others (for example, those in "Youth") are ironic; but others, especially those addressed to the narrator's audience, are devices for the articulation of the critical discourse. In the above passage, for example, it is not the "intelligibility" of Marlow's actions or his "sincerity" that are vindicated, but the validity of his interpretation of Jim's story. Marlow does not spin his yarn in a void, but in a highly polemical context, where his interpretation is in conflict not only with the impersonal narrator's presentation of Jim, but also with that of the other internal narrators.

The conflict, as Conrad contrives it, is not over Jim's guilt or innocence but over the uncomfortable questions raised by his fateful jump. Marlow is Conrad's main device for forcing the reader's involvement. This effect is achieved mainly through the narrator's self-questioning and his uncovering a progression of paradoxes, the only figure of speech which can insert a doubt in the initial condemnation Conrad himself suggested. Marlow, to this end, adds as a further comment: "In this transaction, to speak grossly and precisely, I was the irreproachable man; but the subtle intentions of my immorality were defeated by the moral simplicity of the criminal. No doubt he was selfish, too, but his selfishness had a higher origin, a more lofty aim" (153). Jim's determination to face the court's verdict will touch off Marlow's most eloquent vindication of the young man's value. By the end of the *Patna* section, this determination will establish him in the captain's eyes as a most strenuous believer in the sea code. By then, Marlow's authority as a narrator will have been established definitively. His apparently uncalled-for paradoxes turn out to be the only possible rationalization of the internal conflict triggered by Jim's case.

II

Marlow's reflections, which disclose a reading alternative to the language of facts, are not set in a purely discursive form. They are part of a rhetorical structure that brings together conflicting interpretations of Jim's case. This combination of critical discourse and narrative structure keeps alive that conflict between Marlow's interpretation and the omniscient narrator's judgment; and it is this conflict that forces the reader continually to take sides. Conrad uses a gallery of internal narrators or figures to articulate this conflict, by juxtaposing them to Jim physically or bringing them forth through Marlow's mnemonic associations. Like fragments of a broken glass, they refract the impersonal narrator's position, either by confirming Jim's image sketched in the first chapters or casting a negative light on his personality. Marlow absorbs their testimony into the flow of his own narrative, thus breaking through that division between frame and fictional tale which had characterized the narrative frame in "Karain" and "Heart of Darkness." This apparently rambling organization of Marlow's narrative up to the Patusan section thus allows Conrad to reveal from different angles the lights and shadows of Jim's personality.

In the "analytic" section of *Lord Jim* the conflict of points of view typical of the narrative frame is dissolved into Marlow's narrative. This change in Conrad's use of the technique advances understanding of the continuity of his different narrative forms after *Lord Jim*. Later, in works such as *Nostromo* and *The Secret Agent*, he was able to conflate in an ironic and detached narrative voice those conflicts he had dramatized through narrative frames in "Karain" and the early Marlow tales. There is no one single model of narrative frame in these tales. Instead the frame in each short story or novel is the result of an attempt to balance the creating of a fictional world with the establishing of a communication with the audience. This attempt at communication is basically a translation of fictional language in order to reach an English audience. In "Karain," the frame narrator quite literally translates a story told in Malay. In "Heart of Darkness," Marlow tells his audience of former seamen the effect on himself of his encounter with the Other in the African wilderness. And in so doing, he relies on Kurtz's translation into English of the wilderness' appeal. The same does not occur in *Lord Jim*. The novel lacks the spatial unity provided by the *Nellie*; the audience is not individually characterized; time shifts continually and the third person narrator is not a polemically involved listener. Rather, one of the novel's most remarkable features is that Marlow never explicitly questions the position adopted by the impersonal narrator. Certainly, he carries on a highly polemical vocal exchange with his audience, quite similar to the one in "Heart of Darkness." Here, though, it is somehow secondary to the silent contest which contrasts the negative reading of Jim's personality set forth by the impersonal narrator in the first three chapters. Rather than emphasizing this contest by having Marlow voice it, Conrad uses the figures juxtaposed with Jim to translate into action the conflict of points of view.

In terms of narrative economy the characters that allow Conrad to articulate contrasting readings of the *Patna* case have different roles. Some are internal narrators with the function of helping to unravel the story. Archie Ruthvel ("as his story goes . . ."; 37), Captain Elliott ("As he used to tell me . . ."; 39) and Mr. Jones ("His grey-headed mate . . . would tell the story with tears in his eyes"; 59) help Marlow piece together various sources of information. Other figures are introduced through Marlow's mental associations or memories to give, as Robert Haugh notes, "a three-dimensional depth to the moral implications of the event":[19] the Malays who kept on steering the *Patna*, Captain Brierly or Bob Stanton. The evidence they contribute refers not only to the story itself but also to the underlying discourse. At the story level the light these characters cast on Jim's attitude reflects an effect similar to that which Conrad aimed at when he had the impersonal narrator open the narrative: the other seamen's behavior – even to the extent of committing suicide – qualifies Jim's act as inexcusable cowardice. Any seaman could cast the first stone at him.

All these characters are elements of the narrative frame. They are juxtaposed not only to Jim, but also to the complexities Marlow is trying to bring to the surface: their damning evidence is promptly countered by a glimpse of the not-quite-so-simple meaning of the acts. The notion of critical discourse provides a context for these figures which runs counter to that linear progression leading from the impersonal narrator to Stein: the scrutiny into the fracture between reality and illusion revealed by Marlow's interpretation.

When viewed in this light, the evidence produced by the characters juxtaposed to Jim appears much more contradictory. The passage that reveals most clearly the complexity of the narrative structure connecting submerged themes across the literal surface is Marlow's encounter with the most striking and authoritative figure in the *Patna* case, the French Lieutenant. This character is introduced at the end of Chapter 12 (137), where the account of his thirty hours aboard the *Patna* fills a gap in Marlow's knowledge of what actually happened between Jim's jump and the arrival of the ship in Aden. His use as an eyewitness neatly fits in with the unraveling of Jim's story on the verandah. By the time the long night talk has reached Chapter 12, Jim's account is over, and he is telling Marlow how exposure had come as a relief for him because it had allayed the sight and sounds of the dying pilgrims which had beset him ever since abandoning ship.

Conrad shifts the account from Jim to the Frenchman in an extremely telling way. Jim's hallucinations are shown in the light of the inquiry; the original conflict which had launched Marlow's involvement is re-enacted at this point by recalling how Jim and the other *Patna* officers had been sure that the ship's light disappeared shortly after they abandoned the *Patna*. An old skipper sitting next to Marlow in court summarizes what all the persons attending the trial were thinking: "Of course they would lie" (135). Brierly, however, comes out with a rational explanation: "when the squall struck [the *Patna*] a little on the quarter, she swung head to wind as sharply as though she had been at anchor. By this change in her position all her lights were in a very few moments shut off from the boat to leeward" (136). However, the explanation itself only increases the dizziness and unreality prompted by the debate. It is therefore a relief when, in the account of the morning after the desertion, a French gunboat bound homeward from Réunion enters the story.

The French Lieutenant gives at first the impression of being a reliable narrator. This impression is confirmed by Marlow's comment at the end of the episode: he felt as though he "were taking professional opinion on the case" with "an expert in possession of the facts ... to whom one's perplexities are mere child's-play" (145–146). The interpretation Marlow had been gradually articulating during his personal inquiry – at first in parallel with, and later in opposition to, the first segment's impersonal narrator – seems to be demolished under the sabre-edged remarks of this professional reader of facts. Jim's weakness appears more concrete than the alternative suggestions which have been building a different effect on the readers. However, before jumping to one of the alternative conclusions reached by most commentators (is the French Lieutenant honorable or obtuse?),[20] one should pay a little more attention to the warnings Conrad gives the reader against simplifications which could too easily play down the ambiguous effect created by the Jim–Lieutenant juxtaposition.

In this episode Conrad is addressing the facts-versus-illusions theme outlined by the threefold segment structure of the novel. Seen in this perspective, the critical discourse in this episode semantically connects syntactically unrelated narrative segments to provide a different effect, which eventually builds up a momentum that reaches its climax in the Stein interview. The connections thus established set forth a carefully laid out patchwork of narrative voices, juxtaposed figures and semantic levels which significantly alters the impression created by a first reading. First, the episode's narrative context raises a number of questions. If Conrad had really intended to emphasize the officer's honor in opposition to Jim's cowardice, why does he have Marlow resume the conversation at the point where Jim displays his fidelity to an abstract code of behavior by turning down Brierly's (and later Marlow's) offer of some money to run away? And, how can one explain the positioning of the Little Stanton digression, right between the French Lieutenant interview and Jim's refusal? Could Stanton's self-sacrifice really add extra punch to the Lieutenant's words? The complicated interplay of the issues discussed in the Sydney café, once uncovered, illustrates that the elements at work in the French Lieutenant episode are the outcome of Conrad's own confrontation with the paradoxical nature of Jim's predicament.

The officer's character (and narrational role) takes on a more ambiguous sense at the beginning of Chapter 13, after his account of the *Patna* rescue. Marlow and the Frenchman are silent for a while. It is the Lieutenant's remark, "*Mon Dieu!* how the time passes!" that breaks the silence and begins the second part of the interview. The shift in the effect of a character's dictum, by an echo cast in figurative language, is characteristically Conradian, and Marlow's reaction is emblematic of his function: "Nothing could have been more commonplace than this remark; but its utterance coincided for me with a moment of vision." Before referring to what he has seen, he explains the kind of insight these revelations provide:

It's extraordinary how we go through life with eyes half shut, with dull ears, with dormant thoughts. Perhaps it's just as well; and it may be that it is this very dulness that makes life to the incalculable majority so supportable and so welcome. Nevertheless, there can be but few of us who had never known one of these rare moments of awakening when we see, hear, understand ever so much – everything – in a flash – before we fall back again into our agreeable somnolence. (143)

Marlow's "revelations," in narrative terms, are a rather unsatisfactory technique, since they are the most mechanical of the devices Conrad uses to advance the work's underlying themes. Among Marlow's performances as deconstructor of language, though, they do achieve an altogether special effect: reaching down into the deepest recesses of commonplace words, they connect fictional passages with human experience. This is the effect hereby realized by Conrad and which Marlow recalls:

I raised my eyes when he spoke, and I saw him as though I had never seen him before. I saw his chin sunk on his breast, the clumsy folds of his coat, his clasped hands, his motionless pose, so curiously suggestive of his having been simply left there. Time had passed indeed: it had overtaken him and gone ahead. It had left him hopelessly behind with a few poor gifts. (143)

Among these gifts, one later learns, is a spotless honor, the reality of which Marlow doubts when he sees the effect of time on this ideal seaman.

It is with this revelation that Marlow then fills in the missing parts of the story. On hearing these, the French Lieutenant gets the gist of the whole matter: "And so that poor young man ran away along with the others." This observation brings Marlow to feel that he is "taking professional opinion on the case" (145), soliciting an opinion which goes beyond the mere facts. The Frenchman's next remark is rich with verbal resonances: "'Ah! The young, the young,' he said, indulgently. 'And after all, one does not die of it.' 'Die of what?' I asked, swiftly. 'Of being afraid'" (146). When the Lieutenant then embarks on a disquisition on the naturalness of fear, Marlow feels emboldened to say: "I am glad to see you taking a lenient view . . . His [Jim's] own feeling in the matter was – ah! – hopeful" (148). This proves to be a terrible mistake, prompted partly by Marlow's urge to find a confirmation of his view in the officer's experience and partly by the earlier revelation. What hope could there be for Jim? The Lieutenant turns upon Marlow a look "like a razor-edge on a battle-axe":

Allow me . . . I contended that one may get on knowing very well that one's courage does not come of itself . . . There's nothing much in that to get upset about. One truth the more ought not to make life impossible . . . But the honour – the honour, monsieur! . . . The honour . . . that is real – that is! (148)

With this the French Lieutenant rises, leaving Marlow so confused that he dares suggest that the whole problem could be reduced to not being found out. Nothing in Marlow's behavior to that point could explain this suggestion. Evidently, his integrity as a character must be sacrificed to the clarification of the underlying theme. The righteous Frenchman altogether dismisses the least possibility of a retort – "This, monsieur, is too fine for me – much above me – I don't think about it" – and walks out, leaving Marlow "alone and discouraged" (149). The French Lieutenant apparently confirmed Marlow's own "lenient view" by affirming that one need not die of being afraid. But when the Lieutenant stressed that only honor is real, Marlow's hope that the old seaman would share his own sympathy for Jim's youthful illusions is crushed.

If Conrad's main concern in outlining Marlow's own interpretation were the illustration of his psychology, then his revelation would only prove how unperceptive the narrator can be. If instead his mind is seen as part of the tale's critical discourse, the words and themes the writer uses in the revelations will be referable to similar passages in which the narrator's insights make explicit the underlying thematic structure. The revelation that signs off the long scene on the verandah of the Malabar hotel, for example, introduces the themes Marlow and the French Lieutenant will discuss a few pages later.

A few pages before the French Lieutenant episode, at the end of Chapter 10, Jim confesses, in a passing remark, that while in the boat he had wished to die. He had not worried at all about not having a hat on under the blazing sun: "The sun could not make me mad . . . Neither could it kill me . . . *That* rested with me." Marlow's interjection tries to add a tragic (and momentous) relief to these words: "'Did it?' I said, inexpressibly amazed at this new turn." Then he asks, "in as impenetrable a tone" as he could command: "Do you mean to say you had been deliberating with yourself whether you would die?" (126). This shocking opening gives Marlow that glimpse which will reveal the "fellowship of . . . illusions" which he discovers between himself and the young man (128). This revelation evolves into a praise of sea life, in which "illusion [is] more wide of reality." Only at sea, he adds, "is the beginning *all* illusion – the disenchantment more swift – the subjugation more complete" (129). By using "illusion" to include the bond uniting all seamen, Marlow is hinting at a reading of Jim's case which could be made by those who live according to the sea code. Jim then continues his story and the motif fades into the narration.

Marlow's insight into the power of youthful illusion, as it shapes Jim's reaction to his shame, surfaces again when Marlow reads into the French Lieutenant's decrepit aspect the "disenchantment" common to seamen. Marlow has just noted how age has acted on the officer's aspect, when the officer remarks on Jim's case: "Ah! The young, the young . . . And after all, one does not die of . . . being afraid" (146). No further references to the contrast between Jim and the French Lieutenant will be made. The two figures will remain, apparently, radically divided by the officer's belief in the reality of honor. The text, however, with its characteristic sinuosity, generates contrasting refractions which undermine irreconcilable opposites. After the Lieutenant's testimony, Marlow remains discouraged about Jim's case. Yet, to justify the fact that after three years it is still so important to him, he relates that he has seen him "only very lately" (149). This opening, which does not advance the story, leads instead to Marlow's digression on Little Bob Stanton, who drowned while he was trying to save a girl in the *Sephora* disaster. And after Stanton's story one of Marlow's mental associations, occurring after the French Lieutenant has left, brings the tale back to the night talk in the gallery of the Malabar House.

Once the thread of the conversation with Jim is picked up again, the respective positions of Marlow and Jim have changed, but the transformation does not seem to reflect the lesson which the Lieutenant's case could have provided. Marlow tries to convince Jim to accept Brierly's scheme before the sentencing. Marlow's proposal is the equivalent of reducing the whole question to not being found out, the improbable suggestion he had made to the

Frenchman. At this point Jim, already cast in a negative light by the redoubtable seaman, utters the most strenuous defense up to this point of his honor, a reaction which will deepen Marlow's understanding of Jim's belief in the value of the principles contained in the sea code.

At the outset of his narrative Marlow shares the basic beliefs of the impersonal narrator, yet struggles in his search for an elusive truth. This search becomes the major dynamic element in the analytic section of *Lord Jim*, as Marlow articulates an interpretation of Jim's case alternative to the omniscient narrator's outright condemnation. A reading of the "revelations" technique makes apparent how the dynamism impressed on the narration by its underlying intellectual quest uncovers new aspects, while giving way at the same time to an increasing momentum which carries forward the effect of basic motifs. The critical discourse is an effect of this complex orchestration. The enlightenment which the verbal resonances and thematic specularity in the French Lieutenant episode bring to the narrative context, however, is not completely clear until the revelation which Marlow undergoes during their talk is perceived in the perspective of the reality/illusion theme. Marlow's vision of the French Lieutenant's appearance mirrors his earlier "distinct glimpse" (128) of the sense of fellowship he feels with Jim's youthful illusions. Both the Lieutenant and Jim are united by a common faith in the reality of honor for which they are willing to sacrifice their lives.[21] Though on the level of factuality they are opposites, in the world of possibilities that Marlow's interpretation gradually unveils the French Lieutenant is only a variation of the Jim-pattern.

The French Lieutenant episode provides the climax for the narration of the long night talk between Marlow and Jim, which ends a few pages later after the former's proposal that Jim should run away. In the following chapter of *Lord Jim*, the last before the Stein interview, the meeting on the night after the sentencing serves the purpose of strengthening the two men's relationship. In this case it is Chester, the "strange idealist" (172), who provides the voice of an underlying theme to create a contrapuntal effect. Chester claims that one must "see things exactly as they are" (162). As a matter of fact, Chester turns out to be juxtaposed not so much to Jim as to Marlow. He would like to take advantage of a Jim deprived of his certificate, to pack him off to a guano island with forty coolies.

Marlow refuses to help him convince Jim, and Chester retorts "Oh! You are devilish smart . . . but you are like the rest of them. Too much in the clouds. See what *you* will do with him" (168). Marlow will later inform his listeners, with some satisfaction, that Chester's expedition ended in a disaster.

Throughout the long scene in Marlow's room during the storm, the vision of the despicable Chester and his partner Robinson keeps intruding on the blank pages of the letter Marlow is writing to find help and sympathy for Jim. Marlow's commitment is based on his interpretation of Jim's appearance and words. At this crucial moment, which Jeremy Hawthorn sees as dramatizing Conrad's "decision not to terminate his tale at this point,"[22] Marlow starts wondering about the power of a word: "There is a weird power in a spoken word . . . And a word carries far – very far – deals destruction through time as the bullets go flying through space" (174). Ill forebodings assail Marlow when he hands Jim the letter he has written. Marlow realizes the presence of an irreconcilable split between his own intention and what Jim makes of the opportunity he has been offered:

I had forced into his hand the means to carry on decently the serious business of life, to get food, drink, and shelter of the customary kind . . . and – behold! – by the manner of its reception it loomed in the dim light of the candle like a big, indistinct, perhaps a dangerous shadow. (184–185)

The candlelight will grow brighter and brighter, the shadow receding into a corner, as Jim's illusions will seem to take on a reality. As the young man leaves the room, Marlow hears him proceeding with "the unhesitating tread of a man walking in broad daylight" (185). The light–darkness opposition, not properly a theme as in "Heart of Darkness," serves here as a metaphor for the very different optics of the young and the old. Marlow melancholically notes:

But as to me, left alone with the solitary candle, I remained strangely unenlightened. I was no longer young enough to behold at every turn the magnificence that besets our insignificant footsteps in good and in evil. I smiled to think that, after all, it was yet he, of us two, who had the light. And I felt sad. (185–186)

Light is necessary and yet deceiving. In those Dark Powers lurking beneath the surface of everyday life Marlow recognizes a "jeering intention" (105). They are invisible in the youth's dream of the future. Only experience can make them visible.

That optimistic light soon fails Jim during his disastrous wanderings: "all his recklessness could not carry him out from under the shadow." And, in trying to assess whether Jim's leaving his various jobs was "shirking his ghost or ... facing him out," Marlow realizes that he himself must strain his "mental eyesight" (197). Only then does he "perceive dimly that what [Jim] wanted, what he was, as it were, waiting for, was something not easy to define – something in the nature of an opportunity" (201–202). Marlow's personal involvement is accompanied by a growth in his understanding of the different issues involved in Jim's story. He is moving from an external view – "I had given him many opportunities, but they had been merely opportunities to earn his bread" (202) – to a truer understanding of Jim's personality.

From the very beginning of his narrative, Marlow is aware that his query into understanding is taking the form of a struggle with an instinctive adherence to the community's condemnation of Jim. As he goes along, he gradually internalizes the debate, especially after he recognizes his own participation in Jim's youthful illusions. His inability to understand what kind of opportunity Jim wants is an intellectual shortcoming caused by his persisting resistance to giving up completely: Marlow hopes to avoid grappling with the ghost of Jim's illusion. Marlow recognizes this reservation in his commitment, and wonders what more could have been done than offer Jim a chance to survive. At this point, Marlow's mental associations reveal once again their narrative function. The conscious Marlow is at a loss – "The position struck me as hopeless" – but a phrase comes to his mind: "poor Brierly's saying recurred to me, 'Let him creep twenty feet underground and stay there.'" "There and then," he recalls, "I had made up my mind to go and consult Stein" (202).

III

Stein enters the narrative as a solution for Marlow's inadequacies. With his appearance the cumulative effect built up throughout the first section of Marlow's narrative becomes apparent through a discursive development of the themes envisaged in motifs and structural appositions. Thus, Marlow's brief presentation of Stein's physical appearance and life serves the specific purpose of pointing out those characteristics which give him the authority to pass definitive word about Jim.

Stein is a living paradox. An adventurer with a tragic past, he still has a student's face, as though he were still keeping alive the illusions of his youth. He is also, according to Marlow, "one of the most trustworthy men" he has ever known (202). Stein is characterized as well by a courage "completely unconscious of itself" (203) and consequently of a kind opposite to Jim's. As Benita Parry remarks, Stein "is shown to be a paradigm of the effective romantic who had translated his aspirations into reality, dissolving in his own history as youthful radical and later as honourable adventurer and confidant of native rulers in the East, the artificial dichotomy between imagination and performance."[23]

As an entomologist, Stein has a name as a learned collector of beetles and butterflies, the lowest and most ethereal of creatures made equal by death. Marlow is eager to point out that those in Europe who revered Stein as a scholar would not be concerned about his life and character. This is precisely what makes Stein so important to Marlow, who remarks in the last lines of the chapter: "I, who knew [his life and character], considered him an eminently suitable person to receive my confidences about Jim's difficulties as well as my own" (203). This passing remark increases the intellectual suspense for how Stein will evaluate the relationship between Marlow and Jim.

Stein's Javanese servant ushers Marlow into a truly Conradian scene. Patches of light and darkness are the setting Marlow and Stein move in, a darkness containing catacombs of beetles, and glass cases of dead butterflies. During their talk Stein moves in and out of the light, the effect of his movements changing the sound of his voice, "as if these few steps had carried him out of this concrete and perplexed world" (213). Stein's first words stress the visual effect: "So you see me – so" (204). Marlow then narrates Stein's story. At twenty-two he had to escape from Bavaria because he was about to be arrested for revolutionary activities, and he eventually reached the East after a series of older men helped him out of various adventures. The first protector, in Trieste, was a republican and must have sympathized with his ideas. A Dutch traveller he meets in Tripoli engages him as an assistant and initiates him as a naturalist. When the Dutch naturalist leaves the Archipelago where they had travelled together Stein stays on with an old Scottish trader who literally adopts him, presenting him as his own son and bequeathing him his position, his goods and a fortified house. A man like Stein will certainly be willing to share with Marlow the responsibility for Jim's future.[24]

Marlow continues Stein's story; the tragic deaths of his best friend, his wife and daughter, and Stein's survival to become a rich merchant and an admired entomologist. The narration returns to the room where Stein is absorbed in the examination of a dead butterfly,

as though on the bronze sheen of these frail wings, in the white tracings, in the gorgeous markings, he could see other things, an image of something as perishable and defying destruction as these delicate and lifeless tissues displaying a splendour unmarred by death. (207)

Is this a case of empty rhetoric, or does Conrad somehow manage to communicate what it is that Stein can perceive and which is at the same time perishable and defying destruction?

Conrad has Stein utter first what he had been thinking about while looking at the butterfly, a manifestation of nature's Platonic harmony. It is not the beauty of the butterfly's wings itself that fascinates him, but "the harmony . . . the balance of colossal forces . . . in perfect equilibrium" which makes them a "masterpiece of Nature – the great artist" (208). Marlow interrupts Stein's reflections; his friendly banter submerges this theme, and what Stein was seeing in the design of the wings is lost for the time being. Stein seems to relax and starts talking about how he captured the butterfly, a story of adventure, betrayal and the unassuming courage Marlow has already indicated as one of the man's characteristics. The story's end, however, has Stein running after a butterfly, the shadow of which he had seen passing over the forehead of a dead foe. Once he captures it, his coolness gives place to an overpowering excitement and he drops on the ground. The emotion of capturing the butterfly he had once "dreamed" of in his "sleep" is far more real than killing three men.

Marlow again puts aside the butterfly theme in order to relate Jim's story to Stein. The simplicity of Stein's diagnosis – "I understand very well. He is romantic" – startles Marlow into asking for a possible cure. The reply – "There is only one remedy! One thing alone can us from being ourselves cure," death – seems too simple for Marlow, who persists: "'Yes,' said I, 'strictly speaking, the question is not how to get cured, but how to live'" (212). Stein agrees with Marlow and rewords the problem as "How to be" (213).[25] He then addresses the question by comparing men and butterflies, in such a way that the earlier meditation on the butterfly he was holding begins to dovetail with the whole argument: "We want in so many different ways to be," he begins, then adds, man "wants to be a saint, and he wants to be a devil – and every time he shuts his eyes he sees himself as a very fine fellow – so fine as he can never be . . . In a dream . . ." (213). Saint and devil are opposite aspects of the same dream. Jim is romantic because, in his case, how to live and how to be coincide. Stein is well placed to pass a judgment on Jim's case: he too has known the reality of dreams, and he pursues that ideal balance in nature which alone can reconcile the opposites ruling the lives of men.

As in the episode of the French Lieutenant, Conrad is extremely careful to make clear in the text what gives the character the authority to express an opinion on Jim. He uses all the devices of his craft for this purpose, in such a way that his dramatic use of the physical setting integrates the purely discursive content with the effect of Stein's voice, the central element in Conrad's use of a character in the critical discourse. Though Conrad outlines very carefully the characteristics which give Stein authority to give the final word about Jim in the analytic section, the theatrical scene he sets up as a context for the German's oracular response interferes or belies the expectation of a straightforward statement. Rather, what is being suggested is a kind of knowledge which eludes a linguistic simplification. This does not mean that the famous "destructive element" paradox in this passage is left intentionally shrouded in the mists of Stein's broken English. Conrad suggests, in one of the most forceful instances of the effectiveness of his prose, how Stein's statements bear on Jim's case by having words interact with the narrative context. The physical setting and Stein's movements while he is speaking underline the contrast between what the German is saying and the silences signaling the points when he can no longer find the words. If, then, one takes Marlow's remarks as stage directions, illustrating how the visual effect acts upon the meaning of words, Stein's interruptions become just as telling as his stated thoughts.

Stein utters his speech on the destructive element while he is in the dark, a "shadow prowling amongst the graves of butterflies" (214).[26] The passage is divided into three parts, each introduced in an assertive manner. Immediately after his remark on saints and devils as opposite aspects of the same dream, Stein moves out of the light into darkness. Here, his form seems "robbed of its substance" and "his voice, heard in that remoteness ... [is] no longer incisive." His words seem "mellowed by distance" (213). And a laugh is heard from the darkness as Stein thinks about what fine fellows men consider themselves to be, just as they discover that this high concept of themselves turns out to be a dream: "Yes! Very funny this terrible thing is. A man that is born falls into a dream like a man who falls into the sea. If he tries to climb out into the air as inexperienced people endeavour to do, he drowns." And he continues, "No! I tell you! The way is to the destructive element submit yourself, and with the exertions of your hands and feet in the water make the deep, deep sea keep you up. So if you ask me – how to be? ..." At this point Marlow steps in to give one of his stage-direction commentaries: "His voice leaped up extraordinarily strong, as though away there in the dusk he had been inspired by some whisper of knowledge" (214).

As if enlightened by this darkness, Stein exclaims: "I will tell you! For that, too, there is only one way." But, instead of disclosing his inspiration, Stein moves into the light, where Marlow can see him again, and he is no longer laughing. Now his appearance seems threatening to Marlow. His hand looks like a gun aimed at Marlow's breast, his eyes seem to pierce through him, and "his twitching lips uttered no word." The magic moment is gone, and Marlow remarks that "the austere exaltation of a certitude seen in the dusk vanished from his face." Stein's appearance changes again, as if he realizes his defeat; the hand which had seemed so menacing is now laid on his friend's shoulder in a gesture of simple friendship. The man who had been laughing at the dreams of his fellow man has changed radically: "There were things, he said mournfully, that perhaps could never be told, only he had lived so much alone that sometimes he forgot – he forgot. The light had destroyed the assurance which had inspired him in the distant shadows." He finally sits down, and Marlow is careful to point out how he rubs his forehead at first, then speaks with one hand on each side of his face while he resumes his speech (though in "a subdued tone"): "And yet it is true – it is true. In the destructive element immerse . . . That was the way. To follow the dream, and again to follow the dream – and so – *ewig – usque ad finem*" (214–215).

Identical words can have entirely different meanings. It had seemed at first that Stein would have enough authority to resolve the enigma of Jim's personality. He is an old man who has chosen to seek the harmony of nature among dead creatures. Indeed, from the darkness he looks with contempt on the efforts of his fellow men. What the old adventurer and scholar comes to realize, suddenly, is that his wisdom is based on his personal experience, and what he thought he could put into words and pass on is actually something he still has within himself: he moves from laughter to mournfulness, from darkness to the crude light, and from a rhetorical present tense to the past tense of his memory: "That *was* the way. To follow the dream . . ." (214–215; emphasis added). Stein's voice had sounded "extraordinarily strong" in the dark, then became "subdued," until, as he recollects how he too had followed a dream, it is barely a whisper, the "whisper of his conviction" (215).

This whisper, however, is enough to bring about another of Marlow's revelations: it "seemed to open before me a vast and uncertain expanse" illuminated by "a charming and deceptive light, throwing the impalpable poesy of its dimness over pitfalls – over graves." Stein had never faltered in the pursuit of his ideals and passions, and this possibly saves him (and explains why Conrad has created in this case his only positive German character: he is an Idealist philosopher). But Marlow cannot abstain from commenting on the images he formed out of Stein's words. The "great plain" under this light, he observes, remains "very desolate." No one could be "more romantic" than Stein, Marlow concludes (215), making clear the egotism underlying Stein's and Jim's romanticism.

On a first reading, Conrad appears to have set in motion too many paradoxes at the same time in the destructive element passage. Coming to life is equated with falling asleep, the sea is like a dream, and breathing – that is, emerging from the sea-dream or waking up – is like drowning or dying. In the second half of the passage, however, the notion of the destructive element brings a certain balance to the spinning paradoxes: the notion is equivalent to self-forgetfulness, the condition which enables one to follow an ideal while gaining strength from the potential destructiveness of its content. The particular tone the narrative context gives to this concept – partly through Stein's inability to transform it into a golden rule, and partly through the painful awareness of his own past which Jim's story arouses in Stein himself – ultimately clarifies Stein's judgment. Stein's authority is not based on his being a philosopher but on the fact that he has been able to put his ideal into practice, to live out the paradox. This is the inheritance which he will try to pass on to Jim.

The continuity in the ideas which run through the German trader's reflections is important for an understanding of not only what the destructive element means but also how Conrad was elaborating his own convictions during the writing of *Lord Jim*. When Marlow enters Stein's study the latter is busy examining a butterfly. Marlow perceives – and Stein's words confirm his insight – that the old man is not fascinated by the beauty of the wings, but is trying to grasp what, in them, is "perishable and defying destruction" (207). Stein then starts to talk about nature's harmony, "the balance of colossal forces ... the mighty Kosmos in perfect equilibrium." Apparently his reflection on what he finds in the beautiful specimen is lost in the following discussion. But, in effect, the destructive element passage is nothing more than the same argument turned upside-down. Stein calls nature "the great artist" in the earlier passage because it manages to establish a "perfect equilibrium" between "colossal forces" (208). It is a creator of harmony out of conflicts and contradictions. This harmony is indeed the ultimate purpose of art, as Conrad had continually stressed since the preface to *The Nigger of the "Narcissus."* Nowhere does Conrad set this concept out more explicitly than in the letter to *The New York Times Saturday Book Review* (August 2, 1901), one year after the completion of *Lord Jim*:

Fiction, at the point of development at which it has arrived, demands from the writer a spirit of scrupulous abnegation. The only legitimate basis of creative work lies in the courageous recognition of all the irreconcilable antagonisms that make our life so enigmatic, so burdensome, so fascinating, so dangerous – so full of hope. They exist! And this is the only fundamental truth of fiction. Its recognition must be critical in its nature, inasmuch that in its character it may be joyous, it may be sad; it may be

angry with revolt, or submissive in resignation. The mood does not matter. It is only the writer's self-forgetful fidelity to his sensations that
matters. But, whatever light he flashes on it, the fundamental truth
remains, and it is only in its name that the barren struggle of contradictions assumes the dignity of moral strife going on ceaselessly to a
mysterious end – with our consciousness powerless but concerned sitting
enthroned like a melancholy parody of eternal wisdom above the dust of
the contest. (*CL* II, 348–349)

Conrad uses "fidelity to his sensations" in his non-fictional writings to emphasize the aesthetic implication of his commitment to
FIDELITY. The added qualification of "self-forgetful" expresses the
subjective condition necessary for giving a representation of the
irreconcilable contradictions underlying existence – a reality
which, reproduced in logical verbal structures, would give place
to an endless series of paradoxes. "They exist" is the central
conviction which must guide a novelist in his effort to illuminate that which in his character will be meaningful for his
readers. The moral tension which sustains any search for truth in
writing fiction is derived from a "consciousness powerless but concerned." This phrase fittingly describes Marlow's reminder that
the world in which men and women must live remains "desolate" even when enhanced by the "impalpable poesy" of Stein's
idealism (215).

The scene at Stein's brings to an end the analytic section of
Marlow's narrative segment. Here Marlow finally lays down the
burden of the uncomfortable reality of Jim's case. Why was Jim so
important to him? Marlow's ruminating mind cannot answer this
question, which he had hoped Stein could help him solve. But
Stein's oracular response is unsatisfactory. Marlow seems ready to
move forward at this point, after another of his revelations has
recontextualized Stein's barren idealism. But Conrad instead gives
an abrupt change to the narration. This change could appear to
end the metaphysical abstractions, but it actually extends the discussion one step further. Marlow has just told Stein that "no one
could be more romantic than himself," at which the old German
scholar shakes his head and remarks that all this talk is useless:
instead of wasting time they should be seeking a "practical
remedy" (215). Stein's sudden appeal to a practical remedy holds a
wonderful irony. At the beginning of their discussion he had sug-

gested that death would be the only possible cure for Jim's romanticism. However, the personal memories brought to the surface have shown how a romantic nature can live out the conflict between idealism and the material world. Now Stein is willing to provide Jim with the opportunity to project his own self-image on the world. Thus, the practical "coda" to the Stein interview turns out to be Patusan, the stage for the romance of Jim's adventurous exploits.[27]

In spite of this practical turn, Marlow's narrative seems in no hurry to close the scene and move on to an account of the momentous decisions of the following morning. Instead, while Stein is accompanying Marlow to his room, the ironic play on being "practical" is allowed to pause a little longer over the themes discussed in the chapter. All of a sudden, Stein repeats, "He is romantic – romantic . . . And that is very bad – very bad . . . Very good, too." Marlow does not have much patience left for Stein's perplexing musings and interrupts him: "But *is he*?" His friend's reply brings out a possible ambiguity in Marlow's question: "Evident! What is it that by inward pain makes him know himself? What is it that for you and me makes him – exist?" (216). Is Jim romantic? Does Jim exist? Only in the context of the Stein interview could these two questions "evidently" coincide. There lies beneath these questions the knowledge Stein and Marlow have come to share about the pangs of growing awareness.

As usual, it is the effect of a word on Marlow that serves to clarify an obscure utterance by placing it within its discursive context. At first he notes that it was difficult to believe in Jim's existence. Focusing on the issue of his existence rather than his being romantic, Marlow goes on to add: "but his imperishable reality came to me with a convincing, with an irresistible force! I saw it vividly, as though . . . we had approached nearer to absolute Truth, which, like Beauty itself, floats elusive, obscure, half submerged, in the silent still waters of mystery" (216). Marlow has finally "approached Truth" after the revelation of Jim's reality has come to him filtered through the young man's illusions. His moral judgment about the jump does not lie in a condemnation or acquittal of Jim, but in the recognition that he cannot dismiss the doubts raised by the investigation simply by denying the reality of the conflicts it raises. Marlow's analytic method, which had seemed to isolate different interlocking themes – youth/maturity, reality/illusion, life/dream – has undergone a significant transformation during the Stein interview. The vivid dramatization given to the effect of light on Stein's scathing assuredness is the best comment on the paradox he makes out of these themes. Stein's passage from darkness to light dramatizes the German's recognition that he is still living the paradoxes inherent in these themes, and therefore he cannot portray them to Marlow in words. The detachment from human affairs that Stein had gained by living apart from other human beings is shattered by the recognition of a common tie between his story and Jim's.

The mirror pattern which Conrad achieves between Stein's pondering at the beginning of the interview and Marlow's revelation confirms that in the Stein scene there emerges a parallelism between Marlow's interpretation of Jim's case and the writer's discussion of his own concerns about fiction in the 1901 letter to *The New York Times*. When Marlow interrupts Stein's examination of the butterfly, the latter cheerily says, "I have been this rare specimen describing . . . Na! And what is your good news?" Marlow's answer is only apparently humorous: "'To tell you the truth, Stein,' I said with an effort that surprised me, 'I came here to describe a specimen . . .'" Stein replies to this apparent joke by asking whether it is a butterfly; but when Marlow, assailed by doubts, rejoins – "Nothing so perfect . . . A man" – Stein becomes "grave" and says, "Well – I am a man, too" (211–212). The uncomfortable reality of Jim's story is weighing on the buoyancy Marlow had assumed when he interrupted Stein in his contemplation of the work of "the great artist" nature, as embodied in the butterfly's wings. This change in Marlow's mood is an apt corollary to the introduction of the destructive element passage. By playing on the sense of insecurity which Marlow suddenly feels in putting the two specimens on the same level, Conrad can connect the submersion of Stein's discourse with both its upside-down paradoxical *doppelgänger* (that is, the harmony established through self-forgetfulness) and Marlow's final revelation. Just as Stein had been able to see "an image of something as perishable and defying destruction" (207) beyond the gorgeous markings of his specimen, Marlow is made to discover signs of an "absolute Truth, which, like Beauty itself" is shrouded by mystery in the "imperishable reality" (216) of his own specimen.

The equivalence between harmony and self-forgetfulness

appears at different levels. It not only connects an author's creativity with an ideal harmony achieved by giving a representation of the conflicting forces regulating our perception of the material world; it also lays out the only way in which it can be possible to live the paradoxes of living, by accepting those different levels of reality which a work of art can integrate. Where can life and dream, actuality and possibility, defeat and victory coexist if not in a fictional tale that goes to the deepest sources of one's perception of the material world? In a novel the "existence" of a fictional character is the first step toward leading the reader to accept the claims which "the barren struggle of contradictions" has on the conscious response to a story, the last step being a recognition of the "existence" of the same paradoxes in his or her life, thus making the fictional world a part of the reader's own reality.

When Marlow, after his revelation in this scene, tells Stein that he is at least as much a romantic as Jim, his German friend answers "Well – I exist, too" (217). That these simple words can be so surcharged with the meanings embedded in the narrative context of the scene, and the novel, is the surest justification of the method Conrad adopted in the first segment of Marlow's narrative. Marlow's revelation follows the pattern already established by Conrad in the novel: the narrator experiences the effect intended for the reader, making explicit his response to it in words which can then be connected in a verbal structure running through the critical discourse. With this technique Marlow can repeat, in the following chapter, the same concepts in a more explicit form, in a direct address to his audience. He returns here to the issue of Jim's existence after having introduced Patusan and after an elaborate peroration on Jim's value. Marlow asks how could he "tell" at the time of his interview with Stein how Jim would have turned out? Stein himself "could say no more than that he was romantic," and all Marlow knew was that "he was one of us." Marlow's next question revives for a moment the discussion in Stein's study, "And what business had he to be romantic?" It would seem that the themes related earlier are emerging again. He stops and tells his listeners:

I am telling you so much about my own instinctive feelings and bemused reflections because there remains so little to be told of him. He existed for me, and after all it is only through me that he exists for you. I've led him out by the hand; I have paraded him before you. Were my commonplace fears unjust? I won't say – not even now. You may be able to tell better, since the proverb has it that the onlookers see most of the game. (224)

At Stein's Marlow realized that Jim is real for him precisely because he is romantic. Now the narrator's "feelings" and "reflections" will no longer guide the reader in the slow uncovering of his own coming to terms with the problem of Jim. The young man has been provided with a stage on which to act out his own play and, as Marlow tells Jim, "it would be for the outside world as though he had never existed"; "Never existed – that's it, by Jove!" is Jim's enthusiastic comment (232).

Marlow's address to his audience echoes the concluding paragraph of the dream-/life-sensation passage in "Heart of Darkness." After his famous speech in the short story about the difficulties of conveying the essence of a dream and of one's memory, there is a pause in Marlow's narrative, followed by an apparently unrelated afterthought: "Of course in this you fellows see more than I could then. You see me, whom you know" (*Y*, 83). The almost identical phrasing in the two passages situated at the culminating point in the critical discourse of the respective tales can help set in relief a metaphorical reference to the concerns Marlow voices in both texts. In "Heart of Darkness," Conrad suggests that Marlow is re-enacting his subjective experience by juxtaposing the "seeing" of a story and the "hearing" of a tale. The question lying at the core of *Lord Jim*, though related, is quite different, however. After the author's unsuccessful attempt to solve the problems he faced while writing the African tale, he addresses the question: in what way can a reader be affected by the "reality" of a fictional character? This question connects the narrative and thematic structures of the novel. The illusion/reality theme and Marlow's discussion of Jim's existence pose the question. Conrad will provide an answer at the end of the Patusan romance.

CHAPTER 5

Lord Jim *(II): the narrator as reader*

The Patusan romance is an adaptation of the narrative form to the conclusions of Marlow's analytic inquiry. Conrad's highest achievement in the use of the narrative frame, Marlow's probing of Jim's case, had been launched as an attempt to make explicit those words that Jim could not utter. To this purpose, Conrad articulated a symbolically suggestive language decodable through a rhetorical commentary which made possible a direct line of communication between author and reader. As it turns out, however, once the internal narrator discovers why the young man matters to him, the truth of these unutterable words comes to be warranted by the reality of Jim's (and Marlow's) illusions. The interpretation of the issues raised by Jim's fateful jump evolved in such a way as to reveal that only by increasing the fiction's fictionality could the author force on the readers a sense of the protagonist's "existence." Thus, the content of the analytical discourse itself comes to support the basis of fiction: the potentiality of human acts is no less true than the "naked fact" (35) which is their actuality. This is why Conrad will not use Marlow in Patusan as a device for questing after that right word which could disclose Jim's subjective point of view. Instead, the narrator becomes an ideal reader whose reality has been touched by the truth of Jim's illusion.[1]

Conrad's creation of a fictional stage on which Jim can act out his illusions provides a striking insight into the way auto-interpretation grounded his artistic evolution.[2] Marlow's sending Jim to Patusan enacts the author's decision to create a fiction-within-the-fiction which would impress upon the reader the possibility of finding an expression of one's illusions in a fictive alternative to historical actuality.[3]

I

In two passages at the end of the analytic section, Conrad presents Marlow's most explicit plea for the value of Jim's illusions and then challenges his audience's Philistinism. The position of these two passages is a clear indication of the mechanism at work in the launching of the Patusan section. Here, the "practical remedy" which Stein and Marlow came up with is charged with the personal commitment the narrator is willing to take on for Jim's success. It is because of this commitment that Marlow states his view in the first passage with an explicitness possible only after his interview with Stein. Marlow is telling the story after his visit to Patusan has confirmed his claims; and so he feels confident enough to declare that his "last words about Jim shall be few": "I affirm he had achieved greatness" (225).

This confidence, though, is checked by Marlow himself when he points out why he is afraid his audience will be incapable of understanding the greatness of Jim's achievements in Patusan: "but the thing would be dwarfed in the telling, or rather in the hearing. Frankly, it is not my words that I mistrust but your minds. I could be eloquent were I not afraid you fellows had starved your imaginations to feed your bodies" (225). In three consecutive sentences, "telling" and "hearing," "words" and "minds," being "eloquent" and starving one's "imagination" are juxtaposed in such a way that this final address in the analytic section cannot be explained away as a quirk in Marlow's personality. Rather, in this passage the author is establishing a relationship between the difficulties of writing and a morality underlying the act of reading.

Marlow's provocation is aimed at deciding between the two points of view, the pro or con in Jim's case, which have clashed throughout Marlow's inquiry; and, at the same time, he is trying to remove the distance between narrator and audience which results from the former's inability to put the shift in outlook determined by the revelation at Stein's into a logical verbal sequence. Marlow's affirmative attitude has been determined by the fact that Jim's belief in the illusions guiding his life makes him real in Marlow's eyes. Such an insight can be gained only inwardly, Conrad avers, by coming to terms with the extent to which one has been able to follow one's illusions. Only acceptance of an interplay between reality and illusions can provide a possible synthesis between the narrator's defective language and the audience's dormant mental faculties, thus re-establishing the flow of understanding between narrator and listeners/readers. Having remarked on his audience's starving their imagination to feed their bodies, Marlow adds:

I do not mean to be offensive; it is respectable to have no illusions – and safe – and profitable – and dull. Yet you, too, in your time must have known the intensity of life, that light of glamour created in the shock of trifles, as amazing as the glow of sparks struck from a cold stone – and as short-lived, alas! (225)

In "Heart of Darkness," the frame narrator's intervention which allows Conrad to define how to read the short story immediately follows Marlow's statement that his audience can see the story because they see him, "whom [they] know" (Y, 83). In Lord Jim, which lacks the narrational concern about storytelling that characterizes "Heart of Darkness," Conrad challenges the mental apathy which limits the reader's response instead of suggesting a particular reading model.[4] If the reader can find a common tie with Jim's deceptive self-image, not only the gap in understanding but also that between the narrator and his audience can be bridged. The shift in narrative form at this point in Marlow's account is consistent with the change in his attitude after the Stein scene. But, in order to launch the story of Jim's fictional achievements, he must make the reader realize in what way the character is granted a higher degree of reality in the romantic setting. Marlow's final provocation seeks to awaken his audience's capability to share a fictional reality, and in order to do so he makes an appeal to an extra-literary solidarity.

The second passage interweaves the themes underlying the analytic section with the ones at work in the Patusan romance. Marlow's reflection raises already familiar themes and integrates new ones. He is about to go back home, whence Jim had come, like a man "under a burden in a mist." The departure signals a realization of the depth of his attachment to Jim. Precisely because of the young man's inscrutability Marlow is brought to reflect: "the less I understood the more I was bound to him in the name of that doubt which is the inseparable part of our knowledge" (221). Marlow has at this point already established himself as an irrepressible doubter, fascinated with the impalpable shades of Jim's personality. And he begins to elaborate about a "spirit that dwells within the land . . .

[to which] . . . one must return with a clear consciousness." Why should he transform the emotions of homecoming into a "spirit"? He promptly counteracts his audience's resistance: "All this may seem to you sheer sentimentalism; and indeed very few of us have the will or the capacity to look consciously under the surface of familiar emotions" (222). These emotions form the web of human relationships usually associated with home, but Marlow is trying to uncover an underlying vital principle.

This spirit is not an abstract idea. Rather, it is a reality not given to everyone to perceive:

I think it is the lonely . . . those who return not to a dwelling but to the land itself . . . who understand best its severity, its saving power, the grace of its secular right to our fidelity, to our obedience. Yes! few of us understand, but we all feel it though, and I say *all* without exception, because those who do not feel do not count. (222)

The "spirit of the land" theme will play a central role in Patusan, where it will come to signify the complex relationship between Jim and the land outside history. When Conrad introduces this theme at the end of Marlow's inquiry, he is trying to bring to the surface a feeling which the audience circumscribed by "us" is familiar with, if only unconsciously. Of course, "the lonely" are not merely a hypothetical projection. Conrad knew what he was talking about. He is talking here of the loneliness acutely felt by those who need an ideal correspondence with the rest of mankind in order to keep rank. He is echoing his commitment to FIDELITY, to an ideal, and to his belief in the solidarity which "knits together the loneliness of innumerable hearts . . . the solidarity in dreams, in joy, in sorrow, in aspirations, in illusions, in hope, in fear, which binds men to each other" (*NoN*, viii).[5] It is in the name of this solidarity that Marlow can overtly affirm Jim's value:

I don't know how much Jim understood; but I know he felt, he felt confusedly but powerfully, the demand of some such truth or some such illusion – I don't care how you call it, there is so little difference, and the difference means so little. The thing is that in virtue of his feeling he mattered. (222)

By jumping, Jim has betrayed both the fidelity to those who embodied for him the spirit of the land and the solidarity fundamental to his calling. However, his awareness of a permanent separation from his ideal community makes him even more important than those who can go back without understanding or feeling what that ideal is. In Patusan he will have the opportunity to turn his illusion into a binding relation with another spirit of the land. And in putting fidelity and solidarity into practice, he will meet his own, Marlow's and Stein's great expectations.

Patusan is introduced to the audience as an insubstantial, surrealistic place seen in moonlight. Marlow remarks on the spectral quality of that setting when he describes Jim after they "had watched the moon float away above the chasm between the hills like an ascending spirit out of a grave" (245). The houses along the river are like "a spectral herd of shapeless creatures pressing forward to drink in a spectral and lifeless stream." Moonlight, he notes, "robs all forms of matter – which, after all, is our domain – of their substance, and gives a sinister reality to shadows alone." Conrad uses this setting – so similar to "the landscapes of Gothic fiction"[6] – to underline an opposition between Jim and his surroundings. Jim's solidity stands out from the shadows "as though nothing – not even the occult power of moonlight – could rob him of his reality in my eyes" (246).

This apparently casual observation leads to an even stranger one: "Perhaps, indeed, nothing could touch him since he had survived the assault of the dark powers" (246). When Marlow had told his audience about the long night-talk during which Jim had given his account of the jump, he had often hinted of an evil agency which had brought about the disaster. He had specifically pointed out the presence of "the Dark Powers whose real terrors, always on the verge of triumph, are perpetually foiled by the steadfastness of men" (121). However, never until this point has he admitted that Jim survived the "assault" of this agency. When Jim expressed his desire to die after the jump, Marlow had remarked: "He had found *that* to meditate about because he thought he had saved his life, while all its glamour had gone with the ship in the night" (129). The glamor of heroism lost forever, Jim had kept himself alive by the light of his illusion that an opportunity would sooner or later come around. But this could only occur in a place outside life altogether. During the Stein interview, the German scholar–adventurer had suggested death as the only cure for human illusions. The novel's conclusion will vindicate the rightness of this diagnosis; but already at this stage of Jim's ordeal the illusory quality of his having "at last mastered his fate ... nearly" (324) lends Patusan a ghostly character. Marlow seems at this point to hang on to the concreteness of Jim's presence, thereby unwittingly stressing to what extent his reading of Jim's achievements is a projection of his own imagination. The remoteness of the setting sounds like a bass chord reminding the reader of the fateful reality of this make-believe world: the price one pays for acquiring reality in this land of illusion is death.

Marlow presents Patusan as nothing more than "a totally new set of conditions for [Jim's] imaginative faculty to work upon," in terms which stress the continuity between the issues of the analytic and fictional sections of his narrative. The radical otherness of this remote place makes it a kind of "heavenly body" for Marlow and his European audience (218). And Conrad makes it immediately clear that Patusan's dimension outside history is apt for the unconventional romance he is creating: all that Jim will achieve among the people of the village, "love, honour, men's confidence ... are fit materials for a heroic tale; only our minds are struck by the externals of such a success, and to Jim's successes there were no externals" (226). If Jim had become a hero to his own community, the distinction between illusion and reality established during Marlow's inquiry would have been blurred. Jim is significant for Marlow because the way in which he lives his situation questions the adherence of principles to reality. He has been judged and found guilty for a fact he cannot dispose of, and yet he goes on believing in, and suffering for, the very ideal which that fact belies. If Jim had been able to do so in an environment familiar to Marlow's audience, he would have become a hero – that is, he would have reasserted a coincidence between reality and illusion. Instead, Jim will struggle for the ideal aspect of the "fit materials," intentionally escaping the external world.[7] Presenting Patusan as a land where Jim "can, ostensibly, structure reality to fit his needs,"[8] Marlow can assert the absolute, universal value of Jim's pursuit of his dream without ever making this dream real. As Marlow remarks, Jim is not seeking any personal advantage. In sending him to Patusan, Stein and he "had to deal with another sort of reality" (230).

The narration of Jim's "successes" is articulated in three themes, each concerned with one of the materials fit "for a heroic tale." Through a series of time shifts, Conrad weaves into the narrative accounts of the honor conferred on Jim by his military prowess, the absolute faith of the natives in his word, and the love story. This elaborate structure belies Guerard's charge that the adventures narrated in Chapters 22–35 "have nothing to do with the essential Jim."[9] These three themes have the effect of extricating the *essentials* from the "externals" of the "heroic tale" (226), and, at the same time, allow Conrad to discuss the same issues of the analytic section in a different form.

In the story of Jim's military exploits, Marlow pits against each other the two forms of authority Jim has acquired in Patusan. The story begins in Chapter 27, which is devoted to the taking by storm of Sherif Ali's fort. The account of the last phases of the assault unfolds in a succession of frames similar to that of film editing. The action is seen both "historically" and through the "popular story" (270) gifting Jim "with supernatural powers" (266). Jim's disclaiming of the legend leads to his account of an apparently unrelated episode: a journey to a village to settle a family feud over three brass pots (268–269). From the way Marlow amalgamates and isolates the different elements in the episodes of the brass pots and the assault, a common denominator emerges: the power of his word. What is important is not the physical courage Jim has shown, or the admiration he has commanded, but that those "people had trusted him implicitly. Him alone! His bare word" (268). He has recovered the balance between facts and ideal that only a name can give.

The people in Patusan take his word for anything and everything, and for Jim the old man who comes to ask his advice about the three brass pots is just as important as the assault. In both cases it is the responsibility that matters: "had it been three lives instead of three rotten brass pots it would have been the same." Marlow reads into these words "the moral effect of his victory in war" (269). And because this moral effect is more important than the actual victory, Conrad elaborates on it before the account of the final assault.

The end of Jim's recital of his triumph produces an unexpected effect. When Marlow notes that he must have enjoyed it, Jim's reaction startles him: "'It was . . . immense! Immense!' he cried aloud, flinging his arms open. The sudden movement startled me as though I had seen him bare the secrets of his breast . . . 'Immense!' he repeated for a third time, speaking in a whisper, for himself alone" (271). At this point Marlow reverts to what had been his most characteristic role in the analytic section, that of enlarging Jim's concise expressions. Yes, he concedes, his achievements were truly immense; but, he warns his listeners, all this "gets dwarfed in the telling." He cannot "with mere words" convey "the impression of his total and utter isolation" (272). Marlow has warned his audience that they would be unable to grasp the nature of Jim's greatness, but the inadequacy-of-words trope he employs here gives a particular meaning to the warning. He cannot find the words to communicate Jim's greatness because it is based on the alienness his young friend has gained from the world the audience lives in: "this isolation seemed only the effect of his power. His loneliness added to his stature" (272). This does not mean that Jim lives in a void. The authority of his words, illustrated in the pages leading to Marlow's comment, has defined the territory in which he has achieved greatness: "his fame, remember, was the greatest thing around for many a day's journey." The communications media of the native society carry this fame, just as the "telegraph cables" and "mail-boat lines" (282) spread the power of the white men: "You would have to paddle, pole, or track a long weary way through the jungle before you passed beyond the reach of [his fame's] voice" (272).

Although Marlow can relate his impressions of the greatness Jim has achieved, he cannot translate Patusan's reality into the language he shares with his audience. In a way Marlow is in the same predicament in which he found himself in "Heart of Darkness," when he entered the upper reaches of the river. The voice of Jim's fame, he says, "took its tone from the stillness and gloom of the land without a past, where his word was the one truth of every passing day" (272). In the land outside history Jim's world coincides with his name. He appears as he sees himself, and his self-image is projected unchecked, forcing other lives to adapt to his reality. His fame, however, cannot be expressed without the accompanying spectral stillness of Patusan. The digression about the misinterpretation of Jewel's name illustrates the distortion which an eventual report of the "essentials" in Jim's achievement would undergo.

After he has underlined the ideal value of Jim's achievement by relating the power that his word has in Patusan (268–272), Marlow mentions for the first time Jim's love story (275). However, Marlow does not immediately proceed to his account of Jim's love in Patusan. Having anticipated why this will not be a conventional love story, he embarks on a digression on the name Jim has given to the girl, Jewel (277–282). Through this digression, Conrad emphasizes the continuity which underlies the thematic shift. The critical discourse he articulates in Jim's naming of Jewel, in fact, elaborates on the reason why Marlow's tale will get "dwarfed in the telling" (272).

Appropriately for a Conradian hero, Jim, as Axel Heyst in *Victory*, gives a new name to his woman: "Jim called her by a word that means precious, in the sense of a precious gem – jewel" (277). Marlow concedes that he "was struck by the name," and this thought allows him to act out his most characteristic role of establishing narrative connections through his mental associations: "it was not till later on that I connected [the name] with an astonishing rumour that had met me on my journey, at a little place on the coast about 230 miles south of Patusan river" (278). The punctiliousness with which Marlow specifies how many miles away the place was from Patusan is the best indication that this connection serves to bring the tale back to the real world, where time and space are accurately measured.

At the "wretched locality" Marlow finds a Dutch third-class deputy-assistant resident whom Conrad depicts as the epitome of vileness, greed and stupidity. As soon as the Dutchman learns that Marlow is going to Patusan, where "some sort of white vagabond had got in," he also starts hinting at an obscure report he has heard: "'Well, then, there might be something in the story, too, after all ... Look here,' says he, mysteriously, 'if – do you understand? – if he has really got hold of something fairly good – none of your bits of green glass – understand? ... You just tell him I've heard the tale'" (279). This embodied outpost of progress, "perspired, puffed, moaning feebly, and scratching himself with such horrible composure that [Marlow] could not bear the sight long enough to find out" (280) what this tale was about.

The next day Marlow finds out that the Dutch deputy-assistant resident's greed had been awakened by a legend the natives of the coast were passing along – "about a mysterious white man in Patusan who had got hold of an extraordinary gem – namely, an emerald of an enormous size." The "amazing Jim-myth" is referred to him by a "purblind ... scribe" who adds a further piece of mythical lore: "such a jewel ... is best preserved by being concealed about the person of a woman" (280). The scribe relates how he has heard that "the white man could be seen with her almost any day; they walked side by side, openly, he holding her arm under his – pressed to his side – thus – in a most extraordinary way," which could only mean that "there could be no doubt she wore the white man's jewel concealed upon her bosom" (281). Jim's care and affection for Jewel are construed as proof of the invented story's veracity.

On the next page, Marlow draws his audience's attention to the contrast in his own mental associations:

But do you notice how, three hundred miles beyond the end of telegraph cables and mail-boat lines, the haggard utilitarian lies of our civilisation wither and die, to be replaced by pure exercises of imagination, that have the futility, often the charm, and sometimes the deep hidden truthfulness, of works of art? Romance had singled Jim for its own – and that was the true part of the story, which otherwise was all wrong. (282)

Once the illusory grasp on reality offered by the communications media no longer sustains the ideology of civilization, the pursuit of material interests turns out to be the only motive of the white men's self-appointed historicizing authority. The reality of Patusan and its "old mankind, neglected and isolated" by the "stream of civilisation" (226) is unperceivable to Europeans. As Marlow remarks, "to the Western eye, so often concerned with mere surfaces, the hidden possibilities of races and lands over which hangs the mystery of unrecorded ages" are usually lost (262). Patusan, then, shares its unreality with the world of art, which appears ever more futile as the utilitarian outlook permeates society. When Marlow compares with works of art the pure exercises of imagination which gave rise to the Jim-myth, he is drawing the logical conclusion of his digression: the external world is incapable of deciphering the romantic meaning of the name Jim gives to Jewel.[10]

The love story which follows will pose a number of questions for Marlow's recognition of an artistic quality in the Jim legend.

During his inquiry, Marlow anticipated that Jim would have "captured much honour and an Arcadian happiness (I won't say anything about innocence) in the bush" (175). The legend-digression provides a generic frame to this "Arcadian happiness." The Patusan romance has a function in *Lord Jim* similar to that which masques have in Shakespeare's comedies. As Agnes Latham writes in her introduction to *As You Like It*, on "the stage a masque has the function of a play-within-a-play. Its heightened illusion makes the rest of the play seem momentarily more real."[11] Even though Patusan cannot be said to mirror the external world, Conrad introduces in his portrait of the land certain features which illuminate the meaning of the distortions resulting from its alienness. Basically, Patusan's remoteness is akin to death; and it will be the love story itself which will reveal the romance's dark side, thus helping Marlow understand in what way the fiction he is living in Patusan turns out not to be a romance at all. The forest around Patusan is not the forest of Arden, the Malays and Bungis are not shepherds and shepherdesses: Jim's romance is not a pastoral comedy.

The "artistic" nature of the land outside history suggested by Marlow sidetracks the theme it should be individuating. This is the first time in the novel that the rhetorical structure appears redundant or contradictory. Could it be that Marlow is stressing the "romantic" aspect of the story because he has believed in it from the beginning, but the story is now moving in another direction? Only after the final disaster will Marlow realize that Patusan is a masque *manqué*.

In his explanation of why Jewel's name had been misinterpreted, Marlow appealed to imagination as the means for perceiving the artistic truth of Patusan. The underlying discursive context, however, sets in relief a far more disquieting content. Jim's narcissistic self-absorption, once set in the spectral reality of Patusan, has been charged with an active valence; that is, from a personality inhibited in its potentiality for action by his self-image, he has become a mythopoeic figure projecting a self-perpetuating authoritative image among people who still believe in myths.[12] This is indeed a great achievement, but a frightening one quite distant from an Arcadian happiness in the bush. The love story will eventually throw light on Jim's cruelty in his pursuit of "the call of his exalted egoism" to which he sacrifices Jewel (416).

Marlow launches the theme of love, which completes his account of Jim's successes, by making it clear – as he has already with honor and "men's confidence" – that this is not a conventional story. He does so by linking the love story to an anguishing reminder of the suffering caused by love. The theme is introduced rather roughly by Marlow once he has told the story of Jim's military exploits. The narrative has reached Marlow's last evening in Patusan, and he now starts uncovering the themes interwoven in the fictional section. When he mentions "And this brings me to the story of his love," Marlow points out defensively, "I suppose you think it is a story that you can imagine for yourselves" (275) – one of those stories so concrete that they make one doubt the sentiment exists at all. But this case is different:

Yet I don't know. To tell this story is by no means so easy as it should be – were the ordinary standpoint adequate. Apparently it is a story very much like the others: for me, however, there is visible in its background the melancholy figure of a woman, the shadow of a cruel wisdom buried in a lonely grave. (275)

What makes Jim's love story actual is that pervasiveness of death which haunts the whole Patusan romance. Marlow's "standpoint" is the coincidence between his own heightened subjectivity and the reality Jim has acquired in the spectral moonlight in the land of illusions.

The uninhibited rhetorical tone in which Marlow enlarges upon the grave's meaning in the love story signals a change in the way Conrad uses his critical discourse in the Patusan romance. After having described the grave itself, Marlow acknowledges that "whether the shadow [of a cruel wisdom] is of my imagination or not, I can at all events point out the significant fact of an unforgotten grave." The tone is not relinquished when he adds that Jim himself worked at the rustic fence, for which "you will perceive directly the difference, the individual side of the story." It is difficult to understand at this stage of the narrative why it is so important for Marlow to make this point. It may be partly for the light this love casts on Jim: "There is in his espousal of memory and affection belonging to another human being something characteristic of his seriousness. He had a conscience, and it was a romantic conscience" (276). There certainly is in Jim a sentiment which goes beyond passion, a capacity for feeling which would make his love story different from the ones Marlow's audience would immediately think of. What Conrad is actually doing is launching what

should be the most "romantic" portion of the fictional tale so that
its eventual use will illuminate how removed the whole narrative is
from romance.

Marlow's warning about the difficulty of telling the love story
launches the theme which will turn out to be at the core of
Patusan's fictionality: in the world of make-believe the narrator
will be made to perceive as he had never before the atrocious
reality of human suffering. As Marlow realizes in the interview
with Jewel which unveils the conflicting drives at work in the love
story, her relationship with Jim is shaped by her already knowing
how it will all end. On the last evening, first in Jewel's words and
then in the darkness close to her mother's grave, he gains the
insight which grounds the narrative standpoint, making the love
story different from the romances his audience could expect. But
the two experiences also lead Marlow to the clearest revelation
concerning his role as narrator of the story, thus illustrating the
centrality of the love theme. Indeed, Jewel's genetic foreknowledge
of how inevitable Jim's betrayal will be – and how inhuman his
faithfulness – vindicates the concreteness of Patusan's "fictional"
world.

In the long scene between Jewel and Marlow (307–319) Conrad
returns to the two narrative devices he had used for Marlow and
Jim's night-talk on the Malabar Hotel's verandah – reversion to
figurative language as a solution for the inadequacy of words, and
use of semi-poetic rhetorical commentary[13] to amplify the effect of
a concise expression. Jewel is afraid Marlow has come to Patusan
to take Jim away and is trying to shield her lover from an appeal
the captain is bringing from the external world. Marlow knows
this is not the case and, to reassure her, tells her that nobody
wants Jim because he is not good enough. Marlow's attitude is
somewhat patronizing. He stands as an envoy from the larger
world, looking down on the poor girl who has lived in Patusan all
her life: "She had grown up there; she had seen nothing, she had
known nothing, she had no conception of anything. I ask myself
whether she were sure that anything else existed" (307). He is
moved by the impression ("it is all I can give you" [308]) of the
anguish the girl is feeling. He is unable, however, to convey this
impression. "She made me believe her," he remarks, "but there is
no word that on my lips could render the effect of the headlong
and vehement whisper, of the soft, passionate tones, of the sudden

breathless pause and the appealing movement of the white arms
extended swiftly" (308). Conrad's explicit references to the
inadequacy of words should not be read as capitulations but as
indicators of how the figurative language suggests rather than
states. In this case, certainly the most successful in *Lord Jim*, he will
use figurative language to render not Jewel's words – nor the
pauses between them – but the visual effect of the movement of her
arms:

They fell; the ghostly figure swayed like a slender tree in the wind, the pale
oval of the face drooped; it was impossible to distinguish her features, the
darkness of the eyes was unfathomable; two wide sleeves uprose in the
dark like unfolding wings, and she stood silent, holding her head in her
hands. (308)

Conrad's attempt to achieve a poetic use of fictional language is
closely related to the emergence of his concerns about writing and
fiction. The intellectual tension giving rise to the critical discourse,
far from being opposed to the creative effort, is actually an attempt
to interpret it.

The reality of the grave permeates Jewel's reluctance to believe
the man she loves. As Marlow comments, "there was nothing
lighthearted in their romance: they came together under the
shadow of a life's disaster." This is why they seem to Marlow like
"knight and maiden meeting to exchange vows amongst haunted
ruins" (311–312). He is being half-ironic and half-sentimental, but
the blow of Jewel's words makes him lose his detachment. By the
end of the talk Marlow will be stunned by the depth of knowledge
Jewel has reached through suffering. The change in his attitude is
presented in a dialogue between Marlow and Jewel in which the
words that will smash his superiority are delivered in a single
sentence: "I didn't want to die weeping" (312). Conrad carefully
prepares the devastating suggestiveness of this utterance, by setting
in relief Marlow's reaction and then distilling, word after word, the
sentence's effect on him. At first he is surprised, not quite sure of
what he has heard. But when she adds, "My mother had wept
bitterly before she died" (312), his defenses fall:

An inconceivable calmness seemed to have risen from the ground around
us, imperceptibly, like the still rise of a flood in the night, obliterating the
familiar landmarks of emotions. There came upon me, as though I had felt

myself losing my footing in the midst of waters, a sudden dread, the dread of the unknown depths. (312)

What could a girl who has always lived in Patusan know? Someone unable even to imagine the reality of the outside world? And instead, her experience cancels the distinction between the two worlds. Like Gabriel Conroy, the protagonist of James Joyce's "The Dead," who is made to discover at the end of the story that he has never loved his wife as much as a young boy who had let himself die for her,[14] Marlow will attain his epiphany once he realizes that Jewel's suffering far exceeds all his experiences.

When Jewel goes on to describe the scene of her mother's death, an account ending with the words "The tears fell from her eyes – and then she died," the trespassing of these "familiar landmarks of emotions" leads Marlow to a more self-conscious experience. The girl's "monotone," he says,

had the power to drive me out of my conception of existence, out of that shelter each of us makes for himself to creep under in moments of danger, as a tortoise withdraws within its shell. For a moment I had a view of a world that seemed to wear a vast and dismal aspect of disorder, while, in truth, thanks to our unwearied efforts, it is as sunny an arrangement of small conveniences as the mind of man can conceive. (313)

"Landmarks of emotions" and "conception of existence" both stand for the protection afforded by negation of the darker side of human experience. These defenses break down under the onslaught of Jewel's story. In this passage Conrad is even more scathing toward the narrowness underlying an identification between these protections and reality. He is far more explicit here than he had been in "Heart of Darkness,"[15] where Marlow had undergone a similar experience in his last moments with Kurtz – perhaps because in Patusan it is the victims who speak for themselves.

The revelation is soon over ("I went back into my shell directly. One *must* – don't you know?" [313]), and Marlow returns to his usual role, picking up the thread of the conversation between Jim and Jewel. But before his return to a rational unraveling of the love story, one last insight is set forth, questioning the basis of his narrative. On regaining his control, Marlow recalls, "I seemed to have lost all my words in the chaos of dark thoughts I had contemplated for a second or two beyond the pale. These came back, too, very soon, for words also belong to the sheltering conception of light and order which is our refuge" (313). The following events, and the words he uses to relate them to his audience, await Marlow on his return from the chaos of dark thoughts. He has had a glimpse of what lies under the surface of Jewel's love, but his figurative language will at most trace the boundary delimiting its inexpressible depths, which can be communicated only approximately but nothing more.

Marlow, of course, is not able to assuage Jewel's fears, and she eventually lashes him with two words spoken in the native dialect, "You lie!" (318). Jim arrives, looking for them, and Marlow slips away. At this point in his narrative, Marlow interrupts his tale. The frame narrator relates that his listeners "seemed startled" and one or "two sat up as if alarmed." Marlow seems to be looking "at them all with the eyes of a man returning from the excessive remoteness of a dream" (320). The frame narrator's interruption reminds the reader that the dream-like quality of Marlow's re-enacting of his past is mirrored in an undermining of the rational order of the verbal sequence.

Marlow then picks up again the thread of his tale by recalling the nocturnal walk which will lead him to Jewel's mother's grave. He finds himself at first in a spot where the ground has been recently cleared. Here Jim intends to start a coffee plantation, an example of his energy and enterprise. The talk with Jewel, however, has deeply affected Marlow's projection into the reality of Jim.[16] Consequently, he can no longer claim that "nothing – not even the occult power of moonlight – could rob him of his reality in my eyes" (246). On raising his eyes, he undergoes an ascent-of-Snowdon experience when he sees the moon and comments that nothing "on earth seemed less real now than [Jim's] plans, his energy, and his enthusiasm" (322). The spectral moonlight seems to have sprung to life on this last night in Patusan, after the shock of Jewel's story. From the hill it seems as if the moon has rolled to the bottom of the chasm; its "eclipse-like light" gives to the flowers decorating Jewel's mother's grave "shapes foreign to one's memory." Patusan's nature is bare at last: the moonlight and silence give the impression that "the earth had been one grave" (323). The scene is ready for the last revelation, among the *fleurs du mal* "grown not in this world" (322).

It seems almost as if Conrad had to set the climaxes of his critical discourse in a narrative context riddled with paradoxes. Marlow himself had some difficulties in extricating himself from the web of paradoxes spun by Stein during their interview. Now, having escaped Jim and Jewel, he is facing the uncanny vitality of the spectral setting. The earth is a grave, and he starts thinking of the "living ... buried in remote places out of the knowledge of mankind." This could be an uncontroversial enough assertion – were it not that he has discovered the reality of Patusan only after he has perceived the memory of the dead mother lingering in the living daughter. The best way he can express the reality of the Patusan people is by employing a phrase rich with resonances from "Heart of Darkness": "The human heart is vast enough to contain all the world" (323). In "Heart of Darkness" Marlow had recourse to a temporal image to explain the kinship he felt toward the natives ("The mind of man is capable of anything – because everything is in it, all the past as well as all the future" [Y, 96]). In Lord Jim, Marlow's experiences on his last night in Patusan enable him to perceive how people unknown to him share in mankind's "tragic or grotesque miseries ... [in] its noble struggles" (323). As a result of his final revelation, he comes to question spatial and temporal distances and suggests they may be illusions contradicted by the vastness of the human heart.

He cannot explain what happened to him. He apologizes – "I suppose I must have fallen into a sentimental mood" (323) – as if aware that the verbal rendering of the experience he is about to relate can only convey a superficial meaning. But in his effort to relate it, he expresses very synthetically all the major themes at work in Lord Jim. At first he recalls his "sense of utter solitude" (323). This disquieting sensation affects him to the point that all he has seen and heard in Patusan, "and the very human speech itself, seemed to have passed away out of existence, living only for a while longer in [his] memory," as though he had been "the last of mankind." The sense of solidarity with all mankind is contracted spasmodically in those few seconds in which Marlow is his own memory without being able to share it. It seems as if Marlow has lost for a moment the detachment of his role, becoming a witness rather than a narrator. He then continues: "It was a strange and melancholy illusion, evolved half-consciously like all our illusions, which I suspect only to be visions of remote unattainable truth, seen dimly." He has not returned yet at this point to the sheltering conception of light and order which shapes his narrative and his role itself. Instead, he lingers, as it were, in the twilight zone between reality and illusion.[17] When Marlow resumes his tale he is talking from the standpoint of the self-conscious narrator setting the reality of Patusan in the perspective of his own intention. Patusan, Marlow says,

was, indeed, one of the lost, forgotten, unknown places of the earth; I had looked under its obscure surface; and I felt that when to-morrow I had left it for ever, it would slip out of existence, to live only in my memory till I myself passed into oblivion. I have that feeling about me now; perhaps it is that feeling which had incited me to tell you the story, to try to hand over to you, as it were, its very existence, its reality – the truth disclosed in a moment of illusion. (323)

Marlow brings back from the revelation he has had next to the grave a dimly perceived truth, the most precious half of which is the reality of the men and women living in the land outside history. Marlow establishes before his audience an explicit relation between the reality of Patusan and the reality of the fictional romance within the tale he has generated.[18] The tale's truth lies in Patusan, the land of make-believe conjured up by two old men for the illusions of the young romantic. What Marlow understands in Patusan *is* the narrative standpoint from which he relates his account of his inquiry into the *Patna* case. The two sections of his oral narrative are thus integrated: as he relives his experience before his audience, Marlow is fulfilling the commitment he made on his last night in Patusan.

At the end of the first narrative segment, the impersonal narrator described Marlow's physical attitude as he recalled Jim's story: "with the very first word uttered Marlow's body . . . would become very still, as though his spirit had winged its way back into the lapse of time and were speaking through his lips from the past" (33). At the end of his oral narrative, however, the remoteness which gives place to the tale's specularity is apparent. Without Patusan, Marlow could not have told the story of his analytic inquiry in the way he does. The fascinating ambiguity given the narrative by the tension between the contrasting readings of Jim's act is possible only because Marlow's belief in the potential reality of Jim's illusions – and of his value – is sustained by the existence of Patusan.

The graveside revelation assesses correctly the issue of Patusan's reality, but does not seem to affect Marlow's perception of Jim's reality in the land. Patusan had been unreal in Marlow's eyes as long as it was only a setting for Jim's opportunity. The impossible love story has changed the narrator's perspective: Jewel's knowledge of past suffering gives her the authority to foresee the outcome of Jim's illusions. Jim is caught in the middle. He cannot recover in Patusan the reality he has tried to leave outside, back in the real world. In the last chapter of the Patusan section, Conrad elucidates how the last revelation bears on Marlow's final statement about Jim.

Conrad renders Patusan's slipping "out of existence" (323) in Marlow's last farewell to the village, as if his narrator were a reader closing an adventure story he had just finished reading. The way in which Marlow presents his departure mirrors Jim's enthusiasm when Stein had given him Doramin's ring as "a sort of credential" (233). At the time the young man had remarked appreciatively that it was "like something you read of in books" (233–234). The ostensible comparison Marlow makes while he is leaving Patusan is with painting: "next morning . . . all this dropped out of my sight bodily . . . like a picture created by fancy on a canvas, upon which, after long contemplation, you turn your back for the last time." As he approaches the sea, Marlow feels he is "going back to the world where events move, men change, light flickers," where he "would have enough to do to keep [his] head above the surface." What he had anticipated the night before is now happening: the human beings he is leaving behind will never change, the picture will remain "in the memory motionless, unfaded, with its life arrested, in an unchanging light." The feelings and motivations, the drama of love and hate will all remain in Marlow's mind, "intense and as if for ever suspended in their expression" (330) – a state similar to the "suspended animation" (*PR*, 15) of the figures Conrad evoked in *Almayer's Folly* before his first reader read the manuscript.

When Marlow begins to distinguish signs of the sea's vivifying presence, Conrad imparts an abrupt quickening to the prose's rhythm (similar to the one the sea gave to the fictional language in *The Nigger of the "Narcissus"*), amplifying in this way the effect of the thematic opposition between the two worlds. The particular kind of vision Marlow acquires in Patusan is shown when he remarks that he is certain of the Patusan characters because they "exist as if under an enchanter's wand" (330). However, the clarity of the fictional picture is blurred around Jim. He cannot be immobilized by a "magician's wand." He is alive, he is "one of us" (331). The distinction established by this phrase in *Lord Jim* does not run along a racial division line, for the whole Patusan episode runs counter to such a distinction. Rather, it refers to the kind of reality Jim partakes of. His enigmatic personality cannot be fictionalized. Just as the actual determination of his potentialities is inadequate for assessing his value, ultimately only his death can make him real, as Stein had always known.

Jim's non-fictional status seems to disarrange the carefully set-up departure from Patusan. Marlow will not be able to leave behind a world of fiction because Jim will show at the last moment that he has fulfilled Marlow's and Stein's expectations. The light under which Marlow sees Jim at the end will be the moral viaticum which, along with the memory of the nocturnal revelation in Patusan, will transform the captain into a narrator.

The clear light of the open sky and the vastness of the sea have an opposite effect on Marlow and Jim. Whereas the former feels "like a man released from bonds" (331), the latter does not dare raise his eyes, as if "afraid to see writ large on the clear sky of the offing the reproach of his romantic conscience" (332). The reproach looms over the last moments they spend together, even as two fishermen come up to Jim with a complaint, seeking his protection from the overbearing men of Patusan's Rajah. It is a case of stolen turtle eggs, but it provides a last instance, for Marlow, of Jim's achievement: he has given these men security and peace. Jim knows very well that the moment he leaves the country all this would be over: "'I must go on,'" he declares, "'go on for ever holding up my end, to feel sure that nothing can touch me. I must stick to their belief in me to feel safe and to – to' . . . He cast about for a word, seemed to look for it on the sea . . . 'to keep in touch with . . . you, for instance'" (334). Marlow, who is going back to the "impeccable world" (331), is humbled by Jim's words: "I felt a gratitude, an affection, for that straggler whose eyes had singled me out, keeping my place in the ranks of an insignificant multitude" (334). Jim's "singling out" in the courtroom had launched

Marlow's involvement, but here the narrator seems to be referring to an enlargement of Jim's appeal. Through Marlow, Jim will try to keep in touch with the whole "multitude" in which he could not keep his place. Jim, the captive of the "spirit" of this remote land, will act according to that illusion Marlow had referred to in vindicating his value at the end of the analytic section. Now, at the end of the fiction-within-the-fiction, Jim is demonstrating how he has put into practice those ideals which Stein and Marlow had perceived in his internal conflict.

The words Jim utters at the very last, "as if he had found a formula – 'I shall be faithful'" (334), constitute for Marlow a clear moral victory. Fidelity to an ideal relationship binding all men is the closest one can get to an explicit positive statement in Conrad's critical discourse. Jim can pronounce these words at the end of the Patusan romance because of the preceding analytic narrative which, in fact, constitutes the utterance's discursive frame.[19] Marlow is quick in picking up the connection between the light these words cast on Jim and that interpretation of his personality he had reached at the end of his inquiry only with Stein's help: "Ah! he was romantic, romantic," he comments, and adds: "I recalled some words of Stein's ... 'In the destructive element immerse! ... To follow the dream, and again to follow the dream – and so – always – *usque ad finem* ...' He was romantic, but none the less true" (334). The urgency of the critical discourse forces the author to remove the fictional disguise from the internal narrator's figure. Marlow is not simply referring to what Stein had said; he repeats his words as they were pronounced, maintaining the wrong syntax, only translating "*ewig*" (215) into "always" (334). Marlow is made to be as explicit as possible in establishing the extent to which Jim has fulfilled in Patusan the two older men's interpretation of his case. Jim's faithfulness to the ideals he shares with his mentors makes him true and real, in Marlow's eyes, having lived out the potentialities they had detected in him.

If *Lord Jim* had ended at this point, one could have concluded that Marlow is voicing Conrad's own convictions. The dark side of Jim's personality has been illuminated by the victory over the ambiguous shades of the world of fiction's "form of imagined life clearer than reality" (*PR*, 15). But this is not the case, and Marlow's emergence from his role only leads to Conrad's preparing a unique denouement: the internal narrator's subjective point of view was based on his own illusions. These pages are the end of Marlow's three-hundred-page-long yarn. When Marlow will resume his narrative, Conrad will show him in the light of a puzzled witness without a final answer.

The most telling aspect of this shift in Marlow's role is the way he comes to be contained within the hinges of the mechanism regulating the passage from the second to the third narrative segment. He who has for the past three hundred pages glossed upon every single word pronounced by Jim does not offer any comment about Jim's mysterious behavior at the very end. Both men know this will be the last time they meet, and Jim, almost as an afterthought, asks Marlow, "Will you be going home again soon?" Marlow, half-jocularly, replies, "In a year or so if I live," at which Jim unexpectedly shouts after him:

'Tell them . . .' he began. I signed to the men to cease rowing, and waited in wonder. Tell who? The half-submerged sun faced him; I could see its red gleam in his eyes that looked dumbly at me . . . 'No – nothing,' he said, and with a slight wave of his hand motioned the boat away. (335)

Marlow goes on to describe the sunset, and his yarn ends without his having commented on Jim's words.

Throughout Marlow's narrative his voice has been the means for the critical discourse's articulation of that investiture which he had unwittingly accepted in the courtroom: his willingness to "remember [Jim] at length, in detail and audibly" had been connected by the impersonal narrator with Jim's "deliberate opinion that speech was of no use to him any longer" (33). So important is the interpretative key provided by that "investiture," that Conrad uses its re-enactment to seal off the story it had served to launch. Jim's unvoiced appeal, in fact, evokes the same agony he had been feeling while standing in the witness box. He is unable until the very end to translate his feelings into words. But at this point Marlow is satisfied with what he has heard and seen: Jim will be faithful; and even though he remains enigmatic, it is with this assuredness that Marlow can go back – and it is with the same feeling, of course, that he narrates Jim's story. When Marlow will refer back to Jim's "'Tell them . . .'" in the third segment, the discourse Conrad has set up to illuminate the implications for his art of the reality of fiction will reach its logical conclusion. But already at this point a reader who has recognized the pointers indicating the author's discourse can foresee that the eighty pages left are irreconcilable with the splendid isolation in which the narrator has left his hero.

II

At the beginning of the next chapter, the impersonal narrator takes over the narrative to describe the audience dispersing "under [Marlow's] abstract, pensive gaze" (337). The shift from one narrative to the next is very abrupt, but the impersonal narrator does not try to bridge the gap. Quite the contrary: he seems to dwell upon it. The listeners move away, "without offering a remark, as if the last image of that incomplete story, its incompleteness itself, and the very tone of the speaker, had made discussion vain and comment impossible" (337). The white figure on the beach provides a visual image of the story's incompleteness, both because the enigma of Jim's personality has not been solved and because the protagonist has not been able to frame a message which would explain what he has in common with the audience of Marlow's tale. Marlow's narrative continues, but in a different form – a packet, containing three letters and a manuscript, which he sends to one of the listeners of his yarn, the "privileged man" (337) as the impersonal narrator calls him. The fragments of information given by the impersonal narrator outline the personality of this privileged reader. Marlow will then echo each of these fragments in the letter which explains why he has chosen this particular listener.

The packet's effect on the privileged man begins the subtle orchestration which will set in the foreground this figure's function in the metamorphosis that Marlow's narrative is undergoing. As soon as he opens the packet he lays it down, goes to the window and draws the curtains, shutting out the view of the city. He was once a wanderer, and Marlow's packet has the same effect that the news of uprisings in the Archipelago had on "Karain"'s narrator: it "brought back the sounds, the visions, the very savour of the past" (338). No longer, as the narrator informs the readers, does the privileged man struggle forward "in the hot quest of the Ever-undiscovered Country over the hill, across the stream, beyond the wave" (338). The man gives the impression of living in solitude in the city described as a billowing sea, alone in the "highest flat of a

lofty building" (337), compared by the impersonal narrator to "the
lantern of a lighthouse" (337). All these elements envisage an
authoritative person who has outgrown his romantic past and
ostensibly denied it, but is, nonetheless, painfully aware that with
the end of his wandering days the glamor and excitement of his past
is over. Then, "He sighed and sat down to read" (338).

Once he starts reading Marlow's letters, he tries to control his
growing excitement and, "checking himself, thereafter read on
deliberately, like one approaching with slow feet and alert eyes the
glimpse of an undiscovered country" (338). Marlow's packet is a
Pandora's box out of which buried memories come back to life; and
the reading process proves to be similar to those wanderings the
privileged man thought were over for good. At first, Marlow
addresses him, explaining why he has been selected as the only
listener who will hear the last of Jim: "You alone have showed an
interest in him that survived the telling of his story" (338). If this
were actually the case, *mutatis mutandis*, Marlow's tale in the following pages would be substantially the same: he would have chosen a
sympathetic audience for the decoding of Jim's romantic achievement. This is not the case, however, and the interest shown by the
privileged man turns out to have consisted of disparagements of
Jim's achievement in Patusan. Marlow is therefore addressing in
his letter that part of his audience which most forcefully had denied
the ideas he had projected into his oral narrative. Through the
impersonal narrator's melancholic portrayal of the price paid by
the privileged reader for his denial, Conrad can now attack the
possible hostility to the news of the defeat of Marlow's illusions he
can expect from the larger audience.

By having the impersonal narrator contribute elements which
bring to an end the polemical interventions interspersed throughout the oral narrative, Conrad can, here at the opening of the
written account, compound the analytic and fictional portions of
his novel. The privileged reader's comments, coming as they do at
the end of Marlow's elaborately faceted treatment of the themes
clustered around Jim, appear as signs of a defensive refusal of the
implications of Jim's case. Marlow reminds him that he had proph-
esied for Jim "the disaster of weariness and of disgust with acquired
honour, with the self-appointed task, with the love sprung from pity
and youth," and had commented that he knew very well "'that
kind of thing,' its illusory satisfaction, its unavoidable deception"

(338–339). The "privilege" seems a little suspicious: the "interest" shown by the privileged man stands unequivocally for the kind of response specular to the polemical discourse carried on by Marlow.[20] The list of the comments the reader had made continues, confirming his scapegoat function. Marlow then recalls that:

> You said also – I call to mind – that 'giving your life up to them' (*them* meaning all of mankind with skins brown, yellow, or black in colour) 'was like selling your soul to a brute.' You contended that 'that kind of thing' was only endurable and enduring when based on a firm conviction in the truth of ideas racially our own, in whose name are established the order, the morality of an ethical progress. (339)

The ironic tone of this passage (especially from the pen of the author of "An Outpost of Progress," "Heart of Darkness" and *Nostromo*) could not be easily missed. The glaring contrast between the privileged reader's "truth of ideas racially our own" and the "truth disclosed in a moment of illusion" (323) which had grounded Marlow's narrative could not be more clear.

Whatever has happened between the time of Marlow's narrative and his letter, he has not changed his mind about the general issues he discussed in his narrative. On the contrary, he starts out by going over again the polemical threads interwoven in his tale. However, something has happened. He uses Jim's case again to make his point in opposition to what the reader had said. But this time he refers to the past not to suggest the universality of Jim, but the uniqueness which sets him aside from the rest of mankind. As he writes to his reader: "The point, however, is that of all mankind Jim had no dealings but with himself, and the question is whether at the last he had not confessed to a faith mightier than the laws of order and progress" (339). At the time Marlow is writing, he knows that Jim is dead. Marlow's letter to the privileged man – which, as Arnold Davidson observes, "he probably wrote after he had finished the second narration and which therefore well might be his last words on his different accounts of Jim and his deeds"[21] – helps us to understand the basic difference between his narrative standpoint in the written and oral segments. The written and oral narratives are not different for some particular linguistic feature. What distinguishes them is that Marlow's illusions no longer will shape words and events – to the point of transforming words into events as Stein and he had done with their practical remedy.

Conrad intentionally undermined Marlow's authority as a narrator when he chose not to have him know about Jim's death. He manages in this way to structure organically the analytic inquiry and the fictional representation of the whole spectrum of Jim's potentialities, both as a fictional character and a "real" person (in Marlow's eyes the distinction is never very clear). Both sections of Marlow's oral narrative resound with the practical solution that Stein and the narrator contrived for Jim; his rhetorical exchanges with, and exhortations to, his listeners reflect his conviction that Jim's case has been given a rational solution. If Marlow had known about Jim's tragic end beforehand, he would not have told the story.

Marlow's involvement is guided by an ideal tension, an illusion sustained by that conviction of the Patusan romance's reality ingrained in the memory of his last revelation. One wonders how the fictional tale could demonstrate its reality without setting forth a representation of that moral imperative which, prompted by values such as fidelity or solidarity, motivates the writer to envisage an ethically defined world alternative to the one he lives in. Only by moving first beyond the limited view of deterministic objectivity and moral relativity can one act. Thus Marlow in the letter to the privileged man shows how, in the face of his audience's scorn, he still believes in the value of Jim's achievement.

Marlow is partly apologetic for having been carried away by his involvement, and restates at this point the words he had said at the end of the analytic section ("I affirm he had achieved greatness" [225]): "I affirm nothing. Perhaps you may pronounce – after you've read" (339). But it is through the critical discourse that Conrad illustrates the changes the narrative has undergone. Only now does he have Marlow comment on Jim's "Tell them . . ." (335). The formal investiture Marlow had apparently dismissed at the end of the Patusan tale has been accepted. But now he goes back to the scene on the beach with the knowledge that Jim was not able to voice his appeal, not even at the end. The reader does not yet know of Jim's death but is told that what had come to him was "perhaps that supreme opportunity . . . for which I had always suspected him to be waiting, before he could frame a message to the impeccable world" (339). On a second reading of the novel, the ineffable tinge given to "opportunity" has a truly disquieting effect.

Renewing the narrative from Jim's appeal at the end of the Patusan tale, Marlow offers the comment he had abstained from when he originally related the beach scene. Marlow writes: "That was all then – and there shall be nothing more; there shall be no message, unless such as each of us can interpret for himself from the language of facts, that are so often more enigmatic than the craftiest arrangement of words" (340). The circle opened at the end of the first narrative segment comes to a close at this point. Marlow, the only man among the onlookers of Jim's ritual sacrifice in the courtroom who seemed able to articulate a language which could move beyond the factual aspect of the jump, steps back. He can only interpret along with the readers the enigmatic language of facts. It is not in his power to explain this language with a narrative metalanguage. The whole message ingrained in the tale is numbed.

The language of facts had been deconstructed by Marlow, at first, in an attempt to illuminate the universality of Jim's case. The crafty "arrangement of words" in the Patusan tale had gone one step further than the analytical investigation into the causes of Jim's jump. On the basis of their interpretation of the ugly fact – Jim's jump – Stein and Marlow had decided that Jim's illusory self-image had to be given some confirmation in actuality. Theirs was an attempt to set up a fiction which could build an alternative reality, based on potentiality rather than specific determination, by giving Jim the opportunity to live out his ideal conception of himself. Jim's acting out his potential character would have confirmed the validity of their own interpretation. What had been configured as "illusion" throughout the analytical portion of Marlow's narrative had come true in Patusan, and Marlow could feel satisfied at the end of the "romance": the crafty arrangement of words which had re-created his interpretation had been a success. Jim's achievements and ideal faithfulness had turned into a fact. Jim's death, however, puts an end to the illusory projection which had guided Marlow's storytelling, and the narrative becomes ostensibly a written chronicle. Marlow will now relate the facts without developing an antithesis to the historical verdict.

Marlow's bitterness only enhances the extent to which he had invested emotionally and ideologically in Jim's success. In a first comment on what happened in Patusan, he writes that even though the story of the events is incredibly romantic, there is to his mind "a sort of profound and terrifying logic in it, as if it were our imagination alone that could set loose upon us the might of an overwhelming destiny." Whose imagination it was that sent Jim to his tragic fate is not to be asked. But there is certainly a shade of self-reproach in Marlow's next sentence: "The imprudence of our thoughts recoils upon our heads; who toys with the sword shall perish by the sword" (342). The hermeneutical architecture of Stein and Marlow has collapsed, and the storyteller can no longer arrange words into a fiction, or throw at his Philistine audience the implications of a word or an event. At this point Marlow will recede into the niche of a chronicler. He will write as though he "had been an eyewitness," begging forgiveness because his "information was fragmentary."[22] In writing his account he has simply "fitted the pieces together, and there is enough of them to make an intelligible picture" (343). The emphasis Conrad gives to the narrative shift does not point out a change, but an absence, in the surface of the written account that follows. There will no longer be a story of events configuring a fictional world, an illusory stage for human values not necessarily related to the language of facts. Conrad gives this absence an importance quite disproportionate to the difference in fictional language between oral and written narrative. This is understandable in view of the tension built up throughout the critical discourse. Marlow is being used to point out the lesson his creator has learned in the process of writing his last "paper boat." Though fiction shares with reality the minimal common denominator of words, the possibility it expresses cannot sustain an alternative to the merciless logic of actuality – Marlow's dramatic handing down of the burden as interpreter of the "language of facts," then, foreshadows Conrad's relinquishing of a central consciousness as narrative medium.

Jim's death and the elegiac passing on to the written chronicle marks the end of that artistic "dream" which freights Conrad's "paper boats." The tension which Conrad dramatizes in *Lord Jim's* storytelling – through Marlow's emotional involvement and his attempt to make illusions become reality on a fictional stage – reflects the end of a corresponding illusion on the author's part: that he could create his intended effect by conflating the narrative-frame technique and a poetic use of fictional language. Marlow's narrative of Jim's effort to explain himself was accompanied by the reminiscence of the effect Jim's story had on him. The re-creation of that effect brought forth the figurative language which characterizes *Lord Jim*; and, the echo that Marlow's interpretation provided for Jim's figurative expressions gave reality to the illusions common to both men. Now that facts have crushed all illusions, however, he will write down the last, tragic events without trying to find those words which could suggest alternative interpretations.[23] He cannot but wonder, however,

how he would have related it himself. He has confided so much in me that at times it seems as though he must come in presently and tell the story in his own words, in his careless yet feeling voice, with his offhand manner, a little puzzled, a little bothered, a little hurt, but now and then by a word or a phrase giving one of these glimpses of his very own self that were never any good for purposes of orientation. (343)

Those "glimpses" had been such only for Marlow, and Conrad had tried to use his narrator's interpretation of Jim's words to articulate a fiction which could vindicate the young man's unvoiced appeal. The interpretation resulted in neither "orientation" nor any other answer, and Jim is left to pass away, as enigmatic as he had appeared at the beginning.

Already in the letter to the privileged reader it is clear that Conrad is still using Marlow as he did in the oral narrative. The strident notes accompanying the shift in narrative form have nothing to do with a change in Marlow's narrative voice. In Chapter 37, where he presents his sources of information, far from piecing together the eyewitnesses' account, he stresses the significance of the picture he creates from the words of his informers. He begins with Gentleman Brown dying in a "wretched hovel." The sound itself of Brown's words is revolting, but Marlow is at work again, interpreting the pauses between the words: "He talked feverishly; but in the middle of a word, perhaps, an invisible hand would take him by the throat, and he would look at me dumbly with an expression of doubt and anguish. He seemed to fear that I would get tired of waiting and go away, leaving him with his tale untold, with his exultation unexpressed" (345). Marlow's eagerness to know is strong enough for him to face the agent of Jim's disaster. It is Marlow who informs

Brown that Jim is dead as a consequence of the raid, and the dying cutthroat's exultation allows Conrad to cast a particular light on the leader of the "emissaries with whom the world" (385) pursued Jim. He gasps: "I could see directly I set my eyes on him what sort of a fool he was . . . He a man! Hell! He was a hollow sham" (344). Brown is an internal reflector, similar to those which Conrad had used in the analytic inquiry.

Marlow relates in the same chapter how he first knew about Jim (he will not say explicitly that he is dead, until the very end): it had been eight months before, at Stein's. It is there that he meets his other three sources of information, Jim's servant Tamb' Itam, one of Doramin's Bugis, and Jewel. The contrast between Brown's words and Jewel's reticence prepares the reader for the painfulness of the following story. She speaks "quietly" (348), "whispering to herself." Jim has done exactly what she had always known he would do: "He has left me," but "He shall have no tears from me. Never" (349). The love story is over. The reality of the external world has been conjoined with the reality embedded in Jewel's memory. There was no place for Jim in either and he has gone or, as Jewel says, "fled as if driven by some accursed thing he had heard or seen in his sleep . . ." (349). In the last scene on the beach Jim had indulged in an ill-fated prophecy: "In time [Jewel] will come to understand . . . She trusts me" (335). But now the contradictions dormant in the scene on the beach have exploded. The ideal fidelity which Marlow had detected in Jim and his faithfulness to Jewel's love were irreconcilable.

The scene of the denouement is Stein's house. After Jewel's outburst, Marlow wanders into the garden and sits on "a shaded bench near the ornamental pool" (349). In this recess, so different from the "wretched hovel" in which Gentleman Brown died, he puts on his rhetorical robes again. He writes that the "mournful and restless sound" of the branches of the casuarina trees was "a fit accompaniment" to his "meditations" about Jewel's words. He is aware that "there was no answer one could make her": when she "had said he had been driven away from her by a dream . . . there seemed to be no forgiveness for such a transgression." But Marlow's convictions have not changed even after he has known what Jim had made of his pursuit of his dream, *usque ad finem*. After all, he adds, "is not mankind itself, pushing on its blind way, driven by a dream of its greatness and its power upon the dark paths of excessive cruelty and of excessive devotion? And what is the pursuit of truth, after all?" (349–350). One realizes how appropriate it has been on Conrad's part to set this scene in Stein's house.

Having concluded his meditation upon the darker side of human greatness with a rhetorical question pointing out the ruthlessness of bare truth, Marlow meets Stein and Jewel. When Stein was ushering Marlow into Jewel's presence he had urged him to tell "her to forgive him." Marlow, "exasperated at being in the dark," retorts: "but have *you* forgiven him?" (347). There is a sense of guilt lingering in the two men. Their castles in Spain have collapsed, and Marlow is afraid Stein could resent the performance of the real Jim in the role they had assigned to him. This fear, as it turns out, is unfounded. Marlow at first begs Jewel to forgive Jim: "We all want to be forgiven," even she, who had always mistrusted him. And when Jewel breaks out with her final sentence, "He was false," Stein finally stands up for him: "Not false! True! true! true! . . . You don't understand. Ach! Why you do not understand? . . . Terrible," he says to Marlow, "Some day she *shall* understand." For Marlow the memory of the last scene on the beach, in which Jim had expressed the same hopeful conviction, is still burningly alive, and he turns down Stein's appeal: "'Will *you* explain?' I asked, looking hard at him" (350). Marlow has already claimed to his reader that he will no longer "explain" Jim, and in a way he is moving, at this point, beyond Stein, who seems much older than during the interview. Here Marlow's letter ends, and the pieced-together story begins.

As long as Marlow holds the reins of the narrative in *Lord Jim*, his rhetorical interventions will serve to connect his account of the final disaster with the themes articulated in the preceding segments. When the drama reaches its highest point and Jim convinces "the assembled heads of the people" (392) to let the white men go, their consent prompts Marlow to establish a meaning through verbal connections. He remarks that "most of them simply said that they 'believed Tuan Jim,'" and their touching trust leads him to reaffirm the lesson of Patusan: "In this simple form of assent to his will lies the whole gist of the situation; their creed, his truth; and the testimony to that faithfulness which made him in his own eyes the equal of the impeccable men who never fall out of the ranks." As though the verbal resonances springing from these phrases were not enough, Conrad has Marlow recall Stein's assessment once more: "Stein's words, 'Romantic! – Romantic!' seem to ring over those distances that will never give him up to a world indifferent to his failing and his virtues" (393). Ultimately, on the verge of the narrator's disclosure of the last steps of Jim's ruin, he claims once again the role he had ostensibly abjured: suspended between Jim and the world of men, his vision expresses the truth of the young man:

From the moment the sheer truthfulness of his last three years of life carries the day against the ignorance, the fear, and the anger of men, he appears no longer to me as I saw him last – a white speck catching all the dim light left upon a sombre coast and the darkened sea – but greater and more pitiful in the loneliness of his soul, that remains even for her who loved him best a cruel and insoluble mystery. (393)

Just as the truthfulness of Jim's word was distorted by the third-class deputy-assistant resident, his mercy will be repaid with bloodshed. The emissaries of the external world have entered Jim's enchanted forest, and he has to treat them as he would treat his people; otherwise the ideal basis of this world and its universality would collapse. Marlow recognizes the constancy in Jim's behavior and admits his admiration for the man who was fated to seek human solidarity in an absolute solitude.[24]

Conrad portrays the moment in which Jim realizes that the spell of his exalted loneliness has been broken by having Marlow interpret a concise expression. When Tamb' Itam brings Jim the news of Brown's ambush and Dain's death, Jim immediately starts giving orders to organize a pursuit. But Tamb' Itam does not move. He is afraid: "It is not safe for thy servant to go out amongst the people" (408). This short sentence is all the information Marlow has, and he must caution himself, specifying "I believe that . . ." (408), and admitting "all I know is that . . ." (409). Nonetheless, he can confidently write (without needing any factual evidence) that "Then Jim understood" (408). In the Patusan romance, Marlow's interpretations led at times to an inextricable confusion between his point of view and the story itself, to the point that the tale's fictionality could appear as one subjective truth. But here, Marlow's words, in opposition to the limitations of the factual language, ring unmistakably true.

The living presence of Marlow's personality is expressed also in his reticences. He will not repeat Jewel's account "of the hour or more she has passed in there wrestling with [Jim] for the possession of her happiness." As he writes, "I haven't the heart to set down here such glimpses as she had given me" (410). When, a few pages later, he describes Jewel's last attempts to stop Jim, the scene is terrible. The narrative choice between what can be said and what cannot does not spare the reader's sensibility, but enables Marlow to use the "glimpses" given by Jewel in the way Conrad finds more significant.[25] Marlow himself seems unable to sustain the tension of the writing and interrupts his account at the point where Jewel starts sobbing, holding Jim round the neck. This is one of those scenes which cannot be summarized in critical language. The heart-rending reality of Jewel's suffering is increased by the fact that it is suggested by Marlow's sympathetic imagination.

As though Conrad were seeking relief from his imagination, his writing explodes in an arresting, gory description of Patusan: "The sky over Patusan was blood-red, immense, streaming like an open vein. An enormous sun nestled crimson amongst the tree-tops, and the forest below had a black and forbidding face." But even more striking is the author's rationalizing over the scene his own imagination has created. Conrad has Marlow contribute two pieces of evidence. Tamb' Itam relates how angry and frightening the heavens were that evening, and Marlow confirms this information with a MacWhirrian report on the weather: "I may well believe it, for I know that on that very day a cyclone passed within sixty miles of the coast, though there was hardly more than a languid stir of air in the place" (413). In two paragraphs Marlow has set forth the three different truths which have interacted throughout the tale: the factual, objective truth of the sea captain; the legend, which is true only within a certain system of beliefs; and the poetic truth one can find in the fictional language. None contradicts the others.

Jim dies as he has lived, "with his hand over his lips" (416), but his place in Marlow's memory gives unprecedented eloquence to his enigmatic figure. Conrad uses all manner of verbal resonance to revive in Marlow's envoy the motifs and themes of the novel. In the "tissue of unanswered questions" which is the novel's ending,[26] Conrad assigns a central role to the two tropes of his critical discourse that underlie the novel's thematic structure: FIDELITY and IDEALISM. "Now he is no more," Marlow writes, and there are days when the reality of his existence comes to me with an immense, with an overwhelming force; and yet upon my honour there are moments, too, when he passes from my eyes like a disembodied spirit astray amongst the passions of this earth, ready to surrender himself faithfully to the claim of his own world of shades. (416)

The fidelity Marlow projects onto the radical solitude of death ultimately comes to coincide with what makes Jim still exist in his eyes, and the enigmatic quality of his figure keeps Marlow's involvement alive beyond the tale itself.

Marlow has no intention of consigning Jim to eternal peace. Instead – in particular with the written tale and letter sent to his Philistine reader – he is passing on the awareness of the paradoxical nature of Jim's reality. Stein's prophecy has been borne out: Jim's suspension between the world of reality and the world of his illusions has been resolved only with death. He has thus acquired reality; that is, he has fulfilled the vision underlying his self-image with the final opportunity of keeping his word.[27] His very flight from Jewel is described by Marlow as an act of love. He had gone away, he writes, "from a living woman to celebrate his pitiless wedding with a shadowy ideal of conduct" (416). His act is sanctioned by that idealism which had made him significant for Marlow in the first place.

Marlow the sea captain had courage and imagination enough to test his convictions, those ethical ideals shaping his everyday working life. In the process, however, he uncovered a disquieting similitude between those ideals and the illusions he discovered beneath the surface of Jim's guilt. He had then provided the young romantic with an opportunity to test these illusions, in the hope that Jim would eventually actualize them under the form of the ideals of fidelity, honor, solidarity. No univocal interpretive "orientation" has come from this voyage, except for a deeply rooted awareness of Jim's "existence" or, better still, of the problems posed by Jim's reality. Now that Jim is dead and Marlow has returned to his life, having enough to do to keep his "head above the surface" (330), the reality given to his own illusions by Jim's death will help him keep his bearings in this perplexing world.

Postscript

Most commentators agree that the changes in subject matters and modes of presentation in the tales that followed *The Nigger of the "Narcissus"* signal an improvement in Conrad's fiction which resulted, two years after the completion of *Lord Jim*, in *Nostromo* and the other works of his "major phase." Thus, the shift following the end of *Lord Jim* is viewed as a step forward in Conrad's artistic maturity. However, the use of the word "maturity" to describe the growth of an author's creative power can often be misleading. A pear or an apple is certainly "better" when it is mature. But in the case of a human being – let alone a creative artist – there is a loss in maturity which must be taken into account. Maturity is the result of a person's realization of that loss, as Marlow well knows. What evidence is there in Conrad's works that the fiction written in the twentieth century is more mature? Did Conrad lose his initial naiveté in moving from *The Nigger of the "Narcissus"* to *The Secret Agent*? Is his characterization of the language teacher in *Under Western Eyes* more skillful than his presentation of Marlow in "Heart of Darkness"? Are Jim's feelings for Jewel more melodramatic than those of Nostromo for Giselle Viola in the last pages of *Nostromo*? These generalizations do not work. And it is because they do not work that critics have taken refuge in the notion of an "achievement and decline." The argument for encroaching senility has been advanced to strengthen the lame one for maturity.

The critical discourse uncovered in his non-fictional writing and in his 1897–1900 fiction offers a different perspective for evaluating the evolution of Conrad's work. Having followed Conrad's testing of his "dream" in his "paper boats," it is now possible to understand on what grounds Conrad constantly emphasized in his later statements the continuity of the convictions underlying his fiction.

The change in Conrad's fiction after *Lord Jim* is the consequence of what had already been dramatized in the *Patna*/Patusan split within the novel. Seen in the light of the detached mode of narration and the "simple" language of "Typhoon"[1] – written two months later – the shift from the analytic to the romantic section of the novel appears to have redirected the evolution of Conrad's search for new novel forms.

The relevance of his decision to set up a fictional stage is indeed so important that Frederic Jameson sees it as a crucial event for the understanding of contemporary literature. The "qualitative shift" from Marlow's inquiry to the Patusan romance, according to Jameson, is "a shift between two distinct cultural spaces, that of 'high' culture and that of mass culture." This makes Patusan "a virtual paradigm of romance as such ... the prototype of the various 'degraded' sub-genres into which mass culture will be articulated (adventure story, gothic, science fiction, bestseller, detective story, and the like)."[2] On the surface, this may seem to be a disparaging evaluation of the break in *Lord Jim*. However, once set in the context of the experiments in genre which, after *Lord Jim*, replaced Conrad's earlier linguistic and narrative experiments, the shift pointed out by Jameson helps to link the 1897–1900 "paper boats" and the great novels of the 1900s. *Nostromo*, *The Secret Agent*, *Under Western Eyes* and *Chance* appear then to be as many deliberate rewritings of "'degraded' sub-genres": a historical novel, a spy story, an instant book on terrorism and a love story told by a cynical old salt.

A discourse which connects some of Conrad's later statements in his non-fictional writings reveals the direction of the author's search for new forms. All these statements indicate that, as a result of his reformulation of the aesthetics set to paper in the 1897 preface, the writer endeavored to create fictional worlds which rely for their referentiality on the distortions generated by the narrative structure rather than on the poetic power of words. The gradual transformation of his use of the sea after the early Marlow tales and his subversion of a number of sub-genres to dislocate the meaning of his tales from *Nostromo* on suggest some of the implications that the perspective provided by this book can have for further studies on Conrad's critical discourse in his later fiction.

It is beyond the scope of the present work, much less this Postscript, to fully examine novels such as *Chance*, in which Conrad uses once again the Marlow device, or *Under Western Eyes*, in which the language teacher repeats, almost verbatim, certain key passages of "Heart of Darkness" and *Lord Jim*.[3] The subject of Conrad's critical discourse in the works written after *Lord Jim* is his undermining of the public's expectations in reading what is ostensibly a love story or a thriller. To articulate this discourse he uses a funambulatory control of space, time and point of view, as well as a heavy-handed irony practiced at the expense of his narrators. For all its differences from the critical discourse set forth through Marlow's commentary, however, the discourse of Conrad's later fiction can be seen as a development of that rejection of obscurity and elitism which he had set forth in the preface to *The Nigger of the "Narcissus."* As this Postscript is intended to demonstrate, the organic perspective on the continuity underlying Conrad's experiments with language and sub-genres may provide a final assessment of his theoretical relevance in the formation of the twentieth-century novel.

A testimony from T. S. Eliot can help understand what was involved in Conrad's reformulation of his view of fiction when he transposed his same concern for PRECISION and EFFECT from his quest for a poetic fictional language to a series of experimentations with the narrative structure of his fictional worlds. Eliot was one of the few poets intellectually prepared to acknowledge that "poetry has as much to learn from prose as from other poetry," and to recognize that "an interaction between prose and verse, like the interaction between language and language, is a condition of vitality in literature."[4] Thus, when he comments in "Swinburne as Poet" (1920) that "the language which is more important" to the poets of his own generation "is that which is struggling to digest and express new objects, new groups of objects, new feelings, new aspects, as, for instance, the prose of Mr. James Joyce or the earlier Conrad,"[5] he captures in one illuminating phrase the essence of how the novelist contributed to enlarging the potentiality of the language, especially with "Heart of Darkness" and *Lord Jim*.

Yet the poet and the novelist pursued apparently opposite paths: Conrad, by always remaining faithful to his literary apprenticeship under "the shade of old Flaubert" (*PR*, 3), and Eliot, by directing his efforts towards a greater obscurity in his poetry. Eliot's poetry consciously reflects the sense of *malaise* familiar to artists at the beginning of this century which led them to the conclusion that language could reflect their vision only through its dislocation from denotative referential usage. This dislocation, as their practice and creeds suggest, could be embodied only in an obscure language, in a poetry which Eliot saw as the contemporary counterpart of the Jacobean poets' "task of finding the verbal equivalent for states of mind and feeling." "It appears likely," he adds,

> that poets in our civilization, as it exists at present, must be *difficult*. Our civilization comprehends great variety and complexity, and this . . . must produce various and complex results. The poet must become more and more comprehensive, more allusive, more indirect, in order to force, to dislocate if necessary, language into his meaning.[6]

Is there a contradiction between Eliot's recognition of the importance of the early Conrad and the need for a *"difficult"* language? In what way does Conrad's Flaubertian quest for verbal and visual precision suggest a dislocation of reality into a more comprehensive language? Far from being a contradiction, Eliot's recognition reveals the polarity underlying the "interaction between prose and verse."

Poetry allows a structural complexity by which a poet can express a "dislocated" meaning through a self-contained pattern of rhythm and words whose difference from denotative language is immediately perceptible to the reader. But a Pindaric flight of poetic inspiration in a novel structured as a story would prove ineffectual. Deprived of a poetic pattern, the words of the fictional language would not interact with the reader's imagination as a dislocation of common speech. A reader can experience the language of fiction as different from common speech only if the novelist manages to create, out of that language, a fictional world. The fictional world of the novel acts as a lens through which a reader approaches the verbal structures which are meant to reflect his own reality.

As Conrad had realized by the time he wrote "Books" (1905), "every novelist must begin by creating for himself a world, great or little, in which he can honestly believe"; and, even though "This world cannot be made otherwise than in his own image . . . it must resemble something already familiar to the experience, the thoughts and the sensations of his readers" (*NLL*, 6). The conventions that determine the reader's response to a novel require a transfer of common emotions and feelings from one world to the other. Obscurity would not allow such a performance – let alone, therefore, that dislocation which is as much a part of the novelist's vision as the poet's. Only if the novel's structure "dislocates" the reader from his own expectations can the falsely mimetic prose language attain an effect similar to the verbal suggestiveness of a poem – that is, shed a more intense light on the actual world by creating a mirror effect between the reader's world and the verisimilitude of the characters and events in the novel.

Conrad's importance as an innovator of the English novel lies in his effort to carry on Flaubert's quest for an artistic prose even in his search for narrative forms capable of setting his fictional worlds in a dislocating perspective. The narrative structure of his texts has the same function which "obscurity" has in T. S. Eliot's conception of poetry. Through shifts in "grouping (sequence)" and "changing lights" (to Richard Curle, July 14, 1923; *LL* II, 317), Conrad forces readers to direct their attention towards the new meanings brought out of old words. Eliot's perceptiveness can be invoked again. "Mr. Conrad," he writes in "Kipling Redivivus" (1919), "has no ideas, but he has a point of view, a 'world'; it can hardly be defined, but it pervades his work and is unmistakable."[7] Conrad eschewed a didactic intention and had far too much respect for his readers to impose his ideas on them. But no success could have been greater than the fact that a poet could recognize in the effect which Conrad had created the living presence of his personal authorial strain.

The relevance of T. S. Eliot's comments for an understanding of Conrad's theory becomes clear once they are set within the context of the novelist's testing of new novel forms. As Ford Madox Ford recalls in *Thus to Revisit: Some Reminiscences*, throughout their collaboration, "Conrad's unceasing search was for a New Form for the Novel."[8] His sense of the contribution he could make in that direction changed considerably in the years from "Typhoon" to *Chance*. Writing to Ernest Dawson on December 12, 1902, Conrad expressed his doubts that "greatness can be attained now in imaginative prose work." When it comes, he adds, "it will be in a new form; in a form for which we are not ripe as yet" (*CL* II, 463). However, when he dictated a statement on fiction to Francis Warrington Dawson ten years later he clearly had changed his mind. A sense of achievement is apparent in the long talk he dictated in the summer of 1913 to his American friend, who took down verbatim these remarks:

There is a convention that only six or seven novel forms exist, & all writers are expected to adapt themselves to those forms.

If everybody has agreed to look at a landscape in one way, I don't see why we should not look at it in another. It does not hurt for us to stand on our head to see it, if it has grown stale to us when we look at it standing on our feet.

I am the only one in our generation who seems to be seeking a new form. Not that I deliberately sought it – stories came to me so. I had to have a number of different people seeing others from different angles. I had already adopted the form before I had fully realised it. And then I knew it was essentially mine, so I continue in it.[9]

The "new form" evolved out of the personal sub-genre of the Marlow tales, once he stood on his "head to see" the "six or seven novel forms" recognized by convention. He changed settings, language and narrative techniques to adapt his narrative strategies to the discoveries he made while writing "Heart of Darkness" and *Lord Jim*.

Two insights he offers in *A Personal Record* reveal the theoretical and personal implications of the new awareness which prompted a redirection in Conrad's search for a new form. First, his remark on the novelist's "first virtue," which is "the exact understanding of the limits traced by the reality of his time to the play of his invention" (*PR*, 95). By articulating a meta-narrative discourse to direct his readers to the metaphors of his fictional language, Conrad had tried to bend his medium as far as possible to reach out to them. But once he came to accept that a poetic prose could not overcome the limits dividing reality from fiction, the rhetorical structure of the narrative frame became an obstacle to the launching of his fictional worlds. Thus, starting from the limits imposed by the reading conventions of his time, he set out to manipulate his readers' expectations.

The second insight is offered in his remarks on the Novalis phrase chosen ten years before as an epigraph to *Lord Jim*. This comment can help understand how crucial the Patusan romance was for realizing the potentiality of dislocating fictional worlds in order to articulate one's personal appeal. In his memoirs, Conrad is recalling his first reader, the "young Cambridge man" (*PR*, 15) who read the manuscript of *Almayer's Folly* aboard the *Torrens*. This first communication with a reader had the effect, he writes, of waking "from their state of suspended animation" Almayer and the other characters he had seen in Berau, the village on which he based his fictional Patusan.[10] He then adds,

What is it that Novalis says? 'It is certain my conviction gains infinitely the moment another soul will believe in it.' And what is a novel if not a conviction of our fellow-men's existence strong enough to take upon itself a form of imagined life clearer than reality and whose accumulated verisimilitude of selected episodes puts to shame the pride of documentary history? (*PR*, 15)

It is only natural that Novalis' aphorism should have struck Conrad as germane to *Lord Jim*'s theme. The central word is "believe."[11] How can a novelist have his readers believe in the author's convictions? He cannot persuade them, he can only create a world of "make-believe" in which the author's conviction of his fellow-men's existence acquires reality. In *Lord Jim* he strove to make the reader believe in Jim's "existence" both through Marlow's interpretation and the creation of a romantic fiction-within-the-fiction. When he accepted the limitations of the meta-phorical possibilities of the sea and the Archipelago, his forms of "imagined life clearer than reality" became grounded on a con-scious manipulation of his readers' perception of reality. The result is the change in settings which accompanied more detached modes of narration.

Lord Jim is largely the result of Conrad's drawing on the two physi-cal and existential settings characteristic of his early works – the Malayan Archipelago and the sea – for the subjects of his tales. These settings are highly symbolical, and their metaphorical value has a transparency which makes the underlying critical discourse inseparable from the story's literal surface. Conrad found for the first time in the voyage of the *Narcissus* a setting which enabled him to put in the foreground those values which had shaped the subjec-tive side of his past experiences. As a result of his efforts faithfully to portray his past impressions, he experimented in *The Nigger* with more effective ways of portraying contrasting points of view. In "Karain," then, he applied the narrative form he had elaborated while writing *The Nigger* – the narrative frame – to a tale set in the Malayan Archipelago, the subject of his first two novels, *Almayer's Folly* and *An Outcast of the Islands*. It was the sea that offered Conrad the means to make morally significant the theoretical problems he was facing. And it was Marlow the imaginative sea captain who enabled him to enlarge the universal relevance of Almayer's solitude. Only with the introduction of Marlow was Conrad able to integrate narrative strategies and fictional settings. With the *Patna*/Patusan split in *Lord Jim*, Conrad consequently plays one setting against the other, synthesizing all his work up to that time.

It was Conrad's characterization of MacWhirr, the protagonist of "Typhoon," that opened the way for a different handling of the sea (and, for that matter, of any setting). The sea tale is in many ways complementary to *Lord Jim*.[12] In the light of the conclusion of Jim's story, it is possible to distinguish in the later tale a discourse that uses and subverts the "language of facts" to which Marlow had surrendered after Jim's death. That Conrad selects language and seamanship as signs of MacWhirr's inadequacy emphasizes that this literalist captain and Marlow embody opposite attitudes towards their craft. The sea metaphor, which had helped bring Marlow's musings closer to the reader's sensibility, is set to work here for the opposite purpose: a lack of perceptiveness is described as an inability to see below the surface of the sea. But the author's balancing of negative and positive qualities in MacWhirr's power of vision and his literal mind is also a first indication of the ambiguity his detached ironic narration can impart to his tales, now that narrative techniques share a larger burden in the illustration of the underlying themes in Conrad's fictional worlds.

Marlow's storytelling had been an attempt to re-create his subjective response, by casting his memory of particular visual impressions into a figurative language. MacWhirr, instead, who would have been an ideal magistrate presiding over Jim's trial,[13] is unable to interpret signs which refer to something he cannot see. Words mean something for him only inasmuch as they are a direct translation of facts, "which alone his consciousness reflected"

(*T*, 14). This is why he writes his letters home while sitting on the bridge of his ship, where he is in visual contact with "every-day, eloquent facts, such as islands, sand-banks, reefs, swift and change-able currents – tangled facts that nevertheless speak to a seaman in clear and definite language" (*T*, 15). MacWhirr, like the "good prose" of the Notices to Mariners, is completely "Outside Literature" (*LE*, 39). His failure in seamanship is caused by his inability to interpret a language which speaks of that which lies beyond his senses. Because of this failure, the captain does not become an ideal figure of a seaman able to use language to express metaphorically the things of his trade. When Conrad heavily stres-ses that MacWhirr possesses the sailor's eye to the utmost degree but at the same time does not attach any meaning to words, he makes clear that he has relinquished the figure of the writer/sailor, following his realization that it is impossible to activate the tension between the old words of factual language and the suggestiveness of figurative expression.

However, Conrad's sketch of a sea captain who has a keen eye for his trade but who distrusts words for being "worn-out things" (*T*, 15) cannot be read simply as an ironic portrait of a pitiful brute. MacWhirr is not symbolically stupid, but rather Conrad's first "real" seaman. The captain fails in his seamanship, but his literal-ness turns out to be extremely effective when applied to a problem related to land conditions. The reduction of the sea captain to his actual size is a consequence of the change in Conrad's attitude towards his characters and settings.

The "land entanglements" (to Henry S. Canby, April 7, 1924; *LL* II, 342) which the *Narcissus* could leave behind come to disturb life aboard ship in the short stories Conrad wrote after "Typhoon." Now that his demythologized sea is no longer free from the com-plexities of the "pedestrian shore" (*LE*, 23), it becomes alive with dangers, allurements and disturbing conflicts unknown to "the children of the sea" – chief among them, love between a man and a woman. This testing of new themes in his 1901–1912 sea tales allowed him to first set themes which will then play a major role in the longer novels in the familiar context of ships and skippers. The effect was at times ludicrous – in "The Brute" (1906) the ship kills the captain's fiancée. But this testing, which proceeded along with the creation of new settings, enabled him to conflate the personal novel form of the Marlow tales with the experiments in sub-genres of his later years.

Only a few days after completing "Typhoon,"[14] Conrad started "Falk," his first story of passion between a white man and a white woman. In the Malay tales the lovers were either a white man and a native or a native man and a half-caste woman. "The Return" is the negation of passion, and the story which should have brought together two whites – *The Rescue* – simply could not be written. Instead, the didascalic emphasis which Conrad gives to the primitivity of Falk's passion indicates that the writer is starting to explore here an entirely new field, by stripping love of all its sentimental and ideal aspects. And he does so by describing nautical operations in words which recall at times a rape and at times a beau courting a belle – as when he portrays the towing of a ship in a way which reveals the sexual tension between Falk, the "man-boat" (*T*, 162) centaur, and the nymph of the *Diana*, that "most innocent old ship [which] seemed to know nothing of the wicked sea" (*T*, 149).

The Author's Notes of the two novels Conrad wrote after "Typhoon," *Nostromo* and *The Secret Agent*, focus on the problem of how to find a new setting and transform it into a fictional world. *Nostromo*'s case is particularly interesting because he makes two cryptic remarks in his letters that become decipherable once they are set in the perspective provided by the critical discourse. In the light of Conrad's testing of narrative and linguistic strategies in his "paper boats," the claim he made in 1903 that *Nostromo* "is more of a novel pure and simple than anything I've done since Almayer's Folly" (to J. B. Pinker, August 22; *CL* III, 55) is certainly justifiable. *Almayer's Folly* and *Nostromo* certainly have more in common with each other than with *Lord Jim*. They both are objectively told novels, and they are free of that semantically surcharged language typical of Conrad's "paper boats." But if by 1903 he was able to revisit that Flaubertian ideal which had guided his apprenticeship it was only because of the masterful control over characters and events which remained as a legacy of his efforts to articulate a critical discourse in the Marlow tales.

The underlying continuity between the Marlow tales and *Nostromo* is confirmed by a 1902 letter to John Galsworthy, in which Conrad tells his friend for the first time that he is working on

a new story of which he has "not been able to write a single word –
except the title . . . NOSTROMO." The most interesting anticipa-
tion about this story is that it belongs "to the 'Karain' class of tales
('K' class for short – as you classify the cruisers)" ([October 23,
1902?] *CL* II, 448). What do "Karain" and *Nostromo* have in common? Certainly not the subject matter or the setting. Rather, the
connection between the short story, in which Conrad for the first
time used the narrative frame, and *Nostromo* has to do with the
narrational organization. Conrad had "Karain" in mind while he
was planning *Nostromo*'s structure because the kind of effect he was
seeking would require the transformation of that "distant view"
(*TU*, vii), which he strove after in the Malay tale, into an impersonal narration capable at last of handling contrasting points of
view. Conrad could go back to using Flaubert's omniscient narrator after the experiments of his "paper boats" without capitulat-
ing to the traditional novel form he inherited from the Victorians
because his mastery of his craft enabled him to tell a story in a
personal way even without an involved narrator.

The Author's Note to the South American novel registers a sense
of disorientation at having lost the familiar reference points of his
personal settings. What made this "the most anxiously meditated"
of the novels he wrote after "Typhoon" was the feeling "there was
nothing more in the world to write about." "I don't mean to say,"
he cautions his readers, "that I became then conscious of any
impending change in my mentality and in my attitude towards the
tasks of my writing life. And perhaps there was never any change,
except in that mysterious, extraneous thing which has nothing to
do with the theories of art; a subtle change in the nature of the
inspiration" (*N*, xv). It is no longer a matter of finding an inspiring
story. He starts writing about an episode which suddenly surfaced
from his memory, finding confirmation in a seaman's memoirs. But
finding a story is not enough. He can finally begin to write only
once he envisions a setting which can bring out the complexity of
the action.

The potentials for a fictional world came to his eyes when he had
"the first vision of a twilight country . . . with its high shadowy
Sierra and its misty Campo for mute witnesses of events flowing
from the passions of men short-sighted in good and evil" (*N*, xvii).
The province of Sulaco has rather the same function the sea has in
The Nigger, where the setting stands out as a protagonist giving

eloquence to the numb struggle of the "children of the sea." The significant difference being that the South American landscape, by dwarfing the puppets strutting on the stage of the "historical" events, gives eloquence to the silence of those who in a historical novel usually are the supernumeraries – the losers. Only to Mrs. Gould does Conrad give that sensibility to "come nearer to the soul of the land in the tremendous disclosure of [its] interior" which enables her to see the "suffering and mute" people of Costaguana (*N*, 88).

The 1920 Author's Note to *The Secret Agent* is remarkable for Conrad's explicit discussion of how he had distorted the mechanics of popular sub-genres to tell the story of a tragic "maternal passion." He sets out to reject the accusations of "ugliness" and "sordidness" which reviewers made against the novel,[15] distinguishing among the tale's "subject, treatment, artistic purpose" (*SA*, vii). With his choice of subject, he writes, he certainly was not "elaborating mere ugliness in order to shock . . . [his] readers." In fact, as "anybody can see . . . the whole treatment of the tale, its inspiring indignation and underlying pity and contempt, prove my detachment from the squalor and sordidness which lie simply in the outward circumstances of the setting" (*SA*, viii). His choice of London as a setting reflects the "world of . . . inferior values [he was] lost in" after finishing *Nostromo* and *The Mirror of the Sea* (*SA*, ix). Instead of "South America, a continent of crude sunshine and brutal revolutions," or the sea, "the mirror of heaven's frowns and smiles, the reflector of the world's light," the vision of "an enormous town presented itself, of a monstrous town more populous than some continents and in its man-made might as if indifferent to heaven's frowns and smiles; a cruel devourer of the world's light." This black mirror of the sky became a fictional world when "the dawning conviction of Mrs. Verloc's maternal passion grew up to a flame between [Conrad] and that background . . . *This* book is *that* story" (*SA*, xii). If his readers have confused setting and subject, it is because they have missed his "purely artistic purpose, that of applying an ironic method" to disengage Winnie Verloc's story "from its obscurity in that immense town" (*SA*, xiii).

Perhaps the author is being a little too ingenuous. After all, the tale was serially published with the misleading subtitle, "A Tale of Diplomatic Intrigue and Anarchist Treachery" – a ploy which did not work either when he added glitzy subtitles for the short stories he included in *A Set of Six*.[16] And some reviewers had recognized that he had transformed a story which "in the hands of nine British novelists would have been a mere hash of old improbable plots, sensational incidents, and crude character-drawing" into "a revelation of all human life itself."[17] However, Conrad's claims are justified in the light of what he had expected when he wrote the novel. As he had written to Cunninghame Graham, *The Secret Agent* "had some importance for me as a new departure in *genre* and as a sustained effort in ironical treatment of a melodramatic subject – which was my technical intention" (October 7, 1907; *CL* III, 491). The distinction in the respective roles which subject, treatment and artistic purpose have in his revisitation of the spy-story genre provides the coordinates for his "departure" towards a new form.

There is poetic justice in Conrad's having found that *"public introuvable"* (to Galsworthy, November 1, 1910; *LL* II, 121) he had sought in vain for twenty years only when in *Chance* he took the Marlow device down from the shelf one more time to have that old salt pull a love story inside out. In *Chance* Conrad uses the two strategies which underlie the works written after *Lord Jim*. The story of "The Damsel" and "The Knight," which is usually compared with the early Marlow tales, should in fact be approached as the arrival point both of Conrad's testing of love stories in the sea setting and his experiments with sub-genres.

That Conrad uses most of the tropes of his critical discourse in the Author's Note to *Chance* to comment on the novel's commercial success is a telling indication of the significance the readers' response had for that artistic ideal which guided his literary theory. This success allayed his fears of becoming "a writer for a limited coterie" (*C*, viii), a condition he abhorred for the doubt it would cast on "the soundness" of the convictions he had set to paper in the preface to *The Nigger* and the "Familiar Preface" to *A Personal Record*: his "belief in the solidarity of all mankind in simple ideas and in sincere emotions" (*C*, ix). If he derived pleasure and encouragement from the sudden expansion of his audience, it is because of that respect for the everyday occupations of his readers expressed by the WORK trope. The novel's reception proved that through his writing – "which, strictly speaking, is my proper business" – he had managed "to please a certain number of minds busy attending to their own very real affairs" (*C*, ix).

When he sits down to write, his "intentions are always blameless however deplorable the ultimate effect of the act may turn out to be." In *Chance* his "intention was to interest people in [his] vision of things which is indissolubly allied to the style in which it is expressed." Thus he can take as well the appreciation of the critics – whose "business it is precisely to criticize such attempts to please" – as "a recognition of [his] good faith in the pursuit of . . . this art which, in these days, is no longer justified by the assumption . . . of a didactic purpose." Evidently, none of the "varied shades of moral significance which have been discovered" in his writing "have provoked a hostile manifestation." And if so, this means that he "never sinned against the basic feelings and elementary convictions which make life possible to the mass of mankind and, by establishing a standard of judgment, set their idealism free to look for plainer ways, for higher feelings, for deeper purposes" (*C*, ix–x).

At the heart of Conrad's literary purpose, starting with his decision to become an artist, was his hope that he could voice in his fiction those untimely convictions which constituted his intellectual inheritance. The struggle faithfully to re-create his memories brought the long-time exile in touch with the sources of his creative life. This emotional and intellectual homecoming transformed his quest for more effective ways to communicate with his readers into a moral commitment. And it was because his artistic ideal was founded on a moral commitment that Conrad kept faith with his belief in an "appeal to universal emotions" throughout his search for a personal novel form (*LL* II, 321).

This book has tried to assess the theoretical value of Conrad's "dream" by demonstrating that, in working out his commitment to authorship, the writer's convictions became as many motivations for writing in a form different from that at work in the traditional novel he inherited from the Victorians. The story of this passionate conflict traces his growing awareness that he needed to adjust the personal form of his "paper boats" to the notion of fictionality which binds a community of readers. The same convictions, then, guided his innovative experiments and enabled him to steer clear of the elitism of those "formulas of art" which negate or evade the potentialities – both as medium and message – of fiction. This is why his manipulations of his English audience's expectations effectively link today's post-modernist fiction to those experiments in creating an effect which – from Defoe to R. L. Stevenson, through Sir Walter Scott – shaped the novel's public.

Notes

Page references to Conrad's works are to the Dent 21-volume *Collected Edition*.

INTRODUCTION

1 Douglas Hewitt, *Conrad: A Reassessment* (1952; rpt. London: Bowes & Bowes, 1975), p. 3.
2 In particular, James' emphasis on the dramatic scene and his rejection of the first person narrative in his prefaces have shaped an abstract set of reading expectations. Richard P. Blackmur, in his introduction to Henry James, *The Art of the Novel* (New York: Charles Scribner's Sons, 1934), attempts to give a systematic coherence to James' prefaces, but in so doing he reveals the limitations of reading expectations based on the writer's theorization. In commenting on James' condemnation of the first person ("the darkest abyss of romance . . . a form foredoomed to looseness" [pp. 320–321]), Blackmur notes that "whether his general charge will hold is perhaps irrelevant; it holds perfectly with reference to the kinds of fiction he himself wrote, and the injury to unity and composition which he specifies may well be observed in Proust's long novel" (p. xxix).
3 Hugh Kenner, *Ulysses* (London: George Allen & Unwin, 1980), p. 3.
4 Gérard Jean-Aubry, *Joseph Conrad: Life and Letters* (Garden City: Doubleday, Page, 1927), II, p. 320. Subsequent references appear in the text.
5 David Leon Higdon, "Conrad in the Eighties: A Bibliography and Some Observations," *Conradiana*, 17, No. 3 (1985), p. 216.
6 Samuel Hynes, "Two Rye Revolutionists," *Sewanee Review*, 73, No. 1 (1965), 151–158; rpt. in *Edwardian Occasions: Essays on English Writing in the Early Twentieth Century* (London: Routledge & Kegan Paul, 1972), p. 49. Subsequent references appear in the text.
7 Samuel Hynes, *The Edwardian Turn of Mind* (Princeton, N.J.: Princeton University Press, 1968).
8 Wayne Booth, in *The Rhetoric of Fiction* (Chicago: University of Chicago

Press, 1961), pp. 8–9, argues that the "showing vs. telling" precept which Percy Lubbock (*The Craft of Fiction* [London: Jonathan Cape, 1921]) derived from James' prefaces notably diminishes an imaginative revisitation of pre-Jamesian literature. For an eloquent rejection of an unquestioning application of James' categories to a reading of Conrad, see Ian Watt, "Conrad Criticism and *The Nigger of the 'Narcissus,'*" *Nineteenth-Century Fiction*, 12 (1958), p. 259: "a generation of critics ... have developed, partly from Conrad's technique, partly from the theory and practice of Henry James, and even more from its formulation in Percy Lubbock's *The Craft of Fiction* (1921), a theory of point of view in narrative which has been tremendously influential in providing both the critic and novelist with an until-then largely unsuspected key to the technique of fiction. But there is a vast difference between welcoming a valuable refinement of formal awareness and accepting as a matter of prescription the rule that all works of fiction should be told from a single and clearly defined point of view."

9 E. M. Forster, "The Pride of Mr. Conrad," *The Nation and Athenaeum*, 19 (March 1921), pp. 881–882; rpt. as "Joseph Conrad: A Note" in *Abinger Harvest* (1936; rpt. London: Edward Arnold, 1965), p. 160.

10 Mary Virginia Mitchell, "Joseph Conrad and 19th Century Aesthetic Tradition," dissertation, University of Minnesota, 1969 (Ann Arbor, Mich.: Michigan University Microfilms, 1972), p. ix.

11 Forster, "Joseph Conrad: A Note" p. 160.

12 Frank Raymond Leavis, *The Great Tradition* (1948; rpt. Harmondsworth: Penguin, 1977), p. 201. Subsequent references appear in the text.

13 Hewitt, *Conrad: A Reassessment*, p. 4.

14 *Ibid.*, p. vi.

15 *Ibid.*

16 Frederick R. Karl, in "Joseph Conrad's Literary Theory," *Criticism*, 2 (1960), p. 317, dismisses Conrad's Author's Notes and concentrates, instead, on his early statements of his literary intention because these were made at "a time almost twenty years before the debility set in which marked his last years of creative work and which carried over into the notes written during the same period." René Kerf, "Ethics *Versus* Aesthetics: A Clue to the Deterioration of Conrad's Art," *Revue des langues vivantes/ Tijdschrift voor levende talen*, 31 (1965), p. 240: "My purpose ... is to analyse Conrad's conception of art, as revealed in his articles about literature and in his Author's Notes, and to show that the development of his views may give us a clue to the process of deterioration."

17 Hewitt, *Conrad: A Reassessment*, p. x.

18 Bernard C. Meyer, *Joseph Conrad: A Psychoanalytic Biography* (Princeton, N.J.: Princeton University Press, 1967).

19 Sigmund Freud, in James Strachey (ed. and trans.), *The Interpretation of*

Dreams, Vol. V of *The Standard Edition of the Complete Psychological Works of Sigmund Freud* (London: Hogarth Press, 1953), pp. 359–360, writes: "I should like to utter an express warning against over-estimating the importance of symbols in dream-interpretation, against restricting the work of translating dreams merely to translating symbols and against abandoning the technique of making use of the dreamer's associations. The two techniques of dream-interpretation must be complementary to each other; but both in practice and in theory the first place continues to be held by the procedure ... which attributes a decisive significance to the comments made by the dreamer."

20 Jacques Lacan, in "L'insistenza della lettera dell'inconscio o la ragione dopo Freud," in *Scritti*, trans. Giacomo Contri (Turin: Einaudi, 1974), Vol. I, pp. 504–507, elaborates on Freud's discovery that the unconscious material does not emerge directly from a dream, but from the patient's rendering of that dream in the waking state. Lacan notes that the psychoanalyst must take into account the resistance of which the patient's discourse is only a cover. He suggests that this can be done by focusing on the tropes and figures of style of classical rhetoric, which he finds are still the best labels for the patient's "mechanisms of defense." According to Lacan, these very figures and tropes are "at work in the rhetoric of the discourse which the patient in fact utters" (p. 516, my translation). The pattern unifying Freud's theory and practice as envisaged by Lacan questions critical approaches which try to uncover unconscious segments in literary texts. Ultimately, it is not the individuation of a certain primordial image that can lead to a writer's "pre-conscious" intention. The emergence of material from the author's subconsciousness is more accurately traceable on the literal surface because here the interplay between unconscious material and its interpretation is more apparent.

21 Caroline Gordon, "Some Readings and Misreadings," *The Sewanee Review*, 61, No. 3 (1953), p. 388, as quoted in Bruce Harkness, "The Secret of 'The Secret Sharer' Bared," *College English*, 27 (October 1965), p. 56.

22 Albert J. Guerard, *Conrad the Novelist* (1958; rpt. New York: Atheneum, 1967), p. 1.

23 Ian Watt, *Conrad in the Nineteenth Century* (Berkeley: University of California Press, 1979), p. x.

24 John Bayley, *The Characters of Love: A Study in the Literature of Personality* (London: Constable, 1960), p. 268: "Forster's comments on [Conrad] tell us a good deal about the ethos of the critic but they do not illuminate the author. Not that this matters – criticism of a modern writer may be most helpful when it suggests how he differs from the particular kind of modernity which the critic represents – but its danger lies in creating a language for reflecting on a work of the imagination which

is fundamentally different from the language of the work itself."

25 That Conrad is a *moraliste* in the French tradition is a critical common-place. Christopher Cooper's *Conrad and the Human Dilemma* (New York: Barnes & Nobles, 1970) and R. A. Gekoski's *Conrad: The Moral World of the Novelist* (London: Paul Elek, 1978) have addressed directly the moral significance of his work. G. H. Bantock, in "The Two 'Morali-ties' of Joseph Conrad," *Essays in Criticism*, 3, No. 2 (1953), p. 142, presents a case for Conrad remaining true to both "public morality" and "private order." F. R. Leavis, however, remains the most influen-tial critic in establishing the criteria for evaluating Conrad's works for their moral seriousness by conjoining the writer's aesthetic and moral concerns. Indeed, he includes Conrad in the great tradition of the English novel because, "like Jane Austen and George Eliot and Henry James," he is "an innovator in 'form' and method," and his "concern with art . . . is the servant of a profoundly serious interest in life" (*The Great Tradition*, p. 28). For a dissenting voice, see René Kerf, "Ethics *Versus* Aesthetics," pp. 240–249. Kerf reaches the conclusion, in his analysis of Conrad's statements about his art, that Conrad's "attempt to reconcile ethics and aesthetics was one of the causes that brought about the simplification of his outlook and the consequent deteriora-tion of his art in the later works" (p. 249).

26 Virginia Woolf, "Mr. Conrad: A Conversation," in *The Captain's Death Bed and Other Essays* (London: Hogarth Press, 1950), p. 77. In a similar attempt, Albert J. Guerard, in "The Conradian Voice," in Norman Sherry (ed.), *Joseph Conrad: A Commemoration* (London: Macmillan, 1976), p. 4, describes the effect of Conrad's language by distinguishing between Conrad's style and his "authorial voice."

27 The notion that Conrad made his discoveries about the art of fiction while interpreting his own writing was suggested by a reading of Frank Kermode's "Secrets and Narrative Sequence," *Critical Inquiry*, 7, No. 1 (1980), pp. 83–101. Out of his observation that "Stories as we know them begin as interpretations" Kermode evolves a reading of *Under Western Eyes* which tests his "proposition that there will always be some inbuilt interpretation, that . . . will produce distortions, secrets to be inquired into by later interpretation" (pp. 85, 87).

28 Werner Senn, in *Conrad's Narrative Voice: Stylistic Aspects of His Fiction* (Bern: Francke Verlag, 1980), p. 175, points out that most of the features of his verbal style "can be conveniently if somewhat crudely subsumed under the structuralist notion of 'discourse' (as distinct from 'story'), since they relate, in various degrees of directness, to the problems of communication between narrating medium and reader, and so to the ways in which the story is told and received." Owen Knowles, in "Commentary as Rhetoric: An Aspect of Conrad's Tech-nique," *Conradiana*, 5, No. 3 (1973), p. 7, describes Conrad's commen-

tary as "an amalgam of rhetorical directives, sustaining an implicit dialogue between author and reader. In direct and oblique ways his voice is always active: it guides, challenges, persuades, analyses and often insists that the fictional world cannot be insulated from the common values we all share." Paul B. Armstrong, in "The Hermeneutics of Literary Impressionism: Interpretation and Reality in James, Conrad, and Ford," *The Centennial Review*, 27, No. 4 (1983), sets Conrad's critical discourse in the context of his contemporary literary theory: "James, Conrad, and Ford ... write meta-novels which make explicit the implicit dynamics of projecting a fictional world" (p. 257). Their narrators "tend to call into question our assumptions about interpretation instead of conferring on meaning a quasi-natural stability" (p. 263).

29 To H. B. Marriott Watson; January 28, 1903. In Frederick R. Karl and Laurence Davies (eds.), *The Collected Letters of Joseph Conrad. Volume 3: 1903–1907* (Cambridge: Cambridge University Press, 1988), p. 12. Subsequent references to this volume appear in the text as *CL* III, while *CL* I refers to Frederick R. Karl and Laurence Davies (eds.), *The Collected Letters of Joseph Conrad. Volume 1: 1861–1897* (Cambridge: Cambridge University Press, 1983) and *CL* II refers to Frederick R. Karl and Laurence Davies (eds.), *The Collected Letters of Joseph Conrad. Volume 2: 1898–1902* (Cambridge: Cambridge University Press, 1986).

30 Zdzisław Najder (ed.), *Conrad's Polish Background: Letters to and from Polish Friends* (London: Oxford University Press, 1964), p. 1. Najder himself views his critical work as a contribution to the interpretation of the terms Conrad uses. In the preface to *Joseph Conrad: A Chronicle* (New Brunswick, N.J.: Rutgers University Press, 1983), p. vii, he claims for himself the role of "lexicographer," because in Conrad's case the biographer must establish "the meaning of signs used by the given author by pointing not only at his intentions but, much more important, at his cultural background and resources." The importance of this lexicographical work for an understanding of Conrad's critical discourse is made even more clear by Najder in "Conrad's Polish Background, Or, From Biography to a Study of Culture," *Conradiana*, 18, No. 1 (1986), p. 6: "The motifs of fidelity and solidarity, of obligations, of honor defended or lost, or treason ... are found in abundance in classical Polish literature; and not only in literature, but also in the repository of moral images and exemplary tales passed by word of mouth ... what may have seemed to be a private code, deciphered only by biographical investigations and pointing to esoteric meaning, turns out to be a cultural language, a public system of signs, which carry meaning independently from the reflections of the novelist's own personality."

31 Bruce W. Powe, *A Climate Charged: Essays on Canadian Writers* (Oakville,

Ont.: Mosaic Press, 1984), p. 26: "For McLuhan, a literary work was not defined by theme or genre, but by audiences: the work achieved life only in relation to its effect on receivers and participants. This was, as McLuhan described, Rhetoric."

32 Hugh Kenner, *The Poetry of Ezra Pound* (Norfolk, Conn.: New Directions, 1951), p. 264: Conrad "was, however, as Dr. Leavis has remarked, in many respects a simple soul; it was Ford who was able to disengage technique from intuition sufficiently to make useful statements about narrative procedures." Frederick R. Karl, *A Reader's Guide to Joseph Conrad* (New York: Noonday Press, 1960), p. 21: "Conrad's ... was not a great critical mind and his is certainly not a criticism that can stand aside in separate distinction ... [his] remarks do not afford a profound insight into literature, but at their best ... lead back only to himself." David Goldknopf, "What's Wrong with Conrad: Conrad on Conrad," *Criticism*, 10, No. 1 (1968), p. 54: "the querulous self-vindication [in Conrad's Author's Notes] sometimes takes the form of 'reaching' for criticism; the 1917 note for *Lord Jim*, for example, has this picayunishly defensive tone." William Bonney, *Thorns & Arabesques: Contexts for Conrad's Fiction* (Baltimore: Johns Hopkins University Press, 1980), p. 3: "No ideological system exists in Conrad's works that is validated implicitly through sustained coherences, although critics have persistently concocted a sequence of systemic definitions of Conradian values."

33 Frederick R. Karl, *Joseph Conrad: The Three Lives: A Biography* (New York: Farrar, Straus & Giroux, 1979), p. 88: "It is not so much that the author's notes are trivial as that they are misleading." R. W. Stallman, "Conrad and the 'Secret Sharer,'" in R. W. Stallman (ed.), *Joseph Conrad: A Critical Symposium* (East Lansing, Mich.: Michigan State University Press, 1960), p. 278: Conrad's "disclosures about his literary aims are highly deceptive, often deliberately misleading." Marvin Mudrick, in "Conrad and the Terms of Modern Criticism," *The Hudson Review*, 7 (Autumn 1954), p. 421, warns readers against the "meretricious effects" through which Conrad "tends to divert attention from his genuine gifts." When Conrad betrays "his entertaining narrative," Mudrick adds, this becomes a "contrived exemplum, and the characters bogus-heroic gestures or dispensable emblems, of the author's foggy self-sustaining metaphysic."

34 Letter to Rollo Walter Brown, September 9, 1919. Quoted in Watt, *Conrad in the Nineteenth Century*, p. 77.

35 Kerf, "Ethics *Versus* Aesthetics," p. 249.

36 Donald W. Rude's account of the care with which Conrad wrote the 1924 preface, in "Conrad as Editor: The Preparation of *The Shorter Tales*," in Wolodymyr Taras Zyla and Wendell Marshall Aycock (eds.), *Joseph Conrad: Theory and World Fiction*, Proceedings of the Comparative Literature Symposium, Vol. VII (Lubbock, Tex.: Texas

Tech University, 1974), p. 189, justifies his claim that it is
"unfortunate" that this preface "has been largely ignored by Conrad's
biographers."

37 The first critics to set the terms which recur in Conrad's non-fictional
writings in the context of his entire corpus were Helen Thomas Follett
and Wilson Follett. In "Contemporary Novelists: Joseph Conrad,"
The Atlantic Monthly, 119 (February 1917), they note that, not "being
given to formal definitions, Mr. Conrad phrases his ideal in a few
words that recur with unconscious frequency throughout his books,
such words as Conscience, Service, Fidelity, Honor" (p. 235).

I THE CRITICAL DISCOURSE: FIVE TROPES

1 Karl, "Literary Theory," pp. 317–355. Ian Watt, "Impressionism and
Symbolism in *Heart of Darkness,*" in Sherry, *Conrad: A Commemoration,*
esp. pp. 39–41. Watt, *Conrad in the Nineteenth Century,* pp. 76ff. Eloise
Knapp Hay, "Impressionism Limited," in Sherry, *Conrad: A Com-
memoration,* pp. 54–64. Royal Roussel, *The Metaphysics of Darkness: A
Study in the Unity and Development of Conrad's Fiction* (Baltimore: Johns
Hopkins University Press, 1971), pp. 47–48.

2 John Howard Weston, "*The Nigger of the 'Narcissus'* and Its Preface," in
Robert Kimbrough (ed.), *Joseph Conrad: The Nigger of the "Narcissus"*
(New York: Norton, 1979), p. 339.

3 Karl: "Literary Theory," p. 334.

4 Samuel Hynes, *Edwardian Occasions,* p. 50.

5 Ian Watt, "Conrad's Preface to *The Nigger of the 'Narcissus,*'" *Novel: A
Forum on Fiction,* 7 (1974), p. 103, as quoted in Weston, "*The Nigger,*"
p. 339.

6 Karl, *A Reader's Guide,* p. 22.

7 Karl, *Three Lives,* p. 450.

8 Of particular interest for understanding how Conrad's close study of
Flaubert brought him in touch with the principal tenets of *symbolisme,*
see Donald C. Yelton, *Mimesis and Metaphor: An Inquiry into the Genesis
and Scope of Conrad's Symbolic Imagery* (The Hague: Mouton, 1967), pp.
90–93. Maupassant's influence on Conrad's aesthetic of fiction is
examined in G. J. Worth's "Conrad's Debt to Maupassant in the
Preface to *The Nigger of the 'Narcissus,*'" *Journal of English and Germanic
Philology,* 54 (1955), pp. 700–704. A more general analysis of Maupassant and Conrad is Yves Hervouet's "Conrad and Maupassant: An
Investigation into Conrad's Creative Process," *Conradiana,* 14, No. 2
(1982), pp. 83–111. For a discussion of how Conrad's first novel,
Almayer's Folly, "in its diction and color ... directly reflected much
late nineteenth-century poetry," see Frederick R. Karl, "Joseph Con-
rad: A *fin de siècle* Novelist – A Study in Style and Method," *The
Literary Review,* 2 (1959), p. 565.

9 David Goldknopf, "What's Wrong with Conrad," pp. 55–56.

10 Jocelyn Baines, in *Joseph Conrad: A Critical Biography* (London: Weidenfeld & Nicolson, 1961), p. 187, criticizes this successive qualification when he writes that the preface is "marred by repetitiveness."

11 Joseph Martin, in "Conrad and the Aesthetic Movement," *Conradiana*, 17, No. 3 (1985), p. 199, states that "although Conrad has adopted some stylistic concepts of Aestheticism and his technique displays Aesthetic influence, the fiction nevertheless represents a thematic rejection of Art for Art's Sake."

12 Commenting on the title he gave to the collection *Les Poètes maudits*, Paul Verlaine vindicates the estrangement of these "Poètes Absolus": "notre titre a cela pour lui qu'il répond juste à notre haine ... pour le vulgaire des lecteurs d'élite – une rude phalange qui nous la rend bien." In Paul Verlaine, *I poeti maledetti*, trans. Diana Grange Fiori (Parma: Guanda, 1988), p. 22.

13 As Frank Kermode points out in *The Romantic Image* (1957; rpt. London: Routledge & Kegan Paul, 1961), pp. 115–116, Arthur Symons' chapter on Mallarmé in *The Symbolist Movement in Literature* (1899) shows that, even for a theorist of symbolism such as Symons, "the Mallarméan method holds out little hope of avoiding an obscurity, an impermeability to the ordinary senses of the reader, which may well seem indistinguishable from the vague and indeed the obscurantist."

14 Agostino Lombardo, *La poesia inglese dall'estetismo al simbolismo* (Roma: Edizioni di storia e letteratura, 1950), pp. 39–44.

15 Morton Dauwen Zabel, introduction to *The Portable Conrad* (1947; rpt. New York: Viking Press, 1969), pp. 7–8, remarks that Conrad "saw unmistakably" that the fundamental problem of modern art was that its makers, "Having revolted against the older conventions of omniscience, dramatic artifice, and moral didacticism ... were now falling prey to new formulations – aesthetic, scientific, sociological, technical. They were satisfied with fragments. They objectified their problems in arguments ungrounded in character or action. They evaded their responsibilities by specialized and arbitrary techniques. They were failing, in a new way, to unify principle with substance." Karl, in "Literary Theory," p. 332, clarifies Conrad's position by pointing out the moral commitment underlying his artistic choice: "In trying to travel the rocky literary path between an 1890's 'code' of artistic anarchy and a Victorian code of professed didacticism, Conrad took refuge, as did Flaubert and James, in that devotion to craft wherein art and morality meet in commitment, responsibility, and lawfulness."

16 Ian Watt's recognition of the preface's critical nature, in *Conrad in the Nineteenth Century*, p. 88, stresses the moral link outlined by the present reading: "Conrad's main effort in the preface is not in the ordinary

sense critical at all; it is, rather, to set his own personal feelings about writing fiction within the psychological, moral, and historical perspective of other activities in the ordinary world."

17 Conrad uses the figure of WORK throughout the preface to remind the reader of this moral link. The novelist is called a "worker in prose," a "workman in art," and novels are invariably a "work." Even the deleted passage contains a similar reference: "in art alone of all the enterprises of men there is meaning in endeavor disassociated from success and merit."

18 Most commentators have read Conrad's appeal as a proclamation of impressionistic objectivity. See, for example, Walter F. Wright, *Joseph Conrad on Fiction* (Lincoln: University of Nebraska Press, 1964), p. xii: "the author himself must first see distinctly and render objectively," and Sisir Chatterjee, "Joseph Conrad: 'The Power of the Written Word,'" in *Problems in Modern English Fiction* (Calcutta: Bookland Private, 1965), p. 116: Conrad "suggests that an artist is basically a person who [sees] and not a person who reasons." Other critics, instead, have pointed out the intellectual stimulus implicit in making the reader "*see.*" John Holloway, in *The Victorian Sage: Studies in Argument* ([London] 1953; rpt. New York: Norton, 1965), p. 10, finds that Conrad's artistic purpose is an indication of how certain Victorian intellectuals worked "by quickening the reader to a new capacity for experience." James Hillis Miller, in *Poets of Reality: Six Twentieth Century Writers* (Cambridge, Mass.: Harvard University Press, 1965), pp. 26–27, writes that the "impressions things make on the senses are no more ultimate reality than their interpretation into meanings and objects ... The attempt to render the exact appearances of things is not an end in itself. Its aim is to make the truth of life, something different from any impression or quality, momentarily visible."

19 Edward Said, in "Conrad: The Presentation of Narrative," *Novel*, 7 (1974), p. 119, notes that "the perceptual transformation that occurs when writing or reading result in *sight* is very drastic, even antithetical. So antithetical ... that one tends to forget the whole sentence in which Conrad formulates his primary ambition ... Conrad's narratives thus embody (provide a locale for) the transformation in the act of taking place. Conrad's own efforts, he says, are to employ the power of *written* words, with their origin in the painstaking craft of writing, in order to make his reader experience the vitality and dynamism of *seen* things."

20 Watt, "Conrad's Preface," in Kimbrough, *Conrad: The Nigger*, p. 151.

21 John Dozier Gordan, *Joseph Conrad: The Making of a Novelist* (1940; rpt. New York: Russell & Russell, 1963), p. 237.

22 Najder, *Chronicle*, p. 213.

23 Thomas Lavoie, "Textual History and Textual Notes: The 'Preface,'" in Kimbrough, *Conrad: The Nigger*, p. 150. Subsequent references to

the omitted paragraph appear in the text.

24 An interesting reading of Conrad's discussion of WORK in his fiction is Paul L. Gaston's "The Gospel of Work According to Joseph Conrad," *The Polish Review*, 20, Nos. 2–3 (1975), pp. 203–210. Discussions of this central tenet of Conrad's *Weltanschauung* can be found in Avrom Fleishman, *Conrad's Politics: Community and Anarchy in the Fiction of Joseph Conrad* (Baltimore: Johns Hopkins Press, 1967), pp. 73–75, and in Jeremy Hawthorn, *Joseph Conrad: Language and Fictional Self-Consciousness* (London: Arnold, 1979), pp. 9–10. Paul Bruss, in *Conrad's Early Sea Fiction: The Novelist as Navigator* (Lewisburg: Bucknell University Press, 1979), p. 27, fully recognizes the importance of WORK: "Conrad actually makes work (and its justification) the sine qua non of his early sea fiction."

25 In the same essay, Conrad goes on to remark that the man of letters often forgets that his craft is first of all a work, "especially in his youth," when he is "inclined to lay a claim of exclusive superiority for his own amongst all the other tasks of the human mind" (*NLL*, 7). The "flight of imaginative thought" may very well transcend "moralities current amongst mankind," if the novelist does "think himself of a superior essence to other men" (*NLL*, 9). This detachment may give a novelist the illusion he can find "the promise of perfection for his art"; perhaps in one of "the absurd formulas trying to prescribe this or that particular method of technique of conception." Conrad rejects such a detachment. Rather, he writes, let the young writer "mature the strength of his imagination amongst the things of this earth . . . And I would not grudge him the proud illusion that will come sometimes to a writer: the illusion that his achievement has almost equalled the greatness of his dream" (*NLL*, 10).

26 For a similar interpretation of Conrad's use of his first person narrator, see Carlisle Moore, "Conrad and the Novel as Ordeal," *Philological Quarterly*, 42, No. 1 (1963), pp. 55, 60. Moore asserts that "tests of character" in Conrad's fiction "acquire a special interest . . . because of his own peculiar involvement in them, the involvement of a . . . craftsman for whom the very act of writing was an ordeal analogous to his protagonists'." In particular, he quotes a number of letters to show how in "speaking of his own works Conrad often used the imagery of voyages," and that "his stories of moral failure and success . . . may in one sense be read as emblematic reenactments of his own harrowing problems as a writer in England."

27 Jocelyn Baines, in *Critical Biography*, p. 354, writes that there is "no analysis, no probing below the surface" in *A Personal Record*. Leo Gurko, in *The Two Lives of Joseph Conrad* (New York: Thomas Y. Crowell, 1965), p. 157, reaches the conclusion that Conrad "wished to describe his experiences rather than bare his soul."

28 Guerard, *Conrad the Novelist*, p. 3.

29 Jacques Berthoud, *Joseph Conrad: The Major Phase* (Cambridge: Cambridge University Press, 1978), pp. 5, 7.
30 For a discussion of the difference between autobiography and autobiographical fiction, see Avrom Fleishman, "*The Mirror of the Sea*: Fragments of a Great Confession," *L'Epoque conradienne* (May 1979), esp. pp. 136–142.
31 There have been conflicting evaluations of Bobrowski's influence on his nephew. Avrom Fleishman, in *Conrad's Politics*, p. 20, writes that the Bobrowski side of Conrad's heritage embodies the "democratic–liberal element which Conrad ranks uppermost in the Polish tradition . . . it is significant that he valued so highly this, his Bobrowski heritage." Najder, on the other hand, describes Conrad's uncle and guardian almost as a collaborationist with the Russians: "Tadeusz [Bobrowski] opposed the tradition of resistance . . . his political 'realism' was one-sided" (Najder, *Chronicle*, p. 30). See also Najder, *Conrad's Polish Background*, pp. 17–20.
32 Fleishman, *Conrad's Politics*, p. 10.
33 Raoul Cadot, "Les Traits moraux de la Mer dans l'Oeuvre de Joseph Conrad," *Revue de l'enseignement des langues vivantes*, 50 (1933), p. 400: "dans un ouvrage comme *Le Miroir de la Mer* . . . l'anthropomorphisme de Conrad s'affirme au premier plan, par la continuité du trait, la couleur et le vigoureux relief de ses images du monde."
34 Henry James was one of the first readers who praised the language of *The Mirror*: "I read you as I listen to rare music – with deepest depths of surrender, and out of those depths I emerge slowly and reluctantly again"; quoted in Edward Garnett's introduction to *Conrad's Prefaces to His Works* ([London] 1937; rpt. Freeport, N.Y.: Books for Libraries Press, 1971), p. 29. Rolfe Arnold Scott-James, in "Above the Battle," in *Fifty Years of English Literature: 1900–1950* (London: Longman, Green, 1951), p. 161, also remarks how Conrad's "language recalls the tone of the sea, in sentences short and sharp like small breakers, or in long voluminous sentences like ocean rollers." More recently, Peter Wolfe, in "Conrad's *The Mirror of the Sea*: An Assessment," *The McNeese Review*, 15 (1964), p. 43, has examined the various applications of Conrad's "rhythmic effect" as part of his "trying to catch the monumental roll of the sea."
35 Dale B. J. Randall (ed.), *Joseph Conrad and Warrington Dawson: The Record of a Friendship* (Durham, N.C.: Duke University Press, 1968), pp. 160–161.
36 The deletions Conrad made in the final version of *The Rescue* (1919) to alter the character of Lingard are one of the most striking instances of how revealing of his personality is a seaman's attitude towards his craft. Thomas C. Moser, in *Joseph Conrad: Achievement and Decline* (Cambridge, Mass.: Harvard University Press, 1957), pp. 146–147, points out that although the Lingard of the manuscript of "The

Rescuer" (1896–1898) "is passionately devoted to his ship . . . his devotion seems to be the expression of something different from a perfect love of his calling." In a description of Lingard's performing an act of seamanship, Conrad deleted the original description of Lingard's lack of self-possession "whenever he had to call upon his unerring knowledge of his craft." In another deleted passage, Conrad points out that Lingard expects his brig to answer "without hesitation to every perverse demand of his desire." These deletions show how meaningful the notions involved in the "standard of conduct" remained for Conrad throughout his writings.

37 Commenting on the loss of a sense of community between speaker and listener in modern writers, Edward Said writes in "Conrad: The Presentation of Narrative," p. 125, that "Conrad's personal history made him acutely sensitive to the different status of *information* in the sea life, on the one hand, and in the writing life on the other. In the former, community and usefulness are essential to the enterprise; in the latter the opposite is true. Thus Conrad had the dubious privilege of witnessing within his own double life the change from storytelling as useful, communal art to novel-writing as essentialized, solitary art."

38 Bruss, *Conrad's Early Sea Fiction*, pp. 19–20.

39 Daniel W. Ross, "*Lord Jim* and the Saving Illusion," *Conradiana*, 20, No. 1 (1988), p. 45.

40 Conrad's discussion of the "intended" and "not intended" aspects of his writing sets those remarks about his lack of control over his writings in the perspective of an unceasing struggle after an ideal effect. In particular, his statement, in a letter to Garnett (September 24, 1895) that "all my work is produced unconsciously (so to speak) and I cannot meddle to any purpose with what is within myself – I am sure you understand what I mean. – It isn't in me to improve what has got itself written" (*CL* I, 246–247), and the observation he makes in a letter to David Meldrum – "how mysteriously independent of myself is my power of expression" (August 10/11, 1899; *CL* II, 191) – have led several commentators to overstress the importance of his unconscious production. A rejection of this critical attitude can be found in Edward Said, *Joseph Conrad and the Fiction of Autobiography* (Cambridge, Mass.: Harvard University Press, 1966), pp. 101–102: "narrative method, when it is intensely moving and effective, derives mainly from the fully aware author himself, not exclusively from a technical fussiness, which one would expect the merest apprentice to have outgrown, or from an unconscious over which he has no control."

41 Bruce E. Teets has reviewed the conflicting interpretations of Conrad as a "romantic" or a "realist" in "Realism and Romance in Conrad Criticism," *The Polish Review*, 20, Nos. 2–3 (1975), pp. 133–139. His

study justifies Conrad's awareness of having been misunderstood: "These confused and conflicting comments indicate that for the first fifteen years or so Conrad produced a kind of work which was so new that it . . . could not be precisely classified" (p. 134).

42 Kingsley Widmer, in "Conrad's Pyrrhonistic Conservativism: Ideological Melodrama Around 'Simple Ideas,'" *Novel*, 7, No. 2 (1974), p. 134, offers a different interpretation of "Fidelity" in the context of the "Familiar Preface." Conrad, he writes, "is pushed to his countering 'simple ideas' less by belief or discovery than by reaction against the dangers of radical ideas." The memoirs of Conrad's son, John Conrad, *Joseph Conrad: Times Remembered* (Cambridge: Cambridge University Press, 1981), contribute interesting biographical evidence which critics who have elaborated on Conrad's "conservatism" will find very useful. John Conrad recollects that his father "had a very strong aversion to policemen in uniform and if one came to the door he would shut himself in his study and refuse to come out" (p. 187). The reason for this behavior, John Conrad explains, is that his father distrusted policemen because he associated them with the Russians who deported his parents to Siberia.

43 Randall, *Conrad and Dawson*, pp. 160–161. In a January 28, 1903, letter to H. B. Marriott Watson, Conrad hints at an unidentified source for this phrase: "my method of work . . . is based on truth too, of not a very different order: on fidelity – in the words of a writer now dead – 'remorseless fidelity to the truth of my own sensations'" (*CL III*, 12).

44 Najder, *Chronicle*, p. 28.

45 Unsigned review, *Glasgow News*, October 3, 1907, p. 5, in Norman Sherry (ed.), *Conrad: The Critical Heritage* (London: Routledge & Kegan Paul, 1973), p. 195: Conrad "has imported into English literature a quality, a mood, a temperament which has never appeared in it before . . . this is a new note . . . so new that one does not feel it British at all; it is Slavonic."

46 Najder, *Chronicle*, p. 332.

47 *Ibid.*

48 Gérard Jean-Aubry, *Joseph Conrad: Lettres françaises* (Paris: Gallimard, 1929), p. 87.

49 *Ibid.*

50 George Steiner, "Extraterritorial," in *Extraterritorial: Papers on Literature and the Language Revolution* (New York: Atheneum, 1971), p. 21, quoted in C. B. Cox, *Joseph Conrad: The Modern Imagination* (London: J. M. Dent & Sons, 1974), p. 8.

51 Donald W. Rude, "A Linguistic Reading of Conrad," *L'Epoque conradienne* (May 1979), p. 55: "English, Conrad learned as an adult, at a time he had not been using Polish in everyday contacts for years. Therefore, all of his English vocabulary and grammar must have been, at one period or another confronted with his earlier French

vision of the world – with underlying Polish 'signifiés' – one notable exception being seamanship, for his amateurish tampering with the sea during his French period cannot compare with later professional experience."

52 Conrad refers to the journal in which the article appears as "*Seccolo*," obviously a misspelling of *secolo*, Italian for "century." Since no article appeared in the only Italian journals with that name (*Secolo XX* and *Il Secolo Illustrato*), the only possible explanation is that Conrad is referring to the *Century Illustrated Magazine*, which contains in its May 1923 issue an article on Conrad by Walter Tittle (Walter Tittle, "Portraits in Pencil and Pen," *Century Illustrated Magazine*, 106 (May 1923), pp. 53–61. Tittle does not express the concepts ascribed to the anonymous critic in the letter to Curle. Conrad, however, may be actually referring to the long conversations he had with the artist while he was sitting for him.

53 Eloise Knapp Hay, in "Impressionism Limited," p. 57, underlines the difference between Conrad's impressionism and realism by relating the letter to Curle to the letter to Colvin (*CL* II, 200), and maintains that with his "unconventional grouping and perspective," Conrad is trying to illuminate *les valeurs idéales*, "forcing the reader to look *deeply into things*."

54 Quoted in Watt, *Conrad in the Nineteenth Century*, p. 186.

55 Carlo Angeleri, "Joseph Conrad: una lettera inedita a Carlo Placci," *Paragone*, 8 (1957), pp. 55–58, quoted in Watt, *Conrad in the Nineteenth Century*, p. 186.

56 Arnold T. Schwab, "Conrad's American Speeches and His Reading from *Victory*," *Modern Philology*, 62, No. 4 (1965), pp. 347, 346.

57 *Ibid.*, p. 346.

2 WORKING ON LANGUAGE AND STRUCTURE: ALTERNATIVE STRATEGIES IN *THE NIGGER OF THE "NARCISSUS," "KARAIN" AND "YOUTH"*

1 Ford Madox Ford, introduction to Joseph Conrad, *The Sisters* (Milan: Mursia, 1968), pp. 14–16.

2 Moser, *Achievement and Decline*, pp. 68–69.

3 For a different interpretation of the effect that Conrad's revisitation of the sea scene had on his writing, see William E. Messenger, "Conrad and His 'Sea Stuff,'" *Conradiana*, 6 (1974), pp. 3–18. Messenger concludes his documented reading of the Conrad–Garnett correspondence in 1896 by noting that it is "the complex of attitudes and loyalties described and documented above . . . that led to *The Nigger of the "Narcissus"* being what it is, a flawed masterpiece, virtually a compendium of the conventions and clichés of sea fiction" (p. 15).

4 Joseph Conrad, *The Nigger of the "Narcissus"* (1897; rpt. Garden City, N.Y.: Doubleday & Co., 1925), pp. ix–x. All subsequent references to

The Nigger of the "Narcissus" are to the J. M. Dent *Collected Edition.*

5 *Ibid.*, p. x. John Dozier Gordan's path-breaking examination of Conrad's early works in *Joseph Conrad: The Making of a Novelist* first established the position of *The Nigger of the "Narcissus"* in the writer's canon. His conclusion, that only after completing *The Nigger* was Conrad "emotionally convinced of his ability to produce work undertaken in seriousness and completed despite difficulty" (p. 25), has since become a commonplace.

6 Paul Kirschner, *Conrad: The Psychologist as Artist* (Edinburgh: Oliver & Boyd, 1968), pp. 200–205.

7 Unfortunately, however, Conrad gets his dates wrong in his 1914 note. He did not write the preface right after completing the deep-sea story in February 1897 but at least six months later. In fact, there is no mention of the preface until August 24 of the same year, when Conrad sent a copy of the manuscript to Edward Garnett (*CL* I, 375). Conrad's incorrect dating has been sufficient for commentators to dismiss the relevance of his claims that the novel's completion is connected with the aesthetic of fiction he formulated a few months later. By manipulating the dates, however, Conrad may very well be covering up what he later considered to have been a weakness: his anxiety over the novel's reception. "Karain"'s frame narrator is a first answer to the problems of point of view he had tried to solve in telling the story of the *Narcissus*, but in "The Return" and *The Rescue* he faced the same problems as before. Therefore, as David R. Smith shows in "'One Word More' about *The Nigger of the 'Narcissus*,'" *Nineteenth Century Fiction*, 23 (1968), p. 203, in awaiting publication of *The Nigger* his doubts on whether his audience would understand the significance of the sea tale emerged.

8 Karl, *A Reader's Guide*, p. 108.

9 See David Manicom, "True Lies/ False Truths: Narrative Perspective and the Control of Ambiguity in *The Nigger of the 'Narcissus*,'" *Conradiana*, 18, No. 2 (1986), p. 116: "In the *Nigger of the 'Narcissus'* Conrad ... discovers the considerable virtues of the narrator who is participant *and* interpreter, discovers the way in which this can control both sides of 'inconclusive experience' through the multiplication of perspectives ... What would be advantageous for the increasingly intricate perspectives of the later works was a *character* who actually acts in the way the narrator of *The Nigger of the 'Narcissus'* acts, who is both character and storyteller, inhabitant and constructor of the text. What would be needed was Marlow."

10 Two well-known criticisms of Conrad's handling of point of view in *The Nigger* are Vernon Young's "Trial by Water: Joseph Conrad's *The Nigger of the 'Narcissus*,'" *Accent*, 12 (Spring 1952), pp. 67–81; rpt. in R. W. Stallman (ed.), *Joseph Conrad: A Critical Symposium* (East Lansing, Mich.: Michigan State University Press, 1960), p. 119, and

Marvin Mudrick's "The Artist's Conscience and *The Nigger of the 'Narcissus,'*" *Nineteenth-Century Fiction*, 11 (1957), pp. 291–292.

11 Sanford Pinsker, *The Language of Joseph Conrad* (Amsterdam: Rotopi, 1978), p. 57: "the narrative point of view . . . represents the collective sensibility of the *Narcissus'* crew, complete with all the ambivalences and initiations into complexity which make for the story's tightly balanced tone . . . the unnamed figure who narrates the story cannot connect – or, for that matter, make sense of – the disparate elements which swirl on the *Narcissus'* deck."

12 John Lester, "Conrad's Narrators in *The Nigger of the 'Narcissus,'*" *Conradiana*, 12, No. 3 (1980), p. 171: "Through the seaman–narrator we have endured with the crew the physical trials of the voyage . . . At the same time, the omniscient narrator has shown us the exact inadequacy of the lower deck's point of view." The distinction which Jakob Lothe makes between "authorial" and "personal" narrative in "Variations of Narrative in *The Nigger of the 'Narcissus,'*" *Conradiana*, 16, No. 3 (1984), pp. 215–224, further clarifies how the narrational perspective functions in the novel.

13 Ian Watt's "Conrad Criticism" remains the most effective rebuttal to the various charges of inconsistency made against *The Nigger*.

14 W. R. Martin, "Conrad's Management of Narration," *Conradiana*, 14, No. 1 (1982), pp. 53–56, rightly focuses on the "effect" Conrad was aiming for when he violated the dogma of point of view in the scene between Donkin and the dying Wait. Martin suggests that this effect is "the reader's experience of human 'solidarity'" (p. 53).

15 For an interpretation of Allistoun's decision similar to that suggested here, see H. M. Daleski, *Joseph Conrad: The Way of Dispossession* (London: Faber and Faber, 1977), p. 40. An opposite view can be found in R. D. Foulke, "Creed and Conduct in *The Nigger of the 'Narcissus,'*" *Conradiana*, 12, No. 2 (1980), pp. 113–114: "Before the ship is knocked on her beam ends [Captain Allistoun] has been mortgaging his seamen's judgment for a decent day's run in adverse conditions; afterwards he must insure the safety of life and property as best he can. In the light of these obligations, refusing to cut away the masts is an act of infidelity to the *Narcissus* and her men."

16 Ian Watt, in *Conrad in the Nineteenth Century*, writes that "The solidarity of seamen . . . is essentially provoked by a common enemy; and the essence of Conrad's literary use of the sea is reverence for the heroism of man's 'continuous defiance of what [the sea] can do'" (p. 97).

17 Joseph Warren Beach, in *The Twentieth Century Novel: Studies in Technique* (1932; rpt. New York: Appleton-Century-Crofts, 1960), pp. 349, 352, writes that technically Conrad's interpretation of the subject matter of *The Nigger* "appears as a kind of exercise in story-telling, *in the course of which* only he stumbled upon methods which might come in as a supplement to the mere power of words. . . To experiences which

he had personally lived through he was trying to apply the traditional impersonal manner of fiction, and only as it were in spite of himself fell into the personal manner of one who was there."

18 Karl, *Three Lives*, p. 391.

19 In a January 19, 1922, letter to Pinker, Conrad claims that in fact he had already written a short story in 1886, "The Black Mate," for a competition announced by the weekly *Tit-Bits* (*LL* II, 264). However, Jessie Conrad asserted that she had suggested the idea of the story which Conrad published in 1908. But Najder notes in *Chronicle*, p. 339, that "*Tit-Bits* indeed used to run competitions but not for short stories, only for reminiscences. The manuscript of 'The Black Mate' ... shows no signs of being a reshaped version of an earlier draft. Perhaps Conrad had in fact written something for *Tit-Bits* and later connected it with the artistically primitive tale suggested by his wife."

20 Rosalind Walls Smith, "Dates of Composition of Conrad's Works," *Conradiana*, 11, No. 1 (1979), p. 66.

21 *Ibid.*

22 To John Quinn, December 1911, date unspecified, quoted in R. W. Smith, "Dates of Composition," p. 66.

23 Joseph J. Martin, in "Edward Garnett and Conrad's Reshaping of Time," *Conradiana*, 6, No. 2 (1974), pp. 97–98, points out the similarities between the use of "theatrical metaphors" in Conrad's characterization of Karain and Turgenev's initial description of Harlov, the protagonist of "A Lear of the Steppes." Conrad also used the theater as a structural device in "The Return." Deirdre David, in "Selfhood and Language in 'The Return' and 'Falk,'" *Conradiana*, 8, No. 2 (1976), p. 138, notes that Conrad set up "a tightly ordered narrative structure, broken into three approximately equal sections, and resembling a three act play... This tripartite composition forms a structural analogy to the dramatic experience of Conrad's characters."

24 Bruce M. Johnson, "Conrad's 'Karain' and *Lord Jim*," *Modern Language Quarterly*, 24 (March 1963), p. 14.

25 Conrad uses his last trip aboard the *Loch Etive* as a setting for the episode related in "Initiation." He left this ship on April 25, 1881, and he signed on for a voyage to Bangkok aboard the *Palestine* only on September 19 of the same year. See Najder, *Chronicle*, pp. 69, 73.

3 THE MIRROR EFFECT IN "HEART OF DARKNESS"

1 Henry James has been reported as saying that he "objected to the narrator mixing himself up with the narrative in *The Heart of Darkness*." See Thomas C. Moser, "From Olive Garnett's Diary: Impressions of Ford Madox Ford and His Friends, 1890–1906," *Texas Studies in Literature and Language*, 16 (1974), p. 525; quoted in Watt, "Impressionism and Symbolism," p. 51.

2 Leavis, *The Great Tradition*, p. 204.

3 *Ibid.*, p. 208.

4 John Palmer comments on the paradoxical effect of Marlow's commentary, in *Joseph Conrad's Fiction: A Study in Literary Growth* (Ithaca, N.Y.: Cornell University Press, 1968), p. 43: "It is common to object to 'Heart of Darkness' on the grounds of its evasiveness . . . Yet here again the vagueness and abstract elaboration are the concrete particulars of a represented experience; this paradox, in fact, is one source of the story's irony."

5 Cedric T. Watts, in *Joseph Conrad's Letters to R. B. Cunninghame Graham* (Cambridge: Cambridge University Press, 1969), p. 119, notes that at the time of the letter "the first instalment of 'The Heart of Darkness' had just been published in *Blackwood's Magazine* (CLXV, 193–200, Feb. 1899)."

6 Jocelyn Baines, in *Critical Biography*, dismisses the letter's relevance for an interpretation of the short story: so "wrapped up is [the idea] that one wonders whether Conrad was always clear as to his intention and whether one is justified in trying to unravel the story to the extent of imparting a coherent meaning to it" (p. 224). Other critics, however, have used this passage to explain Conrad's impressionism. Donald C. Yelton, in *Mimesis and Metaphor*, p. 24, finds Coleridgean echoes in this passage. James Hillis Miller, in *Poets of Reality*, p. 26, connects the passage with Conrad's "fidelity to the truth of his sensations" in order to define the "technique of impressionism [which] is the deliberate method of 'Heart of Darkness.'"

7 Chinua Achebe, "An Image of Africa," *The Chancellor Lecture Series 1974–1975* (Amherst: University of Massachusetts, 1976), pp. 31–43; rpt. in *Hopes and Impediments: Selected Essays 1965–1987* (Oxford: Heinemann International, 1988), pp. 1–13. Renato Oliva, "Dalla commedia della luce alla tragedia della tenebra, ovvero l'ambigua redenzione di Kurtz," in Renato Oliva and Alessandro Portelli, *Conrad: l'imperialismo imperfetto* (Turin: Einaudi, 1973), p. 70: "in spite of the precision of certain intuitions and his attempt to be objective . . . [Conrad is] a disenchanted chronicler of colonialistic exploitation who is faithful, however, to the *idea* which could redeem and mitigate it. An imperialist with a bad conscience. An imperfect imperialist" (my translation).

8 Douglas Brown, "From *Heart of Darkness* to *Nostromo*: An Approach to Conrad," in Boris Ford (ed.), *The New Pelican Guide to English Literature* (Harmondsworth: Penguin, 1983), Vol. VII, p. 136: "The novelist himself is among the group of listeners to Marlow's voice, aboard the yawl that night on the Thames. His eyes see Marlow as an object."

9 Seymour L. Gross, in "A Further Note on the Function of the Frame in 'Heart of Darkness,'" *Modern Fiction Studies*, 3 (Summer 1957), p. 169, comments on Conrad's use of the light/darkness opposition to

distinguish Marlow's point of view in the opening scene of the story: "The imagery of light with which the first two pages of the story are studded serves both as an index to the narrator's innocence and as an ironic prologue to Marlow's opening comment."

10 Benita Parry, *Conrad and Imperialism: Ideological Boundaries and Visionary Frontiers* (London: Macmillan, 1983), p. 25: "the imagist manner of [the frame narrator's] presentation . . . is at odds with the conventions of celebratory rhetoric and makes the speaker an active communicator of irony whose very words carry the seeds of their own subversion."

11 Several commentators associate the "outside" with Marlow's language. James L. Guetti, in *The Limits of Metaphor: A Study of Melville, Conrad and Faulkner* (Ithaca, N.Y.: Cornell University Press, 1967), pp. 57–58, remarks that "here we encounter the idea of [Marlow's] language moving over the outside of an 'episode,' surrounding the episode but never penetrating it . . . The emphasis of the passage . . . is affirmative; the narrator implies that the search for meaning can be satisfied, somehow, in a concern with the exterior. And yet the very structure of 'Heart of Darkness' . . . implies that matters of the surface are not enough." Cedric T. Watts, as well, in *Conrad's "Heart of Darkness": A Critical and Contextual Discussion* (Milan: Mursia International, 1977), p. 42, remarks that "certainly the affair of Kurtz depends for its value on the 'outside': on the reflections of Marlow."

12 James Hillis Miller, in *Fiction and Repetition: Seven English Novels* (Oxford: Blackwell, 1982), p. 26, recognizes the tale's function in bringing out the meaning of the episode: "Though the meaning is outside, it may only be seen by way of the tale which brings it out. This bringing out takes place in the interaction of its different elements in their reference to one another."

13 Jerry Wasserman, "Narrative Presence: The Illusion of Language in *Heart of Darkness*," *Studies in the Novel*, 6 (1974), p. 328: Marlow is "the visual focus of the novel. Sitting before his audience and trying to recount his experience through words, Marlow himself embodies his experience."

14 Bruce M. Johnson, "Names, Naming and the 'Inscrutable' in Conrad's *Heart of Darkness*," *Texas Studies in Literature and Language*, 12, No. 4 (1971), p. 678: "The name 'enemies' is no more meaningful and effective than the performance of the 'man-of-war' . . . popping shells into the indifferent immensity of Africa. She is 'incomprehensible' and futile in the same way that the idea of *war* and *enemies* is simply incommensurate with the reality confronting these names."

15 John Palmer, in *Joseph Conrad's Fiction*, p. 43, notes that the story shows in exact terms that "Marlow's experience cannot immediately be comprehended in *specific* terms, that confusion and hypothetical abstractness are part of a civilized resistance to the forces of darkness."

16 For a comprehensive study of the continuity of the silence motif in Conrad's fiction, see Martin Ray, "Language and Silence in the Novels of Joseph Conrad," *Conradiana*, 16, No. 1 (1984), pp. 19–40. See also Wasserman, "Narrative Presence," p. 330: "it is most of all the profound silence of the wilderness itself that reveals to Marlow the poverty of human speech," and Parry, *Conrad and Imperialism*, p. 24: "Marlow occupies the centre of the stage with a practised narrative delivered in the language of a metropolis while reiterating a mistrust of words . . . pointing back to the silent wilderness as the repository of transcendent truth and ultimate reality."

17 As Edward Said points out, Conrad made a similar statement in a letter to Henry James about *The Nigger of the "Narcissus"*: "Il a été vécu. Il est, sans doute, mauvais. Rien de si facile comme de raconter un rêve, mais il est impossible de penetrer l'âme des ceux qui écoutent par la force de son amertume et de sa douceur. On ne communique pas la réalité poignante des illusions!" Quoted in Said, *The Fiction of Autobiography*, p. 90. Conrad's letter to Henry James is reproduced in *CL* I, 414.

18 A recurring attempt to trace Conrad's creative process in terms of his use of memory can be found in two works based on opposite critical approaches: Meyer's *Psychoanalytic Biography*, and Norman Sherry's *Conrad's Eastern World* (Cambridge: Cambridge University Press, 1966). Meyer and Sherry undertake most thoroughly the methods which respectively delve into the unconscious and conscious sides of the author. According to Meyer, the writer's use of his memories serves the function of the patient's conscious dream-associations during psychoanalytic treatment. Therefore, he feels able to interpret both Conrad's memories and the symbolic workings of his unconscious materials (pp. 12–13). On the other hand, Norman Sherry traces the creative process back to events remembered. He envisages a Conradian aesthetics in which a "truth" identified with "facts" is seen as Conrad's artistic aim. As Sherry concludes, "truth is fact for Conrad" (p. 270).

19 Hawthorn, *Language and Fictional Self-Consciousness*, p. 20.

20 *Ibid.*, p. 21.

21 For an opposite interpretation of this passage, see Wasserman, "Narrative Presence," pp. 334–335: "the frame-narrator, can only conceive of understanding Marlow's meaning by listening to his words, though the irony is explicit . . . He cannot visualize this narrative by merely listening. He does not catch the clue, and the momentary illumination sparked by Marlow's insight is quenched by the darkness."

22 Guerard, *Conrad the Novelist*, p. 43. For a reading different from Guerard's, see Joseph Dobrinsky, "From Whisper to Voice: Marlow's 'Accursed Inheritance' in *Heart of Darkness*," *Cahiers Victoriens et Edouardiens*, 16 (1982), pp. 77–78. Dobrinsky takes the listener's words

literally and identifies both the words ("ivory" and "Kurtz") and the sentence ("an accursed inheritance to be subdued at the cost of profound anguish and excessive toil").

23 Jacques Darras, in *Joseph Conrad and the West: Signs of Empire* (Totowa, N.J.: Barnes & Nobles, 1982), pp. 86–87, while interpreting this passage along similar lines, reaches the opposite conclusion: "We must not take Marlow on his word alone. It is in the *silence* of the text that, by reading between the lines, we can *see*. . . Marlow asks his listeners to look beyond the frontiers of his narration. A little as if he were rebelling against the narrow task which had fallen to him to guide the story to its end, he cries out that he is the story's blind spot and asks his listeners to be his witnesses. For that reason we must analyse the images which Marlow brings out from Africa."

24 H. M. Daleski, in *The Way of Dispossession*, p. 52, links Marlow's progress toward Kurtz with Conrad's ongoing artistic quest: "As Marlow struggles to get to the bottom of things, to the underlying truth of the affair, the aesthetic which Conrad enunciated in the preface to *The Nigger of the "Narcissus"* becomes the ethic of 'Heart of Darkness.'"

25 Edward Said, in "Conrad: The Presentation of Narrative," p. 119, comments on the difference between "hearing" and "seeing" in a slightly different context: "If we go through Conrad's major work we will find . . . that the narrative is presented as transmitted orally. Thus hearing and telling are the ground of the story as it were, the tale's most stable sensory activity, the measure of its duration, whereas *seeing*, in marked contrast, is always a precarious achievement and a much less stable business."

26 For a stimulating reading of the meta-narrative implications of the notion of seamanship in "Heart of Darkness," see Barbara De Mille, *"An Inquiry Into Some Points of Seamanship*: Narration as Preservation in *Heart of Darkness," Conradiana,* 18, No. 2 (1986), pp. 94–104. De Mille argues that "Marlow uses his duty of navigator–fabricator–narrator both to evade a direct confrontation with the darkness that has confounded Kurtz and to convert his experience of both Kurtz and the darkness into the symbolic status of memory" (p. 95).

27 Robert O. Evans, "A Further Comment on 'Heart of Darkness,'" *Modern Fiction Studies,* 3 (Winter 1957–58), pp. 358–360, rpt. in Robert Kimbrough (ed.), *Joseph Conrad: Heart of Darkness* (1963; rpt. New York: Norton, 1971), p. 231.

28 Marvin Mudrick, in "The Originality of Conrad," *The Hudson Review,* 11 (1958), p. 553, uses his own imagination to visualize what Conrad leaves unsaid: "Kurtz's vision of 'the horror' tends to dissolve at last into a widescreen panorama of 'unimaginable' orgies at 'midnight dances' with hordes of Hollywood natives howling round pyres of human sacrifice."

29 Marshall W. Alcorn, Jr., in "Conrad, and the Narcissistic

Metaphysics of Morality," *Conradiana*, 16, No. 2 (1984), p. 110, points out the interplay of "seeing" and "hearing" at work in Marlow's attempt to re-create the effect on himself of Kurtz's final cry: "Kurtz's words characteristically combine the power of vision with the immediacy of sound synaesthetically to overburden subjectivity with a sense of 'presence.' We are asked, for example, to 'see' Kurtz's speech as a 'stream of light,' and to 'hear' in Marlow's last 'image' of Kurtz the 'faint ring of incomprehensible words.'"

30 For a particularly interesting reading of Marlow's lie, see Robert S. Baker, "Joseph Conrad," review of *Conrad in the Nineteenth Century* by Ian Watt, and *Joseph Conrad: The Three Lives* by Frederick R. Karl, *Contemporary Literature*, 22, No. 1 (1981), pp. 122–123.

4 *LORD JIM* (1): THE NARRATOR AS INTERPRETER

1 Eloise Knapp Hay, "*Lord Jim*: From Sketch to Novel," in Robert E. Kuehn (ed.), *Twentieth Century Interpretations of Lord Jim* (Englewood Cliffs, N.J.: Prentice Hall, Inc., 1969), pp. 14–34. The essay was originally published in *Comparative Literature*, 12 (Fall 1960), pp. 289–309.

2 Alexander Janta, "A Conrad Family Heirloom at Harvard," in Ludwik Kryzanowski (ed.), *Joseph Conrad: Centennial Essays* (1960; rpt. New York: Folcroft Library Editions, 1972), p. 92.

3 Gordan, *The Making of a Novelist*, p. 260: "Before he went back to *Lord Jim*, he completed 'Heart of Darkness' . . . When he took up *Lord Jim* again, he extended his conception of the story and rewrote what he had already done."

4 Palmer, *Joseph Conrad's Fiction*, p. 6.

5 Najder, *Chronicle*, p. 248: the "story of *Lord Jim*'s birth which Conrad presented in his 1917 author's note to the novel . . . [is] . . . apocryphal and largely untrue."

6 Edward Garnett was the first one to point out a breaking into two of the novel. Conrad acknowledges his friend's criticism in a November 12, 1900, letter: "Yes! you've put your finger on the plague spot. The division of the book into two parts" (*CL* II, 302). However, Conrad's deceptive self-flagellation is balanced by the fact that he encloses in his letter to Garnett an "absolutely enthusiastic letter" (to David S. Meldrum, November 27, 1900; *CL* II, 307) about *Lord Jim* from Henry James.

7 See also Linda M. Shires, "The 'Privileged' Reader and Narrative Methodology in *Lord Jim*," *Conradiana*, 17, No. 1 (1985), p. 21: "While the two main thematic sections (pre-Patusan/Patusan) are reinforced by two symbolic jumps that Jim takes in Chapters 9 and 25, there are three main structural divisions . . . these breaks mark off different narrative strategies." Randall Craig, in "Swapping Yarns: The Oral

Mode of *Lord Jim*," *Conradiana*, 13, No. 3 (1981), p. 185, remarks that the threefold structure of the novel reflects Conrad's "attempts to overcome the impersonality of the literary form . . . by making the reader a part of an increasingly select audience." Thus, the novel's "narrative pattern replicates the rhetorical effect of direct address."

8 Ian Watt, in *Conrad in the Nineteenth Century*, p. 300, remarks that "Marlow's probing mind as it tries both to recollect experience and decipher its meaning" is the source of that "progression of moral understanding" outlined by Conrad's handling of time in the novel. Once one accepts "Conrad's moral and internalised definition of what constitutes the main action," Watt adds, "the structure of the narrative can be seen as a single forward movement."

9 Of course, opposite judgments of the omniscient narrator's reliability imply conflicting evaluations of the interplay between the first and second segments. For example, Benita Parry, in *Conrad and Imperialism*, pp. 78–79, argues that the anonymous narrator's "introduction, despite the air of reliable detachment it affects, turns out to be enmeshed with prejudice," but his "composite image of [Jim] is subtly and irrevocably altered by the substance of Marlow's mediation." On the contrary, according to William Bonney, *Thorns & Arabesques*, p. 237, the "only objectively valid glimpses we get of Jim's character occur in chapters one through four . . . which give the reader, from the third-person omniscient point of view, all the evidence needed to define the character of Jim apart from any of Marlow's enigmatic meditations." Bernard J. Paris, in *A Psychological Approach to Fiction* (Bloomington: Indiana University Press, 1974), p. 216, denies the very existence of this interplay: "the novel falls short of complete thematic coherence because it contains one perspective which is not dramatized, that of the omniscient narrator of the first four chapters and the relativistic perspective which dominates once Marlow becomes narrator. I find it impossible to reconcile them."

10 J. Hillis Miller's comment on this passage in *Poets of Reality*, p. 38, is particularly relevant to the present reading in that he sees it as a further elaboration of the concern with PRECISION which Conrad had already expressed in the "kernel" passage in "Heart of Darkness": "The key to [Conrad's] aesthetic theory is a sentence in *Lord Jim*: 'only a meticulous precision of statement would bring out the true horror behind the appalling face of things' (*LJ*, 30). Through exactly described scenes the horror appears, called by the magical incantation of words, though it is something which cannot be directly defined in words. It is the halo which appears around the reflected light of the moon. In Conrad's fiction an invisible haze is lit up by the glow of bright light, the definite facts, reflected in meticulous words, which make up the action. This, I take it, is the meaning of the famous declaration of the narrator of 'Heart of Darkness.'"

11 Ernest Bevan, Jr., "Marlow and Jim: The Reconstructed Past," *Conradiana*, 15, No. 3 (1983), p. 194.

12 See also James Hillis Miller, "The Interpretation of *Lord Jim*," in Morton W. Bloomfield (ed.), *The Interpretation of Narrative* (Cambridge, Mass.: Harvard University Press, 1970), p. 221: "Many sections of the story . . . are told to Marlow by Jim. In these the reader can see Jim attempting to interpret his experience by putting it into words. This self-interpretation is interpreted once more by Marlow, then by implication interpreted again by Marlow's listeners."

13 Armstrong, "Hermeneutics," p. 252: "Marlow is disconcerted by Jim because he is an anomaly – a part inconsistent with Marlow's expectations given his faith in his community's standard of conduct. Jim defies the set of types by which Marlow customarily composes the world. More importantly, however, by frustrating his interpretive hypotheses, Jim undermines Marlow's confidence in the beliefs on which his typology rests."

14 Miller, "The Interpretation of *Lord Jim*," pp. 216–217, finds that in this passage the "discrepancy" is "between what Jim looks like and what he is," and this "puts in question for Marlow 'the sovereign power enthroned in a fixed standard of conduct.'"

15 Dorothy Van Ghent's comment on another passage, in *The English Novel: Form and Function* (1953; rpt. New York: Harper Torchbooks, 1961), p. 237, is useful for understanding how Marlow's responsibility reflects Conrad's own formal concerns: "the significance of action is significance in the judgments of men . . . *What*, then, *is* the act? The question defines Conrad's method in this book, his use of reflector within reflector, point of view within point of view, cross-chronological juxtapositions of events and impressions. Conrad's technical 'devices,' in this case, represent much more than the word 'device' suggests: they represent extreme ethical scrupulosity, even anxiety; for the truth about a man is at once too immense and too delicate to sustain any failure of carefulness in the examiner."

16 H. M. Daleski, in *The Way of Dispossession*, pp. 78–79, stresses the relevance of this distinction between the "why" and the "how" for understanding the shift from the omniscient account to Marlow's narrative.

17 Yelton, *Mimesis and Metaphor*, p. 111: "In a series of a dozen representative works, spanning Conrad's career from *Almayer's Folly* (1895) to *The Rover* (1923) . . . I find a sharp rise in the average frequency of metaphor from the first novel to the works produced just before the turn of the century (*Youth* and *Lord Jim*), followed by a decline in frequency through *Nostromo* (1904) to *The Secret Agent* (1907)."

18 Craig, "Swapping Yarns," p. 190.

19 Robert Haugh, "The Structure of *Lord Jim*," *College English*, 12 (December 1951), p. 139.

20 For encomiastic readings of the French Lieutenant, see Van Ghent, *English Novel*, p. 231 – "the French lieutenant represents the ethically 'approved' manner of action" – and Haugh, "Structure of *Lord Jim*," p. 138, who considers him a "natural athlete, morally speaking." An entirely different interpretation is suggested by Tony Tanner, in *Conrad: Lord Jim* (London: Edward Arnold, 1963), p. 35. Tanner sees the Lieutenant as being "torpid, stolid, emotionless, and shruggingly inarticulate." For a similar interpretation, see also Bruss, *Conrad's Early Sea Fiction*, pp. 112–113.

21 For an interesting comment on the ambiguity of the notion of heroism in this case, see also Suresh Raval, "Narrative and Authority in *Lord Jim*: Conrad's Art of Failure," *English Literary History*, 48, No. 2 (1981), pp. 393–394: "Contrary to the view of some critics . . . the French lieutenant's conduct does not necessarily undermine Jim's . . . the French lieutenant [seems] heroically to mock Jim, Jim seems to mock [the officer] by a heroic gesture of self-assertion . . . The oscillation of response that occurs in the novel . . . functions at the level of a fundamental questioning of the nature of authority and its relation to Marlow's narration of Jim's story."

22 Hawthorn, *Language and Fictional Self-Consciousness*, p. 54.

23 Parry, *Conrad and Imperialism*, p. 93.

24 Palmer, *Joseph Conrad's Fiction*, p. 30, describes in similar terms Conrad's characterization of Stein: "the extraordinarily artificial framework in which Marlow places him and his incredible thumbnail biography . . . provide precisely the one-step-more away from realism Conrad needs to highlight [Stein's] choral function."

25 Elizabeth Brody Tenenbaum, in "'And the Woman is Dead Now': A Reconsideration of Conrad's Stein," *Studies in the Novel*, 10, No. 3 (1978), p. 340, notes that "Stein's rephrasing changes the focus of attention from behavior (the process of living) to identity (its product)." This paraphrase epitomizes a "fundamental discrepancy in outlook between Marlow, the pragmatic communalist, and Stein, the romantic egoist." The difference between Stein's concern with identity and Jim's, Tenenbaum adds, is that "while Stein chose the perpetual creation of an evolving self at the cost of security, repose, and perhaps loyalty as well, Jim elects to preserve a static self by sacrificing not only his lover's well-being but also his very life" (p. 343).

26 C. B. Cox, in *The Modern Imagination*, p. 38, comments in a particularly effective way on Stein's "vanishing act": Stein "moves into 'shapeless' dusk, as if these few steps had carried him out of this concrete and perplexed world . . . It is as if he hovers in that area of consciousness the other side of the pane of glass, of which Jim became aware when the squall struck the *Patna* . . . Conrad deliberately abandons rational articulation, to create a form of words close to music, or perhaps a

symbolist poem."

27 Royal Roussel, in *Metaphysics of Darkness*, p. 96, remarks on the continuity between Stein's interpretation and the essential quality of Patusan: "Patusan, as Marlow describes it, is associated not only with the heights which are the setting of Jim's early dreams, but also with a kind of art which, Stein suggests, allows the perfect embodiment of these dreams. Patusan is, for Marlow, a 'distant heavenly body' . . . where Jim can leave all his failings behind, but it is also for him a world created by imagination and described in terms which suggest the color and tracings on the wings of Stein's butterflies."

5 *LORD JIM* (II): THE NARRATOR AS READER

1 Ian Watt, in *Conrad in the Nineteenth Century*, pp. 306, 308, describes in similar terms the change in Marlow's function in the Patusan section: "Marlow becomes more a reporter and less a participant." This metamorphosis, according to Watt, is an effect of the fact that in "the second part of *Lord Jim*, Conrad is not dealing with realities that can stand up to three-dimensional scrutiny; he is trapped in an intractable contradiction between the basic terms of his previous, and his present, narrative assumptions."

2 Mario Perniola, in his study on the meta-novel, *Il metaromanzo*, I quaderni di Sigma, 4 (Milan: Silva, 1966), p. 65, remarks on J. Warren Beach's insight into Conrad's discovery of new techniques during the writing of his works. "What is important," Perniola notes, "is that this discovery does not make him re-write the first pages for the sake of order and coherence – a sign that for Conrad the creative process is more important than the results, and that the work speaks more of itself than of its characters" (my translation).

3 For an opposite reading of Patusan, see Joseph Martin, "Conrad and the Aesthetic Movement," p. 206: "As Jim the man is replaced by Tuan Jim . . . the realistic mode (life) must give way to the melodramatic mode (art) . . . even in its basic technique the novel presents a fusion of art and life, but only to assert their essential difference in a fictional world where we witness one man's betrayal of life's possibilities."

4 Owen Knowles points out in "Commentary as Rhetoric," the particular function Marlow has in the critical discourse: "Marlow seems to be involved in a submerged argument, cajoling or bullying his audience into awareness. In an effort to coerce his listeners, he insists upon the uncomfortable facts of Jim's 'case' and demands their interpretation, or throws into question the values we bring to the facts" (p. 24).

5 Owen Knowles comments on this passage – which is a clear example of the motives behind Marlow's comments – in "Commentary as

Rhetoric," p. 22: "Marlow's efforts to understand a person by invoking the general values implied by his conduct are paralleled by the author's desire to 'get at, to bring forth *les valeurs idéales*' (*LL* II, 185)."

6 Barton Thurber, "Speaking the Unspeakable: Conrad and the Sublime," *Conradiana*, 16, No. 1 (1984), p. 49.

7 Jean Raimond, in "Jim et Axel Heyst ou les mirages de l'ailleurs: deux avatars conradiens de Don Quichotte et de Robinson," in *Images de l'ailleurs dans la littérature anglo-américaine* (Reims: Publications du Centre de Recherche sur l'Imaginaire dans les Littératures de Langue Anglaise, 1981), p. 88, comments on Jim's flight to an imaginary world outside history: "le domaine de Patusan est tout de suite perçu par Jim comme l' 'ailleurs' que depuis sa faute il appelait de ses voeux, un 'ailleurs' entièrement conforme à l'idéal d'héroïsme dont son imagination n'a cessé de se nourrir. Parce que, comme Don Quichotte, il ne peut et ne veut plus vivre dans le monde ordinaire, Jim se retranche à l'intérieur du cercle enchanté de Patusan où il va enfin réaliser ses rêves d'adolescent."

8 Bevan, "Marlow and Jim: The Reconstructed Past," p. 199.

9 Guerard, *Conrad the Novelist*, p. 168.

10 Daniel Cottom, in *"Lord Jim*: Destruction Through Time," *The Centennial Review*, 27, No. 1 (1983), p. 17, denies this juxtaposition of external world and Patusan: "Although the creation of this myth might seem to show that in Patusan Jim has found a realm appropriate to him, one that will nurture his romantic character, the irony is that it undercuts his idealism as much as the process of the law-court had ... The distortion of metaphor evident in this confusion of signifier and signified perfectly exemplifies the way that Jim is captive to a rhetoric of knightly ideality that has lost its semantic ground in the world and therefore dooms Jim to be misperceived."

11 Agnes Latham, introduction to William Shakespeare, *As You Like It* (London: Methuen, 1975), p. xxii.

12 Giles Mitchell, "Lord Jim's Death Fear, Narcissism, and Suicide," *Conradiana*, 18, No. 3 (1986), pp. 163–179, demonstrates how central the notion of Jim's narcissistic self-image is for an interpretation of *Lord Jim*.

13 Knowles, "Commentary as Rhetoric," p. 25.

14 James Joyce, "The Dead," in *Dubliners* (1914; rpt. London: Granada, 1982), p. 200: "Generous tears filled Gabriel's eyes. He had never felt like that himself towards any woman but he knew that such a feeling must be love." Joyce describes Gabriel Conroy's condition after his epiphany in terms which recall the state Marlow is in – after his interview with the girl – while he is standing next to the grave of Jewel's mother. Gabriel's soul, Joyce writes, "approached that region

where dwell the vast hosts of the dead. He was conscious of, but could not apprehend, their wayward and flickering existence. His own identity was fading out into a grey impalpable world: the solid world itself which these dead had one time reared and lived in was dissolving and dwindling."

15 Jerry Wasserman, in "Narrative Presence," p. 330, comments on the similarity between Marlow's predicament in Africa and his interview with Jewel, and notes: "To reject language as a façade or a fiction is to open oneself to the possibility of understanding the true mysteries of the heart of darkness. But it is also to invite a kind of madness . . . As long as the white men maintain their shelter of language, they remain 'sane.' But, Marlow sees, it is sanity at the expense of truth."

16 Barton Thurber finds that this scene is the clearest example of Conrad's use of the sublime in *Lord Jim*. In "Speaking the Unspeakable," p. 50, he writes: "Jim, his life in Patusan, his plans and aspirations are all transubstantiated in the moonlight into something both real and not real, true and false, understood and not understood. Jim himself is sublime . . . [he is] beyond the pale, not merely of white civilization but of substance, life, even of Marlow's capacity to describe him."

17 Donald C. Yelton, in *Mimesis and Metaphor*, p. 235, though not referring to this passage, affirms the centrality of the reality/illusion theme in Marlow's commentary in Patusan: "we cannot warrantably single out Marlow's lucubrations on moon versus sun and ignore or dismiss his reflections on reality and illusion."

18 Daniel W. Ross, in "*Lord Jim* and the Saving Illusion," p. 58, in commenting on this passage, observes that "Marlow also learns the significance of illusion. The only truth that matters, Marlow suggests, comes from the narrative, the work of art itself. The moment of illusion (the telling of the story) is the thing which reveals the truth."

19 Benita Parry, in *Conrad and Imperialism*, pp. 90–91, points out as well a connection between these words and Stein, but reaches the conclusion that this statement contradicts the novel's critical discourse. She compares Jim's commitment to fidelity with Stein's decision to bequeath his collection of beetles and butterflies to the German town where he was born. These "uncontradicted articulations of devotion to the nation and the race," she writes, draw "*Lord Jim* back into the orbit of traditional imperialist ideology from which the fiction's discourse on matters moral and metaphysical struggles to escape."

20 Linda M. Shires, in "The 'Privileged' Reader," pp. 23–27, ignores Conrad's negative characterization of the privileged man. Consequently, she concludes that this anonymous reader who is "at once most distanced and yet most sympathetic to Jim, is potentially the best reader of the novel . . . because of certain attitudes and background." Nonetheless, her reading of the privileged man and Stein as the most important pair in the "patterns of characters where each

observer of Jim represents a distinct philosophy or outlook" is perhaps the most interesting interpretation of this crucial passage in the novel. Shires usefully applies the concept of a "dialogue of structural perspectives" (drawn from Mikhail Bakhtin) to Conrad's use of juxtaposed figures in the novel. Thus, both Stein and the privileged man become models for "the reader's own still developing attitudes towards Jim." Through these figures, she concludes, "philosophies engage each other across the chapters and invite the reader to participate in dialogue as ally, antagonist, coordinator, or reviser."

21 Arnold Davidson, *Conrad's Endings: A Study of the Five Major Novels* (Ann Arbor, Mich.: UMI Press, 1984), p. 30.

22 In a July 19, 1900, letter to William Blackwood, the writer describes the method he adopted for the end of *Lord Jim* in terms which recall Marlow's surrender to the "language of facts": "The end of Lord Jim in accordance with a meditated resolve is presented in a bare almost bald relation of matters of fact ... I enlarge a little upon the new character which is introduced (that of Brown the desperate adventurer) so as to preserve the sense of verisimilitude ... but all the rest is nothing but a relation of events – strictly, a narrative" (*CL* II, 283–284).

23 See also Watt, *Conrad in the Nineteenth Century*, p. 308, which instead emphasizes the differences between Marlow's oral narrative and the written account – which Watt finds to be "more distant and more rapid."

24 Davidson's reconstruction of the final crisis in Patusan demolishes the reliability of Marlow's reflection in this passage. "For one thing," he writes, "Jim's 'truth' cannot be, at the end of his career, so readily assumed. And neither can his 'faithfulness' be simply posited. Faithful to what or to whom? ... At one time [Jim] did effectively aid Doramin and his people ... But after encountering Brown ... it almost seems as if Jim has [transferred] his allegiance from the Bugis to Brown" (*Conrad's Endings*, p. 22). Davidson's diminishing of Marlow's reliability emphasizes the effectiveness of the "double focus" produced by Conrad's use of his internal narrator. This technique, Davidson notes, "especially pervades the concluding chapters of the book, for here Marlow's claims for Jim are most at odds with the account of his actions" (*Conrad's Endings*, p. 9). Another reason for the "double focus" appearing more sharply at the end of Marlow's narrative is that Conrad has relinquished his internal narrator as a center of consciousness.

25 Robert F. Haugh, in "Structure of *Lord Jim*," p. 141, ignores the suffering that pervades this scene so as to conclude that Jim "redeems himself magnificently" by not yielding to Jewel's plea, which he sees as a repetition of "the theme previously presented by the three renegades of the 'Patna,' who unwittingly pleaded" Jim to jump.

26 Miller, "The Interpretation of *Lord Jim*," p. 219.
27 See also Bruce M. Johnson, *Conrad's Models of Mind* (Minneapolis: University of Minnesota Press, 1971), p. 64: "At the end of the novel Jim must choose between a nearly selfless love for Jewel (selfless because it will ruin the confirmation of his self-image) and his ego ideal."

POSTSCRIPT

1 Lawrence S. Graver, in "'Typhoon': A Profusion of Similes," *College English*, 24 (October 1962), p. 62. For a rejection of the notion of "Typhoon"'s simplicity, see T. A. Birrell, "The Simplicity of *Typhoon*: Conrad, Flaubert and Others," *Dutch Quarterly Review of Anglo-American Letters*, 10 (1980), pp. 272–295. More recently, Charles I. Schuster, in "Comedy and the Limits of Language in Conrad's 'Typhoon,'" *Conradiana*, 16, No. 1 (1984), pp. 55–71, refutes both the notions of the tale's simplicity and that its language is prosaic. Both articles contain exhaustive bibliographical indications about the critics who argued for "Typhoon"'s simplicity.
2 Frederic Jameson, *The Political Unconscious: Narrative as Socially Symbolic Act* (Ithaca, N.Y.: Cornell University Press, 1981), pp. 206–207.
3 In "Heart of Darkness" Conrad had the frame narrator state that he was listening to Marlow's tale "on the watch for the sentence, for the word, that would give [him] the clue to ... this narrative" (*Y*, 83). In *Under Western Eyes* the language teacher remarks on the difficulty of rendering "the moral conditions ruling over a large portion of this earth's surface; conditions not easily to be understood, much less discovered in the limits of a story, till some key-word is found; a word that could stand at the back of all the words covering the pages." But the "decent mind" of the old language teacher can come up with no better word than "cynicism" (*UWE*, 66–67). Conrad uses again in *Chance* this form of commentary. In the long scene on the sidewalk in front of the hotel in which Flora de Barral is hiding, Marlow notes: "The trouble was that I could not imagine anything about Flora de Barral and [Captain Anthony] ... I should have liked to ask the girl for a word which could give my imagination its line" (*C*, 210–211).
4 T. S. Eliot, "The Use of Poetry and the Use of Criticism," in Frank Kermode (ed.), *The Selected Prose of T. S. Eliot* (London: Faber and Faber, 1975), p. 94.
5 T. S. Eliot, "Swinburne as Poet," in *The Sacred Wood: Essays on Poetry and Criticism* (1920; rpt. London: Methuen, 1969), p. 150.
6 T. S. Eliot, "The Metaphysical Poets," in Kermode, *Selected Prose of T. S. Eliot*, p. 65.

7 T. S. Eliot, "Kipling Redivivus," *Athenaeum*, May 9, 1919, pp. 297–298, as quoted in Leonard Unger, "Laforgue, Conrad, and T. S. Eliot," in *The Man in the Name: Essays on the Experience of Poetry* (Minneapolis: University of Minnesota Press, 1956), p. 230.

8 Ford Madox Ford, *Thus to Revisit: Some Reminiscences* (London, 1921), p. 40, as quoted in Randall, *Conrad and Dawson*, p. 65.

9 *Ibid.*, p. 63.

10 Jerry Allen, *The Sea Years of Joseph Conrad* (1965; London: Methuen, 1967), pp. 189–190.

11 Paul Kirschner, "Some Notes on *Conrad in the Nineteenth Century*," *Conradiana*, 17, No. 1 (1985), p. 35: "what Novalis is insisting on here is the power of belief – of acceptance through faith rather than reason."

12 H. M. Daleski, in *The Way of Dispossession*, p. 107, quotes Bernard C. Meyer's view that "Typhoon" is an "antidote" to *Lord Jim*: "It is as if in telling a story of quiet heroism and undeviating devotion to duty [Conrad] was seeking to cleanse his mouth of the bad taste left there by Jim's neurotic suffering and erratic behaviour" (Meyer, *A Psychoanalytic Biography*, p. 162). Daleski, however, takes a different position: if MacWhirr "is regarded as the protagonist of 'Typhoon,' then the tale would seem to stand in a relation of simple reversal to *Lord Jim* . . . But I would argue that Conrad is as much concerned with Jukes as MacWhirr; and since Jukes is a potential Jim . . . the tale is more a complement than an antidote to the novel."

13 Edward Garnett's juxtaposition of Jim and MacWhirr is set in surprisingly chauvinistic terms, which forces today's critics to raise some serious questions about his reliability as mentor and critic of Conrad. In his introduction to *Conrad's Prefaces*, pp. 16, 19, Garnett writes that Jim "was 'one of us,' 'a gentleman,' who had dishonoured the English name," and identifies himself with Brierly: "Our English attitude to the dishonoured Jim is well illustrated by the behaviour of Captain Brierly." MacWhirr, on the other hand, he finds to be "indeed a Briton to be proud of."

14 On the last page of the manuscript of "Typhoon" Conrad wrote that the story was finished "at Midnight, 10th–11th Jan^y, 1901"; and in a January 23, 1901, letter he informs Pinker that "Falk" "progresses having taken a start since last Monday." See Rosalind Walls Smith, "Dates of Composition," p. 68.

15 The *Edinburgh Review* (April 1908) included *The Secret Agent* in an unsigned article on "Ugliness in Fiction." See Sherry, *The Critical Heritage*, pp. 201–202.

16 In a review in *Country Life* (August 15, 1908, pp. 234–235), Anderson Graham writes that "On first looking at Mr. Joseph Conrad's new book, *A Set of Six*, we thought the author had been making some new studies in style . . . But a little consideration led us to think that the compilation of this list was no more than an essay in the art of literary

window-dressing" (Sherry, *The Critical Heritage*, p. 217).

17 Unsigned review, *Glasgow News* (October 3, 1907, p. 5), quoted in Sherry, *The Critical Heritage*, p. 196.

Bibliography

Achebe, Chinua. "An Image of Africa." *The Chancellor Lecture Series 1974–1975*. Amherst: University of Massachusetts, 1976: 31–43. Rpt. as "An Image of Africa: Racism in Conrad's *Heart of Darkness*" in *Hopes and Impediments. Selected Essays 1965–87*. Oxford: Heinemann International, 1988: 1–13.

Alcorn, Marshall W., Jr. "Conrad, and the Narcissistic Metaphysics of Morality." *Conradiana*, 16, No. 2 (1984): 103–123.

Allen, Jerry. *The Sea Years of Joseph Conrad*. 1965; London: Methuen, 1967.

Angeleri, Carlo. "Joseph Conrad: una lettera inedita a Carlo Placci." *Paragone*, 8 (1957): 55–58.

Armstrong, Paul B. "The Hermeneutics of Literary Impressionism: Interpretation and Reality in James, Conrad, and Ford." *The Centennial Review*, 27, No. 4 (1983): 244–269.

Baines, Jocelyn. *Joseph Conrad: A Critical Biography*. London: Weidenfeld & Nicolson, 1961.

Baker, Robert S. "Joseph Conrad." Review of *Conrad in the Nineteenth Century*, by Ian Watt, and *Joseph Conrad: The Three Lives*, by Frederick R. Karl. *Contemporary Literature*, 22, No. 1 (1981): 116–126.

Bantock, G. H. "The Two 'Moralities' of Joseph Conrad." *Essays in Criticism*, 3, No. 2 (1953): 125–142.

Bayley, John. *The Characters of Love: A Study in the Literature of Personality*. London: Constable, 1960.

Beach, Joseph Warren. *The Twentieth Century Novel: Studies in Technique*. 1932; New York: Appleton-Century-Crofts, 1960.

Berthoud, Jacques. *Joseph Conrad: The Major Phase*. Cambridge: Cambridge University Press, 1978.

Bevan, Ernest, Jr. "Marlow and Jim: The Reconstructed Past." *Conradiana*, 15, No. 3 (1983): 191–202.

Birrell, T. A. "The Simplicity of *Typhoon*: Conrad, Flaubert and Others." *Dutch Quarterly Review of Anglo-American Letters*, 10 (1980): 272–295.

Bonney, William W. *Thorns & Arabesques: Contexts for Conrad's Fiction*. Baltimore: Johns Hopkins University Press, 1980.

Booth, Wayne. *The Rhetoric of Fiction*. Chicago: University of Chicago Press, 1961.

Brown, Douglas. "From *Heart of Darkness* to *Nostromo*: An Approach to Conrad." In Boris Ford (ed.), *From James to Eliot*, Vol. VII of *The New Pelican Guide to English Literature*, 8 vols. Harmondsworth: Penguin, 1983: 131–149.

Bruss, Paul. *Conrad's Early Sea Fiction: The Novelist as Navigator*. Lewisburg: Bucknell University Press, 1979.

Cadot, Raoul. "Les Traits moraux de la Mer dans l'Oeuvre de Joseph Conrad." *Revue de l'enseignement des langues vivantes*, 50 (1933): 399–407.

Chatterjee, Sisir. "Joseph Conrad: 'The Power of the Written Word.'" In *Problems in Modern English Fiction*. Calcutta: Bookland Private, 1965: 112–122.

Conrad, John. *Joseph Conrad: Times Remembered*. Cambridge: Cambridge University Press, 1981.

Conrad, Joseph. *The Nigger of the "Narcissus."* 1897; rpt. Garden City, N.Y.: Doubleday & Co., 1925.

Collected Edition, 21-vol. rpt. London: J. M. Dent & Sons, 1946–1955.

Cooper, Christopher. *Conrad and the Human Dilemma*. New York: Barnes & Nobles, 1970.

Cottom, Daniel. "*Lord Jim*: Destruction Through Time." *The Centennial Review*, 27, No. 1 (1983): 10–29.

Cox, C. B. *Joseph Conrad: The Modern Imagination*. London: J.M. Dent & Sons, 1974.

Craig, Randall. "Swapping Yarns: The Oral Mode of *Lord Jim*." *Conradiana*, 13, No. 3 (1981): 181–193.

Daleski, H. M. *The Way of Dispossession*. London: Faber and Faber, 1977.

Darras, Jacques. *Joseph Conrad and the West: Signs of Empire*. Totowa, N.J.: Barnes & Nobles, 1982.

David, Deirdre. "Selfhood and Language in 'The Return' and 'Falk.'" *Conradiana*, 8, No. 2 (1976): 137–147.

Davidson, Arnold. *Conrad's Endings: A Study of the Five Major Novels*. Ann Arbor, Mich.: UMI Press, 1984.

De Mille, Barbara. "*An Inquiry Into Some Points of Seamanship*: Narration as Preservation in *Heart of Darkness*." *Conradiana*, 18, No. 2 (1986): 94–104.

Dobrinsky, Joseph. "From Whisper to Voice: Marlow's 'Accursed Inheritance' in *Heart of Darkness*." *Cahiers Victoriens et Edouardiens*, 16 (1982): 77–104.

Eliot, T. S. "The Use of Poetry and the Use of Criticism." In Frank Kermode (ed.), *Selected Prose of T. S. Eliot*: 79–96.

"The Metaphysical Poets." In Frank Kermode (ed.), *Selected Prose of T. S. Eliot*: 59–67.

"Swinburne as Poet." In *The Sacred Wood: Essays on Poetry and Criticism.* 1920; rpt. London: Methuen, 1969: 144–150.

"Kipling Redivivus." *Athenaeum*, 9 May 1919: 297–298.

Evans, Robert O. "A Further Comment on 'Heart of Darkness.'" *Modern Fiction Studies*, 3 (Winter 1957–58): 358–360. Rpt. in Robert Kimbrough (ed.), *Joseph Conrad: Heart of Darkness, An Authoritative Text, Background and Sources, Criticism.*

Fleishman, Avrom. *Conrad's Politics: Community and Anarchy in the Fiction of Joseph Conrad.* Baltimore: Johns Hopkins University Press, 1967.

"*The Mirror of the Sea*: Fragments of a Great Confession." *L'Epoque conradienne* (May 1979): 136–151.

Follett, Helen Thomas and Wilson Follett. "Contemporary Novelists: Joseph Conrad." *The Atlantic Monthly*, 119 (February 1917): 233–243.

Ford, Ford Madox. *Joseph Conrad: A Personal Remembrance.* [London and Boston,] 1924; rpt. New York: Octagon Books, 1965.

Introduction to Joseph Conrad's *The Sisters.* Milan: Mursia, 1968: 11–30.

Forster, E. M. "The Pride of Mr. Conrad." *The Nation and Athenaeum*, 19 (March 1921): 881–882. Rpt. in *Abinger Harvest.* 1936; rpt. London: Edward Arnold, 1965: 159–64.

Foulke, R. D. "Creed and Conduct in *The Nigger of the 'Narcissus.'*" *Conradiana*, 12, No. 2 (1980): 105–128.

Freud, Sigmund. *The Interpretation of Dreams.* Vols. IV–V of *The Standard Edition of the Complete Psychological Works of Sigmund Freud.* Ed. and trans. James Strachey. London: Hogarth Press, 1953.

Garnett, Edward (ed.). *Conrad's Prefaces to His Works.* [London,] 1937; rpt. Freeport, N.Y.: Books for Libraries Press, 1971.

Gaston, Paul L. "The Gospel of Work According to Joseph Conrad." *The Polish Review*, 20, Nos. 2–3 (1975): 203–210.

Gekoski, R. A. *Conrad: The Moral World of the Novelist.* London: Paul Elek, 1978.

Goldknopf, David. "What's Wrong with Conrad: Conrad on Conrad." *Criticism*, 10, No. 1 (1968): 54–64.

Gordan, John Dozier. *Joseph Conrad: The Making of a Novelist.* 1940; rpt. New York: Russell & Russell, 1963.

Gordon, Caroline. "Some Readings and Misreadings." *The Sewanee Review*, 61, No. 3 (1953): 384–407.

Graver, Lawrence S. "'Typhoon': A Profusion of Similes." *College English*, 24 (October 1962): 62–64.

Gross, Seymour L. "A Further Note on the Function of the Frame in 'Heart of Darkness.'" *Modern Fiction Studies*, 3 (Summer 1957): 167–170.

Guerard, Albert J. *Conrad the Novelist.* 1958; rpt. New York: Atheneum, 1967.

"The Conradian Voice." In Norman Sherry (ed.), *Joseph Conrad: A Commemoration*: 1–16.

Guetti, James L. *The Limits of Metaphor: A Study of Melville, Conrad and Faulkner*. Ithaca, N.Y.: Cornell University Press, 1967.

Gurko, Leo. *The Two Lives of Joseph Conrad*. New York: Thomas Y. Crowell, 1965.

Harkness, Bruce. "The Secret of 'The Secret Sharer' Bared." *College English*, 27 (October 1965): 55–61.

Haugh, Robert. "The Structure of *Lord Jim*." *College English*, 12 (December 1951): 137–141.

Hawthorn, Jeremy. *Joseph Conrad: Language and Fictional Self-Consciousness*. London: Arnold, 1979.

Hay, Eloise Knapp. "*Lord Jim*: From Sketch to Novel." *Comparative Literature*, 12 (Fall 1960): 289–309. Rpt. in Robert E. Kuehn (ed.), *Twentieth Century Interpretations of Lord Jim*: 14–34.

"Impressionism Limited." In Norman Sherry (ed.), *Joseph Conrad: A Commemoration*: 54–64.

Hervouet, Yves. "Conrad and Maupassant: An Investigation into Conrad's Creative Process." *Conradiana*, 14, No. 2 (1982): 83–111.

Hewitt, Douglas. *Conrad: A Reassessment*. 1952; rpt. London: Bowes & Bowes, 1975.

Higdon, David Leon. "Conrad in the Eighties: A Bibliography and Some Observations." *Conradiana*, 17, No. 3 (1985): 214–249.

Holloway, John. *The Victorian Sage: Studies in Argument*. 1953; rpt. New York: Norton, 1965.

Hynes, Samuel. "Two Rye Revolutionists." *Sewanee Review*, 73, No. 1 (1965): 151–158. Rpt. in Hynes, *Edwardian Occasions*: 48–53.

The Edwardian Turn of Mind. Princeton, N.J.: Princeton University Press, 1968.

Edwardian Occasions: Essays on English Writing in the Early Twentieth Century. London: Routledge & Kegan Paul, 1972.

James, Henry. *The Art of the Novel*. Ed. Richard P. Blackmur. New York: Charles Scribner's Sons, 1934.

Jameson, Frederic. *The Political Unconscious: Narrative as Socially Symbolic Act*. Ithaca, N.Y.: Cornell University Press, 1981.

Janta, Alexander. "A Conrad Family Heirloom at Harvard." In Ludwig Kryzanowski (ed.), *Joseph Conrad: Centennial Essays*: 85–109.

Jean-Aubry, Gérard. *Joseph Conrad: Life and Letters*. 2 vols. Garden City: Doubleday, Page, and Co., 1927.

Joseph Conrad: Lettres françaises. Paris: Gallimard, 1929.

Johnson, Bruce M. "Conrad's 'Karain' and *Lord Jim*." *Modern Language Quarterly*, 24 (March 1963): 13–20.

"Names, Naming and the 'Inscrutable' in Conrad's *Heart of Darkness*." *Texas Studies in Literature and Language*, 12, No. 4 (1971): 675–688.

Conrad's Models of Mind. Minneapolis: University of Minnesota Press, 1971.
Joyce, James. "The Dead." In *Dubliners.* 1914; rpt. London: Granada, 1982.
Karl, Frederick R. "Joseph Conrad: A *fin de siècle* Novelist – A Study in Style and Method." *The Literary Review,* 2 (1959): 565–576.
"Joseph Conrad's Literary Theory." *Criticism,* 2 (1960): 317–335.
A Reader's Guide to Joseph Conrad. New York: Noonday Press, 1960.
Joseph Conrad: The Three Lives: A Biography. New York: Farrar, Straus & Giroux, 1979.
and Laurence Davies (eds.). *The Collected Letters of Joseph Conrad, Volume I: 1861–1897.* Cambridge: Cambridge University Press, 1983.
and Laurence Davies (eds.). *The Collected Letters of Joseph Conrad, Volume II: 1898–1902.* Cambridge: Cambridge University Press, 1986.
and Laurence Davies (eds.). *The Collected Letters of Joseph Conrad, Volume III: 1903–1907.* Cambridge: Cambridge University Press, 1988.
Kenner, Hugh. *The Poetry of Ezra Pound.* Norfolk, Conn.: New Directions, 1951.
Ulysses. London: George Allen & Unwin, 1980.
Kerf, René. "Ethics *Versus* Aesthetics: A Clue to the Deterioration of Conrad's Art." *Revue des langues vivantes/ Tijdschrift voor levende talen,* 31 (1965): 240–249.
Kermode, Frank. *The Romantic Image.* 1957; rpt. London: Routledge & Kegan Paul, 1961.
(ed.). *The Selected Prose of T. S. Eliot.* London: Faber and Faber, 1975.
"Secrets and Narrative Sequence." *Critical Inquiry,* 7, No. 1 (1980). 83 101.
Kimbrough, Robert (ed.). *Joseph Conrad: Heart of Darkness, An Authoritative Text, Background and Sources, Criticism.* 2nd edn. New York: Norton, 1971.
(ed.). *Joseph Conrad: The Nigger of the "Narcissus," An Authoritative Text, Background and Sources, Criticism.* New York: Norton, 1979.
Kirschner, Paul. *Conrad: The Psychologist as Artist.* Edinburgh: Oliver & Boyd, 1968.
"Some Notes on Conrad in the Nineteenth Century." *Conradiana,* 17, No. 1 (1985): 31–36.
Knowles, Owen. "Commentary as Rhetoric: An Aspect of Conrad's Technique." *Conradiana,* 5, No. 3 (1973): 5–27.
Kryzanowski, Ludwik (ed.). *Joseph Conrad: Centennial Essays.* 1960; rpt. New York: Folcroft Library Editions, 1977.
Kuehn, Robert E. (ed.). *Twentieth Century Interpretations of Lord Jim: A Collection of Critical Essays.* Englewood Cliffs, N.J.: Prentice-Hall, 1969.
Lacan, Jacques. "L'insistenza della lettera dell'inconscio o la ragione dopo Freud." In *Scritti,* trans. Giacomo Contri. Turin: Einaudi, 1974. Vol. I: 488–523.
Latham, Agnes (ed.). Introduction to William Shakespeare, *As You Like It.*

The Arden Edition of the Works of William Shakespeare. London: Methuen, Arden Shakespeare Paperbacks, 1975: ix–xcv.

Lavoie, Thomas. "Textual History and Textual Notes: The 'Preface. In Robert Kimbrough (ed.), *Joseph Conrad: The Nigger of the "Narcissus"*: 148–150.

Leavis, Frank Raymond. *The Great Tradition*. 1948; rpt. Harmondsworth: Penguin, 1977.

Lester, John. "Conrad's Narrators in *The Nigger of the 'Narcissus.'*" *Conradiana*, 12, No. 3 (1980): 163–172.

Lombardo, Agostino. *La poesia inglese dall'estetismo al simbolismo*. Rome: Edizioni di storia e letteratura, 1950.

Lothe, Jakob. "Variations of Narrative in *The Nigger of the 'Narcissus.'*" *Conradiana*, 16, No. 3 (1984): 215–224.

Lubbock, Percy. *The Craft of Fiction*. London: Jonathan Cape, 1921.

Manicom, David. "True Lies/ False Truths: Narrative Perspective and the Control of Ambiguity in *The Nigger of the 'Narcissus.'*" *Conradiana*, 18, No. 2 (1986): 105–118.

Martin, Joseph. "Conrad and the Aesthetic Movement." *Conradiana*, 17, No. 3 (1985): 199–213.

Martin, Joseph J. "Edward Garnett and Conrad's Reshaping of Time." *Conradiana*, 6 (1974): 89–105.

Martin, W. R. "Conrad's Management of Narration." *Conradiana*, 14, No. 1 (1982): 53–56.

Messenger, William E. "Conrad and His 'Sea Stuff.'" *Conradiana*, 6 (1974): 3–18.

Meyer, Bernard C. *Joseph Conrad: A Psychoanalytic Biography*. Princeton, N.J.: Princeton University Press, 1967.

Miller, James Hillis. *Poets of Reality: Six Twentieth Century Writers*. Cambridge, Mass.: Harvard University Press, 1965.

"The Interpretation of *Lord Jim*." In Morton W. Bloomfield (ed.), *The Interpretation of Narrative*. Cambridge, Mass.: Harvard University Press, 1970: 211–228.

Fiction and Repetition: Seven English Novels. Oxford: Blackwell, 1982.

Mitchell, Giles. "Lord Jim's Death Fear, Narcissism, and Suicide." *Conradiana*, 18, No. 3 (1986): 163–179.

Mitchell, Mary Virginia. "Joseph Conrad and 19th Century Aesthetic Tradition." Dissertation, University of Minnesota, 1969. Ann Arbor, Mich.: Michigan University Microfilms, 1972.

Moore, Carlisle. "Conrad and the Novel as Ordeal." *Philological Quarterly*, 42, No. 1 (1963): 55–74.

Moser, Thomas C. *Joseph Conrad: Achievement and Decline*. Cambridge, Mass.: Harvard University Press, 1957.

"From Olive Garnett's Diary: Impressions of Ford Madox Ford and His Friends, 1890–1906." *Texas Studies in Literature and Language*, 16

(1974): 511–533.

Mudrick, Marvin. "Conrad and the Terms of Modern Criticism." *The Hudson Review*, 7 (Autumn 1954): 419–426.

"The Artist's Conscience and *The Nigger of the 'Narcissus.'* " *Nineteenth-Century Fiction*, 11 (1957): 288–297.

"The Originality of Conrad." *The Hudson Review*, 11 (1958): 545–553.

Najder, Zdzisław (ed.). *Conrad's Polish Background: Letters to and from Polish Friends*. London: Oxford University Press, 1964.

Joseph Conrad: A Chronicle. New Brunswick, N.J.: Rutgers University Press, 1983.

"Conrad's Polish Background, Or, From Biography to a Study of Culture." *Conradiana*, 18, No. 1 (1986): 3–8.

Oliva, Renato. "Dalla commedia della luce alla tragedia della tenebra, ovvero l'ambigua redenzione di Kurtz." In Renato Oliva and Alessandro Portelli, *Conrad: l'imperialismo imperfetto*. Turin: Einaudi, 1973: 9–70.

Palmer, John A. *Joseph Conrad's Fiction: A Study in Literary Growth*. Ithaca, N.Y.: Cornell University Press, 1968.

Paris, Bernard J. *A Psychological Approach to Fiction*. Bloomington: Indiana University Press, 1974.

Parry, Benita. *Conrad and Imperialism: Ideological Boundaries and Visionary Frontiers*. London: Macmillan, 1983.

Perniola, Mario. *Il metaromanzo*. I quaderni di Sigma, 4 Milan: Silva, 1966.

Pinsker, Sanford. *The Language of Joseph Conrad*. Amsterdam: Rotopi, 1978.

Powe, Bruce W. *A Climate Charged: Essays on Canadian Writers*. Oakville, Ont.: Mosaic Press, 1984.

Raimond, Jean. "Jim et Axel Heyst ou les mirages de l'ailleurs: deux avatars conradiens de Don Quichotte et de Robinson." *Images de l'ailleurs dans la littérature anglo-américaine*. Reims: Publications du Centre de Recherche sur l'Imaginaire dans les Littératures de Langue Anglaise, 1981: 77–95.

Randall, Dale B. J. (ed.). *Joseph Conrad and Warrington Dawson: The Record of a Friendship*. Durham, N.C.: Duke University Press, 1968.

Raval, Suresh. "Narrative and Authority in *Lord Jim*: Conrad's Art of Failure." *English Literary History*, 48, No. 2 (1981): 387–410.

Ray, Martin. "Language and Silence in the Novels of Joseph Conrad." *Conradiana*, 16, No. 1 (1984): 19–40.

Ross, Daniel W. "*Lord Jim* and the Saving Illusion." *Conradiana*, 20, No. 1 (1988): 45–69.

Roussel, Royal. *The Metaphysics of Darkness: A Study in the Unity and Development of Conrad's Fiction*. Baltimore: Johns Hopkins University Press, 1971.

Rude, Donald W. "Conrad as Editor: The Preparation of *The Shorter Tales*." In Wolodymyr Taras Zyla and Wendell Marshall Aycock (eds.), *Joseph Conrad: Theory and World Fiction*: 189–196.

"A Linguistic Reading of Conrad." *L'Epoque conradienne* (May 1979): 45–77.

Said, Edward. *Joseph Conrad and the Fiction of Autobiography*. Cambridge, Mass.: Harvard University Press, 1966.

"Conrad: The Presentation of Narrative." *Novel*, 7 (1974): 116–132.

Schuster, Charles I. "Comedy and the Limits of Language in Conrad's 'Typhoon.'" *Conradiana*, 16, No. 1 (1984): 55–71.

Schwab, Arnold T. "Conrad's American Speeches and His Reading from *Victory*." *Modern Philology*, 62, No. 4 (1965): 342–347.

Scott-James, Rolfe Arnold. "Above the Battle." In *Fifty Years of English Literature: 1900–1950*. London: Longman Green, and Co., 1954: 54–74.

Senn, Werner. *Conrad's Narrative Voice: Stylistic Aspects of His Fiction*. Bern: Francke Verlag, 1980.

Sherry, Norman. *Conrad's Eastern World*. Cambridge: Cambridge University Press, 1966.

(ed.). *Conrad: The Critical Heritage*. London: Routledge & Kegan Paul, 1973.

(ed.). *Joseph Conrad: A Commemoration*. Papers from the 1974 International Conference on Conrad. London: Macmillan, 1976.

Shires, Linda M. "The 'Privileged' Reader and Narrative Methodology in *Lord Jim*." *Conradiana*, 17, No. 1 (1985): 19–30.

Smith, David R. "'One Word More' about *The Nigger of the 'Narcissus.'*" *Nineteenth-Century Fiction*, 23 (1968): 201–216.

Smith, Rosalind Walls. "Dates of Composition of Conrad's Works." *Conradiana*, 11, No. 1 (1979): 63–90.

Stallman, R. W. "Conrad and the 'Secret Sharer.'" *Accent*, 9 (Spring 1949): 131–143. Rpt. in R. W. Stallman (ed.), *Joseph Conrad: A Critical Symposium*. East Lansing, Mich.: Michigan State University Press, 1960: 275–288.

Steiner, George. "Extraterritorial." In *Extraterritorial: Papers on Literature and the Language Revolution*. New York: Atheneum, 1971.

Tanner, Tony. *Conrad: Lord Jim*. London: Edward Arnold, 1963.

Teets, Bruce E. "Realism and Romance in Conrad Criticism." *The Polish Review*, 20, Nos. 2–3 (1975): 133–139.

Tenenbaum, Elizabeth Brody. "'And the Woman is Dead Now': A Reconsideration of Conrad's Stein." *Studies in the Novel*, 10, No. 3 (1978): 335–345.

Thurber, Barton. "Speaking the Unspeakable: Conrad and the Sublime." *Conradiana*, 16, No. 1 (1984): 41–54.

Tittle, Walter. "Portraits in Pencil and Pen." *Century Illustrated Magazine*, 106 (May 1923): 53–61.

Unger, Leonard. "Laforgue, Conrad, and T. S. Eliot." In *The Man in the Name: Essays on the Experience of Poetry*. Minneapolis: University of Minnesota Press, 1956: 190–242.

Van Ghent, Dorothy. *The English Novel: Form and Function*. 1953; rpt. New York: Harper Torchbooks, 1961.

Verlaine, Paul. *I poeti maledetti*. Trans. Diana Grange Fiori. Parma: Guanda, 1988.

Wasserman, Jerry. "Narrative Presence: The Illusion of Language in *Heart of Darkness*." *Studies in the Novel*, 6 (1974): 327–338.

Watt, Ian. "Conrad Criticism and *The Nigger of the 'Narcissus.'*" *Nineteenth-Century Fiction*, 12 (1958): 257–283.

"Conrad's Preface to *The Nigger of the 'Narcissus.'*" *Novel: A Forum on Fiction*, 7 (1974): 101–115.

"Impressionism and Symbolism in *Heart of Darkness*." In Norman Sherry (ed.), *Joseph Conrad: A Commemoration*: 37–41.

Conrad in the Nineteenth Century. Berkeley: University of California Press, 1979.

Watts, Cedric T. (ed.). *Joseph Conrad's Letters to R. B. Cunninghame Graham*. Cambridge: Cambridge University Press, 1969.

Conrad's "Heart of Darkness": A Critical and Contextual Discussion. Milan: Mursia International, 1977.

Weston, John Howard. "*The Nigger of the 'Narcissus'* and Its Preface." In Robert Kimbrough (ed.), *Joseph Conrad: The Nigger of the "Narcissus"*: 339–353.

Widmer, Kingsley. "Conrad's Pyrrhonistic Conservativism: Ideological Melodrama Around 'Simple Ideas.'" *Novel*, 7, No. 2 (1974): 133–142.

Wolfe, Peter. "Conrad's *The Mirror of the Sea*: An Assessment." *The McNeese Review*, 15 (1964): 36–45.

Woolf, Virginia. "Mr. Conrad: A Conversation." In *The Captain's Death Bed and Other Essays*. London: Hogarth Press, 1950: 74–78.

Worth, G. J. "Conrad's Debt to Maupassant in the Preface to *The Nigger of the 'Narcissus.'*" *Journal of English and Germanic Philology*, 54 (1955): 700–704.

Wright, Walter F. *Joseph Conrad on Fiction*. Lincoln: University of Nebraska Press, 1964.

Yelton, Donald C. *Mimesis and Metaphor: An Inquiry into the Genesis and Scope of Conrad's Symbolic Imagery*. The Hague: Mouton, 1967.

Young, Vernon. "Trial by Water: Joseph Conrad's *The Nigger of the 'Narcissus.'*" *Accent*, 12 (Spring 1952): 67–81. Rpt. in R. W. Stallman (ed.), *Joseph Conrad: A Critical Symposium*: 108–120:

Zabel, Morton Dauwen (ed.). Introduction to *The Portable Conrad*. 1947; rpt. New York: Viking Press, 1969: 1–47.

Zyla, Wolodymyr Taras and Wendell Marshall Aycock (eds.). *Joseph*

Conrad: Theory and World Fiction. Proceedings of the Comparative Literature Symposium. Vol. 7. Lubbock, Tex.: Texas Tech University, 1974.

Index

DATE DUE

9 - De			
408			
GAYLORD			PRINTED IN U.S.A.